Jonica Newby's childhood was heavily influenced by four cats, a Scottish Terrier, two mice, several horses, a few stud Herefords and 2000 head of sheep. These, and the discovery at the age of four that she could speak cat language, led inevitably to Murdoch University and a first class honours degree in Veterinary Science.

After working for several years as a vet in mixed practice, Dr Newby joined the Petcare Information and Advisory Service (an autonomous, non-profit organisation funded by the pet food manufacturer, Uncle Bens of Australia) from 1993 to 1998, where she discovered the fascinating new field of the study of human–animal interactions. A trip to Geneva in 1995 to attend an international conference on that subject provided the final inspiration for this book and the associated ABC radio and television series. A former member of the board of the Australian Veterinary Association, Dr Newby now writes and broadcasts about matters animal and scientific on a full-time basis.

THE ANIMAL ATTRACTION
HUMANS AND THEIR ANIMAL COMPANIONS

DR JONICA NEWBY

ABC
BOOKS

This book is dedicated to David Paxton, without whom the ideas would not have come.

Published by ABC Books for the
AUSTRALIAN BROADCASTING CORPORATION
GPO Box 9994 Sydney NSW 2001

First published as The Pact for Survival *in July 1997*
This new edition published in 1999

ISBN 0 7333 0824 4

Designed by Joy Eckermann
Cover designed by Deborah Brash/Brash Design Pty Ltd
Set in 11/14pt Minion
Colour separations by Moose Colour, Adelaide
Printed and bound in Australia by
Australian Print Group, Maryborough, Victoria

ACKNOWLEDGMENTS

This book is the product of hundreds of hours of interviews with some of the world's finest thinkers about our relationship with animal companions. Special thanks to Juliet Clutton-Brock, who invited me to her delightful Cambridge home and served stewed ancestral sheep for Sunday lunch, to Colin Groves, who answered many frantic phone calls about the fashion sense of our ancestors of 80,000 years ago, to John Bradshaw, who suffered two visits and many long-distance phone calls for the simple payment of a bottle of Australian red, and to James Serpell, who likewise answered many phone calls and sent me original transcripts of the witch trials and the draft of his next book. I would also like to thank all the people who gave their time to be interviewed: Robert Wayne, Sophia Menache, Harriett Ritvo, Anthony Podberscek, Stephen Hugh-Jones, Edward O. Wilson, Jared Diamond, Aaron Katcher, Xavier Parizot, Andrew Linzey, Raymond Coppinger, Paul Shepard, Anatoli Ruvinski, Marion Stamp-Dawkins, Daniel Dennett, Tony Juniper, Tim Flannery, Elizabeth Paul, John Guillebaud, Hugh MacKay, Wolfgang Lutz, Alexander Cuthbert, Virginia Jackson, Roland Fletcher, Richard Murray, Andrew Rowan and Andrew Edney. Thanks, too, to the team at the ABC's Science Unit who helped produce the series "Animal Friends" for Radio National. Also to members of ABC TV Science who made the TV series possible—especially Ian Cuming for his enormous support and commitment and spear-making abilities. And most of all, thank you to David Paxton, a veterinarian and lateral thinker who was responsible for opening my eyes to the breathtaking scope of the relationship between human and dog. Many of his ideas are here, and I dedicate this book to him.

Preface

IN THE past few years, I have had the pleasure of exploring humanity's fascinating and often surprising relations with our animal companions in three very different media: radio, television and print. Each offered the opportunity to approach the subject matter from a different perspective. This book, formerly published as *The Pact for Survival*, is not the book *of* the television or radio series, but a complementary volume. It picks up many of the themes of both, concentrating on the closest of our animal companions—our cats and dogs. Readers will find that some of the stories they enjoyed in the television series are not here, but that other ideas have space and depth impossible to explore within the constraints of a half-hour time slot. I hope that those who enjoyed the series find the book an equally intriguing treatment of the Animal Attraction.

Contents

CHAPTER 1

IN THE BEGINNING ...

JULIE IS lying under a delicately patterned cream and yellow quilt in a small room. She's not doing much — just looking out through a window onto the small patch of green outside, and idly recalling a similar scene from her childhood. Actually, to be honest, she can't move much at all these days; every limb feels so heavy and even thinking about lifting them is so exhausting that usually she decides, grumpily, it's all too much effort. She can certainly smile though, and turn her head, which she does now as her companion of the last seven years walks noisily into the room.

"Morning, Max," she says, softly, warmly, and moves her fingers just a little to indicate her welcome. Max's face stretches into what looks suspiciously like a smile, and obligingly he pads over and places his silky golden head under her proferred hand. Tail still wagging slightly, he then walks back to the end of the bed, from where he can launch his not inconsiderable weight bed-ward with minimum chance of toppling Julie in the process. Next, he settles carefully into his customary position, lying full length, head within easy reach of Julie's hand, and within easy nosing distance if he requires a bit of touch and reassurance himself, and tail stretched out, poised ready for the occasional, necessary thump. From here,

1

he will maintain his vigil until late afternoon, when the family comes to take him home.

Julie is 56 years old, and she is dying. She isn't real, although she's based on many real cases. And the scene is very familiar. Not that everyone has had to watch a friend die, but the affection so clearly expressed in her relationship with Max is common. Most of us have experienced it in some way, and even if it hasn't been highlighted personally by hardship, many of us know people for whom it has. Times when the company of an animal was a lifeboat during a period of storm. Why else is it that custody of the pet is often one of the bigger bones of contention in a divorce?

The mystery is not in the strength of that relationship — few of us in the West at least would find it remarkable. The mystery is in the fact that we *don't* find it remarkable. How did it come to be this way? How did humans become so close to another species that when a study asked dog owners to draw a diagram of their significant relationships, more than a third of the subjects drew the dog closer to themselves than any other family member?[1] Not to mention the surveys which have found many people would rather cuddle their pet than their spouse!

Perhaps human culture is so powerful we can force other animals to fit in with our desires (and if that means turning them into cuddly spouse substitutes, so be it). But if that is so, why have so few species succumbed? Sticking just to mammals for the moment, of all the millions of species on this planet, only a handful ever became domesticated. And of those, only two, *Canis familiaris* (whose very name means "of the household or family") and *Felis catus* have made the transition to life in the city.

And the place of the dog is especially intriguing. Even in cultures where dogs are *not* admired, are shunned or eaten, they are still there. There are virtually no human communities today that do not contain dogs. And in nearly all cases, we know that they've been in those communities for at least 10,000 years. Why?

There are many answers to that "why". Almost as many as there are types of dog living in the world today. And many of those "whys" are covered in this book. They range from the simple fact that there are no other animals with which we feel as comfortable having a conversation, to the suggestion pets are playing a critical and barely noticed role in one of the greatest challenges facing mankind: the control of our burgeoning population.

However, it is the original "why" which will concern me first, and which, in trying to answer, will help us to understand all the others. That is — how did it all begin?

MAN-MADE ANIMALS?

We used to think dogs were made for us: by God. As English historian Sir Keith Thomas noted, you don't need to look further than the first chapter of Genesis to see that the Judaeo–Christian God seems to have awarded Man "dominion over every living thing that moveth upon the earth".[2] This not only established human superiority, but made it easier to *use* animals. It was a rationale helped along by incorporating Greek traditions into Christian thought: Aristotle placed every other life form well below humans on the "ladder of life" on the basis of their capacity for rational thought. Then there was the later influence of Descartes, who in the sixteenth century infamously tortured dogs and claimed that as they had no soul, "their cries are but the squeaking of the springs of clocks".

While we no longer think God created dogs to serve humans, the modern idea still puts humans in control. It says that dogs are somehow "man-made". The legend of "man tames wolf" is as entrenched in our culture as the story of Adam and Eve. Our success in breeding dogs of all shapes and sizes makes it even easier to believe they were created through human ingenuity. As many writers have pointed out, the belief that dogs are somehow "artificial" has long inhibited serious scientific consideration of them. Even today, many of the people who are researching human relations with dogs complain it is seen as a "soft" science. A favourite comment came from Dr John Bradshaw, director of the Anthrozoology Institute at the University of Southhampton: "You aren't seen as a real biologist unless you spend half the year knee-deep in mud being dirty and uncomfortable. Studying your subject from an armchair by a cosy open fire doesn't seem to make the grade!"[3] Dogs are simply so entrenched in human culture, it's easy to think we made them.

Even Konrad Lorenz, the Nobel Prize-winning animal behaviourist, was not immune from this oversight. He wrote a wonderful tale of "how it might have started" in his popular 1954 book, *Man Meets Dog*.[4] In it, he gives his hero a "brighter eye" and "forehead higher and more arched" than the other members of a little band of primitive humans. Clearly this is a pretty clever guy who, when the group is so small it can't maintain an adequate watch at night, thinks of leaving meat out to attract the company of a nearby group of jackals. (At this stage, Lorenz was under the mistaken impression that jackals were the ancestors of dogs.) When later generations of jackals start helping the humans in the hunt, the high-browed man's actions are more than vindicated. And it is this entertaining fable that has informed popular opinion ever since.

But was it really a case of "the clever ape" manipulating another species? Or was there something far more subtle, mutual and interesting going on? Is it possible that the coming together of human and dog was less an act of domination made possible by

Homo sapiens' brain power, and more a process of mutually beneficial cooperation? A symbiosis. A "co-domestication", even. In fact, is it possible that as much as we "chose" them, they "chose" us — and there wasn't necessarily a lot we could do about it?

SEARCHING FOR THE BEGINNING

Juliet Clutton-Brock, now retired from her longstanding position with the Natural History Museum in London, is one of the foremost experts on the origins of domestic animals. She helped establish the field of science known as archaeo-zoology. It is a relatively new field — almost brand new when she was drawn to it more than 30 years ago. Prior to then, most archaeologists were far too interested in working out what old bones could tell us about our own species to be overly concerned with the bones of other, definitely non-human species lying around. Except, of course, when trying to work out who had eaten what or whom for dinner. But as time went on and some of the major questions about our own origins began to be settled (such as the sad conclusion that, no, the first human was not an Englishman, despite some very creative attempts to prove otherwise), a few people became interested in these other animal remains for their own sake. The significance of the domestication of animals in our own cultural development began to be discussed more widely, and a handful of enthusiasts began developing a new animal-orientated specialty. Among them was Juliet Clutton-Brock, who went on to write many of the definitive texts.[5]

One of the fundamental problems posed by her science lies in the question of timing.[6] Pinning down the exact date of the earliest association between man and dog, or at this stage *Homo sapiens* and *Canis lupus* (or wolf), is not easy. As everyone trying to piece together the sequence of human evolution is more than aware, the archaeological record is quite sparse and widely scattered in time, with every possibility that relics which would provide clues to key dates or events may never be found. To compound the problem — again — early archaeologists intent on establishing the "missing links" in human ancestry often paid scant attention to non-human remains, and important information was probably overlooked or lost. A notorious example of this sort of short-sightedness (which, admittedly, wasn't caused by scientists) is the case of the cat mummies. The Egyptian practice of revering and then mummifying cats after death resulted in huge caches of desiccated felines, which would have been of great value for study — but when mounds of them were shipped to England in the nineteenth century, most were promptly purchased by an entrepreneur and ground up to be sold as fertiliser.

To make matters worse, given that both humans and wolves are predators, often with similar habitat requirements, when canine bones are found with human bones, there is a dilemma. Were they loosely associated, under human control, or were they dinner? Or did they have nothing to do with each other and just happened to use the same cave one hundred years apart?

So how do scientists like Clutton-Brock work out when the connection first happened? When did *Canis lupus* stop being the terrifying monster of childhood stories, and become plain "Lupus", man's best friend and preferred companion of women (if the surveys rating spouse cuddliness are anything to go by)? The only way they can tell for sure is, first, if they find the typical changes in size and shape of skeleton which characterise the transition from wolf to dog. And second, if they find unequivocal cultural evidence of association which makes it unlikely that the connection was anything other than a socially intimate, even affectionate, one. Both criteria are fulfilled in the crucial excavation at Ein Mallaha, situated near the Huleh lake in the upper Jordan Valley in Israel, a site dated at 12,000 years Before Present (BP)[7].

This period of prehistory is referred to by archaeologists as the Natufian. Twelve thousand years ago and to the north of our site, the ice from the last great cold spell had more or less receded, leaving behind vast, grassy plains and opening the way for future forested stretches. At the time, our ancestors were still hunter-gatherers (or gatherer-hunters, as many modern anthropologists like to put it in recognition of the contribution of plants to human nutrition) taking advantage of the relative abundance of tasty herbivores. They were people, however, on the verge of a dramatic life change; it would not be longer than a thousand years before they would be permanently indentured to that often cruel master, climate, the paramount force once they became committed to agriculture.

The locals of Ein Mallaha were on the cusp of that change. They were clearly no longer completely nomadic, as they lived mainly in small round stone huts and were already utilising what were later to become common crop plants, as evidenced by the basalt pestles and mortars for grinding cereals found with the dwellings. But what is significant is that they also routinely buried their dead in stone-covered tombs. And in one of these, lying in death as she probably so often lay in life, was the skeleton of an elderly woman, her knees curled up as she rested on her side, and her hand cupped over the chest of a puppy. The five-month-old pup, whether tamed wolf or dog (from the skeleton it is hard to tell), lay curled up too, its body just centimetres from the vulnerable face of its companion.

It is hard to imagine a more poignant manifestation of the depth of the bond between two creatures. And it's especially striking when you think about it being formed all that time ago. (Of course, it is sobering to realise that in order to present this tableau, the family of the woman no doubt had to kill the dog so it could lie there so perfectly! But this is hardly to be taken in a modern context, since presumably it was believed that the young wolf or dog would simply accompany its mistress during her long journey through the spirit world.)

The evidence for this affectionate bond between humans and dogs was strengthened by the excavation in the late 1980s of another Natufian burial site in Israel, this time of a man with two adult canids[8]. These finds are certainly not the only ones from around the period which show dogs or wolves associated with human communities, but their setting is particularly significant. While one of the criteria for distinguishing the bones of early domestic dogs from their wild ancestors is their smaller size, the situation is not straightforward. The initial reduction in size of all domesticated animals is probably due to poorer nutrition as they became more dependent on the scraps or largesse of their human associates. But the wild wolf of Western Asia, *Canis lupus arabs*, was already quite small. In fact it was (and still is) the smallest wolf subspecies ranging over the northern hemisphere, probably well within the normal species size of both wolf and dog. If the burial sites didn't so clearly indicate otherwise, we would still not be able to claim for sure that human and dog were genuinely attached this early in our prehistory, despite, perhaps, our best intuition.

There are other distinctive changes which occur to the dog's skeleton as domestication progresses, and these start to show up quite markedly in numerous finds from around the world a little later on. They include the shortened face and jaw and pronounced "stop" which are typical of the modern dog (the "stop" is the angle between the forehead and the nose — in wolves the line from between the ears to the tip of the nose is almost straight, whereas in a Labrador, for example, the domed head meets the straight nose at quite an angle); as well as crowding and shrinking of the teeth. Not to mention a reduction in brain size.

The earliest known canid skull exhibiting a shortened jaw is 14,000 years old, and was found in Germany, making it some 2000 years older and many thousands of kilometres distant from the Israeli sites. A number of others have also been found dated at around 12,000 BP throughout western Asia. Then, from around 9000 to 7000 BP, when the switch to agriculture in the so-called "fertile crescent" of the Middle East was well under way, we start to see dog remains cropping up around the world. These include a 7000-year-old dog in China, a number of 8000-year-old dogs in southern Chile, and the quite recent and exciting discovery of three domestic dogs, found deliberately buried in shallow graves at Koster in the Illinois River Valley, central United States, dated at 8500 years ago.[9]

So this is the archaeological evidence which has convinced Juliet Clutton-Brock and many of her colleagues that the transition from wolf to dog occurred some 12,000 to 14,000 years ago, and probably took place somewhere in Europe and western Asia. But the evidence doesn't tell us *how* or *why* it happened. Or what it meant for both wolf/dogs and humans. Why were dogs so important that before too long, there was virtually not a single human community that lacked them? Why was it that when humans undertook the arduous journeys to new lands, such as crossing the Bering Strait around 12,000 BP to colonise North America or, more recently, paddling the intimidating Pacific in tiny canoes to settle in New Zealand, the dogs came too?

To answer these questions, we have to leave the certainty of solid bones and dates, and shift towards the realms of imagination and speculation. There are a number of theories around. Some of them are highly sustainable, given verifiable fossils and observations of the behaviour of contemporary humans and dogs, including modern gatherer-hunters. Others are more fanciful, with little direct archaeological evidence to back them up. But all should force us to review our current cuddly relationship with dogs, and see that "man's best friend" has had a far greater impact on human development than we have really recognised.

FIRST DOG AS PET

Juliet Clutton-Brock believes the clue is to be found in that remarkable Ein Mallaha tableau. Despite all the "pets are good for you" hype, we still have a tendency today to belittle pet ownership, to think that it is something of a degenerate Western remnant of a once functional relationship. But it could be that pet keeping was precisely the reason for the earliest association of human and wolf.

Picture the scene.[10] The date is some time around 15,000 years before now. The place could be anywhere in Europe or western Asia, but let's say it's in the middle of what is now Israel, perhaps even at Ein Mallaha itself, with our gentle, dog-loving woman still 100 generations or so from being born. We are sitting in a human community of around 30 souls.

Far, far to the north, the ice is still melting, leaving behind its riches of verdant tundra, home to the great herds of large mammals so well suited to this newly grassed world. The weather here, though, is not really much colder than it will be 14,000 years hence. It's a little wetter and, of course, much greener, especially in winter, since the land has not yet been desertified by the voracious demands of nutrient-draining crops and greedy mobs of docile sheep. In fact, the country is quite gentle, with thick bushes dotted over the rolling hills, occasionally interspersed with small clumps of low-lying trees. Many future crop plants grow wild around here; and the women spend much of the day gathering the seed of corn and other cereals, and bringing it back to camp to process in their big stone querns — large rock slabs with a central hollow against which it is easy to grind a small round stone.

There's also plenty of game, an abundance of it, really. Every few days, the men collect up their large stone axes and gather for the hunt. The small stone huts the community builds are really only temporary shelters and the group is still free to follow game and water. Usually the men don't have to travel too far to hunt the gazelle and deer, the wild ass (*Equus hemionus*) and wild sheep, the pigs and goats and cattle which surround them in a swirling sea of life, fecund as the African Serengeti their ancestors left behind.

Of course, life isn't perfect. The rainfall is seasonal and the tribe is often forced to wander long distances in search of good water, especially towards the end of summer as the land turns gold and brown and the soil starts to desiccate. But it's the end of winter that is hardest. At this time, the cereals have long since finished yielding their harvest, and game has become scarce as the grazers move on in response to dwindling supplies of herbage. It is this harsh annual bottleneck which will eventually be a major contributing factor to that notoriously mixed blessing of "civilisation", the development of agriculture.

But, in general, the pattern of community life is fairly stable. Even pleasant. The recent decision to store grains in shallow pits has made quite a difference, easing all but the harshest years; although it's not the whole answer, because there's still a limit to how much grain can be carried around.

There's another change which, surprisingly, seems to have had quite a beneficial impact on community life. Predators, like hyenas and lions, and especially the fearsome leopard, are a constant reminder to everyone to remain vigilant, especially when travelling alone. Particularly troublesome in one season is the arrival near the camp of an unusually fearless pack of wolves. The people decide to band together and the pack is eventually driven away, but in the process a female wolf is killed.

None of this is very unusual, except that on this occasion, a curious young woman of the tribe decides to follow a strange sound. Before long, half hidden by the shrubs in which they sit, she comes across three fluffy little grey creatures, which bristle and growl to warn her off. Their teeth are far too small to hurt, so she promptly gathers them up in her collecting bag and takes them back to camp. It is certainly not uncommon to find the odd young animal and feed it until it dies or runs away, and it is understood that women seem to get particular pleasure out of this, especially those without children. Yet these animals are a little different. Right from the start the youngsters seem positively friendly, unlike any wolf anyone had ever seen, and the group soon becomes quite used to the procession of young woman, three pups, and inevitable troupe of children following behind. There is some trouble when the male pup bites one of the children (a matter discreetly resolved by means of the senior elder's large stone axe), and there are always a few grumbles about these useless creatures who seem to do little but lie around or play and eat precious food, but most people agree they are great at keeping the children occupied. So later on, when the by now fully grown bitch comes back pregnant after a few days' sojourn, there is great competition for the offspring, including from the women of neighbouring tribes. Over time the brood further disperses, some of the semi-tame wolves eventually wandering away from camp, especially when food has been scarce, but on those that remain, the consensus seems to be that the animals have certainly made the community a much more interesting and lively place. And the senior elder's big stone axe doesn't have to be used very often at all.

The idea that the original association of human and wolf was not a functional one at all, but based on affection and the desire to nurture, especially from women, is backed up by studies of modern hunter-gatherers. The South American Indians, for example, are avid pet keepers. As numerous explorers and anthropologists have noted, it is very common for hunters to bring back the young of animals they have killed as presents for the women or children. Similar to our scenario, most of these creatures eventually leave or don't survive. (The case of the Amerindians is interesting because, despite this abundance of wildlife, the dog is the only creature which actually reproduces in human settlements; no other Amerindian "pet" has ever become domesticated.)

But it is not hard to see why the wolf would have been different from other animals brought in as "pets". The Pleistocene period, which started around 1.8 million years ago and was drawing to a close at the time of our putative community scene, was marked by dramatic climatic fluctuations. It encompassed no fewer than 18 ice ages, and it has been estimated that climatic oscillations during this period approached the order of six times the normal. Such instability would have imposed harsh penalties on highly specialised organisms, and favoured those species able to adapt readily to a variety of habitats and food sources.[11] Of course, the master of non-specialisation is humanity.

Our species' success as cooperative, broad-spectrum hunters was not only responsible for the ecological ascendancy of *Homo sapiens*, but probably contributed greatly to our social evolution. Choosing to hunt large ungulates — or animals with hoofs — which are not only bigger but faster than you, requires an advanced ability to integrate activities, as well as considerable communication skills — undoubtedly powerful forces in encouraging the development of human speech and community life. By the end of the last ice age the hunting prowess of *Homo sapiens* had no rival.

But there was a close runner-up. Wolves had also developed a highly sophisticated, broad-spectrum, social hunting strategy. In fact, if you were to take a punt 500,000 years ago, you might have put your money on the wolf, rather than our seemingly less well-endowed hominid ancestors. The sharp teeth of the canid proved to be no match, however, for the developing technology of the big-brained ape, and gradually *Canis lupus* was pushed into second place.

Yet the demands of a similar lifestyle had produced a remarkable congruence of character. Both species had highly developed, nurturing social systems, and spent much of the day engaging in behaviours like grooming and, in the human case, gossiping, which reinforce social bonds.[12] Both, too, were strongly hierarchical, with clear dominance structures helping to minimise intra-group conflict; and groups were at this stage probably quite similar in size. In addition, the ranges and even hunting paths of the two species would have frequently overlapped.

Certainly there were other canids, such as the fox or jackal, which would also have come into contact with humans, but they lacked the communal social behaviours essential for easy integration with human society. (As mentioned earlier, it was Konrad Lorenz who first perpetuated the idea that at least some dogs were descended from jackals; a position he later rescinded in the late 1970s in the preface to *The Wild Canids*[13]. A combination of DNA, behaviour, vocalisation, chemistry and anatomy studies have settled once and for all the debate that dogs are directly descended from wolves.)

So, as a number of writers have pointed out, wolves, perhaps uniquely amongst mammals, were essentially "pre-adapted" (a notion popularised by the evolutionary biologist Stephen Jay Gould, although he preferred the term "exaptation") to life with humans, and it probably did not take much for them to step across the threshold of strangeness and enter our homes.

Take our imagined scene again. You will remember the original wolves were "unusually fearless". This doesn't mean they were particularly aggressive, simply that their flight distance — the distance which they maintain between themselves and potential threats such as humans — was unusually low. Within any species there exists a normal range of expression of behaviours, and fear of "the other", essential for survival (especially in avoiding predators), is one such trait. In social species such as wolves, this wariness is attenuated anyway, since it's very difficult to cooperate if you spend the whole time being nervous of your neighbour. A group of wolves such as this were probably on the "friendly" rather than the "wary" end of the scale. When the pups were raised in different circumstances, this extended to an easier attachment to their new human associates, and a reduction in their tendency to be aggressive.

Of the pups in our scenario, the male did start to show some aggression once he approached adulthood. But this was promptly resolved by means of the big stone axe, effectively removing him from the gene pool. Over time, those less well attached to humans wandered off or were killed, leaving behind only those with an enhanced tendency to associate with humans and a reduced level of hostility. What we call "tameness".

This scenario doesn't require any conscious decision to domesticate. All it requires is a coming together of two essentially compatible species, which first found that there was no particular disadvantage in living together, and then discovered it was mutually beneficial. (It must be remembered that all this took place long before any other creature was domesticated, so there were no models to follow.) It's a very different scenario from the popular "man tamed the wolf to help him in the hunt" theory. When they had no concept of domestication, the idea that a few men noticed how successful wolves were as predators and decided to try to breed some to help them in the hunt, simply doesn't make sense.

As Juliet Clutton-Brock says about the myth of "man tames wolf", "You can't say 'man', it's not politically correct. Humans. And anyway, I firmly believe that domestication was carried out by women!"[14]

FIRST DOG AS SEWAGE SYSTEM

In complete contrast to "first dog as pet" theory is the "dog as latrine" theory.

Raymond Coppinger is an American biologist. His fascination with the evolution of dogs and other domestic animals began early in his 30-year career, and led to a remarkable program over 20 years that introduced livestock-guarding dogs to US flocks. These are the dogs which are raised to "think they are sheep". As small pups, they are separated from their siblings and sent to live with a flock, which essentially becomes their family. As the dogs mature, they become highly effective guards, able to stave off the attacks of wolves and other mutton-seeking predators. In the 1970s, it was estimated that coyotes were responsible for creaming off around 10 per cent of the annual US lamb drop, and Coppinger believes the guarding dog program, which has seen over 1400 of the dogs introduced, was one of the two great innovations in the American sheep industry — the other being the invention of the electric fence![15]

Coppinger doesn't like the "wolf cub as pet" theory — to him it involves too many assumptions. He is particularly wary of putting modern motivations to a people from whom we are separated by 14,000 years, and the idea that they kept pets is for him too speculative. Even if our ancestors did have a sense of "pet keeping", he points out, in order to build a viable breeding population, the poor hunter wanting to give a present to his wife would have had to bring home wolf cubs in their hundreds!

It was far more likely, according to Coppinger, that instead of it being a case of deliberately bringing wolves into our homes, they were actually invaders. And, in the end, getting rid of them proved to be more trouble than it was worth.

With the development of human villages a little over 12,000 years ago came the creation of a new environmental niche. The settlements not only provided novel, often climate-controlled structures in which to reside, but a new source of energy in the form of concentrated wastes. Animals quick to take advantage of these riches included mice and rats, and probably various species of bird. Also, no slouch in the opportunism stakes, would have been the wolf.

Coppinger believes the wolf's original association with *Homo sapiens* was as a scavenger. It was only much later, after co-existing uneasily this way for some time, that the two species became physically close enough for other, less prosaic relationships to form.

Let's revisit our Israeli scene then, only this time it is Raymond Coppinger's imagination that will guide us. The setting is broadly similar to the previous one, although we have fast forwarded 1000 years to around 14,000 BP. The community has become a little more sophisticated about hunting and grain storage, so is now spending much of the year in one place. The one notable difference from our earlier scene, however, is the smell.

On most days, it's not too bad. This is because a rubbish dump for all waste matter has been instituted over a small rise, away from the village, to avoid vermin. It's been a good solution to the waste disposal problem, and it's only at certain times of year, following a period of heat and an appropriate wind, that the stench really pervades the village.

There's a new problem, though. A pack of opportunistic wolves starts to raid the dump. Concerned about the potential danger, several of the villagers gather to discuss what to do. Eventually, a group gets together with sticks and axes and stones, and attacks the wolves, screaming as loudly as possible to frighten them off. But, frustratingly, most of the wolves are soon back.

As time goes by, the animals just seem to be get bolder and bolder. Periodically, more wolf-scaring expeditions are organised, but the wolves always return.

Eventually one comes right up into the village and steals a haunch of gazelle. And one female is even brazen enough to have a litter right in one of the grain stores!

Most of the time, though, they're not much trouble. There is one attack on a person, but the elders organise a hunting group to kill the rogue. Other than that, the wolves are mainly just a nuisance. There comes a point that when the people walk to the dump clattering sticks as loudly as they can, half the wolves barely even lift an eyebrow. It's hardly worth bothering, really.

To appreciate how this scenario might have occurred, you only have to look at the common practice of setting up feeders for birds. The northern winter is a testing time for every creature. With most food sources diminished, and dramatic drops in temperature to contend with, organisms use every strategy available to survive.

Picture, then, the scene outside one of those cosy American homes, complete with wooden balcony, smoke tufting from the chimney and compulsory sauna. The inhabitants have just erected a large bird feeder on the porch and take care to keep it well stocked with grain.

The birds vary in their response to this new bounty. Some are quite bold and feed confidently. Others are shyer and hesitate even to approach. When the owners of the house walk outside, there's a flurry of activity as the birds take flight, but a few birds don't fly very far, and are quick to return once the "danger" has passed. Over the years, the birds seem to grow tamer and tamer, with several regularly coming right up to take food almost from the owners' hands. And when a nesting house is built right next to the feeder, a few of the birds move straight in, and now the owners are anxiously looking forward to next spring and the flutter of little wings.

By providing the bird feeder with a constant supply of grain, the humans have introduced a new energy source into the local ecosystem. Clearly, only those birds less fearful of human settlements will take advantage. This is the first separation of the group. Amongst those who are bold enough to approach the feeder, those birds less inclined to take flight at the approach of humans will waste less precious energy, so the group is further divided. Given the strong selection pressures applied during the annual crunch of winter, it doesn't take many generations for a subgroup best fitted to using the resource to develop. And this subgroup is "tame".

To return to our prehistoric scene, with wolves living off the dumps and refuse of human settlements, a similar process is occurring. For convenience, the scenario condensed what was probably a very long and drawn out process into the space of a few years. To begin with, the community probably wasn't even aware the wolves were around; shy of people, they would have made themselves scarce at human approach, feeding mainly at night. Over time, those with a reduced flight distance would have been advantaged as they wasted less energy and were better able to use the new resource. Eventually, a subgroup of bold or "tame" wolves evolved and, no doubt with some consternation, the people began to be aware of their proximity.

Without knowing it, though, our humans could already have

been benefiting from these scavenging activities. Once *Homo sapiens* stopped travelling and became more or less stationary, disposal of wastes was more of a problem. By reducing the bulk of that waste (and Coppinger suggests this might even have included human faecal matter, giving a possible explanation for that unsavoury doggy habit of eating poo), wolves and other scavengers may have acted as early sewage units, actively limiting the breeding grounds for disease.

Later, when it got to the point of the animals regularly entering human settlements, the stage was set for the final dramatic shift in relations. Once members of this semi-tame subgroup began rearing puppies in the villages, the young would for the first time be exposed to humans during a critical developmental time: the socialisation period. And, as we shall see in later chapters, it is the flexibility of the socialisation period that is one of the keys to our ongoing relationship with dogs.

It is interesting at this point to consider the behaviour of modern wolves. Biologist Luigi Boitano, well known for his studies of free-ranging dogs in Italy, describes a wonderful experiment that shows how much "wild" behaviour is going on around us we are not aware of.[16] Apparently many Italian village dumps have a resident wolf population. Often, the locals aren't even aware of their presence, only noticing their tracks in the snow in winter and saying wisely "Ah yes, the cold has driven the wolves down from the hills". In fact, they've been there all along. One evening, Boitano and his colleagues set a spotlight up at a dump to come on automatically at two o'clock in the morning. The bright light revealed a veritable zoo. There were rats and cats and a village dog. And sure enough, perfectly framed in the sudden glare, was a wolf startled mid-meal, his face full of dribbling spaghetti!

Far from the image of a slavering child-eater, it seems the dog's fearsome ancestor was more at home hunting pasta than people

— figuratively speaking, at least. As for the other fable of humans deliberately domesticating wolves, not only is it unrealistic, but we've probably got it the wrong way around.

Once the niche of human habitation was created — a renewable energy source just waiting to be exploited — the right entrepreneur was bound to come along. Our ancestors were no more able to resist the invasion of wolves, than the good people of Hamlin could resist the salespitch of the Pied Piper, with his unbeatable offer to rid the town of rats.

DOG AS HEARING AID

It is fairly obvious what wolves gained from linking up with humans: a ready supply of food, and even a place to live. (Although nutritionally it was a mixed blessing, because once they became dependent on human scraps it left them open to malnourishment when times were tough. Scientists believe this is why early on in the domestication process, body size drops — smaller animals are favoured because they are better able to cope with nutritional stress.) For better or worse, wolves gained a new ecological niche. But what did humans gain?

Biological theory tells us that we don't willingly give food to others unless we expect something back, so presumably we got something from the arrangement. Was the joy of playful companionship really enough of an answer, or was there more? A successful hunting partnership is one possible benefit; but most modern theorists agree this must have come much later. In fact, anthropological studies have shown that in some communities, dogs are as likely to be a hindrance as a help. Even if we decide the whole thing started because of inadequate pest control, you really can't say wolves are in the same league as rats. For starters, they're much bigger, and easier to find. *Homo sapiens* may not have been able to keep *Lupus* from the dumps, but he could certainly kick him out of his home. Was there something else happening, then, even right at the beginning of the association, which made those human communities infested with dogs better off than those that lived without them?

And it is on this note that David Paxton's fascinating theory comes in. Based in part on his observations of dogs in other cultures while managing agricultural development projects, Paxton, a veterinarian, has come to challenge accepted dates. He is convinced that the first association of human and wolf or dog occurred not 12,000, not 14,000, but perhaps even 80,000 years ago. That during the volatile Pleistocene, two species came together to enter a "genetic contract". And the reason for its success had very little to do with the dog's bite, and everything to do with its bark.

The archaeological evidence for this time frame is at best ambiguous, at worst non-existent. But this is not to say that earlier associations were not possible, or even likely. Anthropologist and author Elizabeth Marshall Thomas has written a wonderful book called *Reindeer Moon*[17] set in the Pleistocene around 20,000 BP, in which, two orphaned girls form a temporary alliance with a lone she-wolf in order to survive a harsh winter. According to Juliet Clutton-Brock, this is a perfectly plausible scenario.[18] Yet evidence for this would never be found in the fossil record. For starters, tame wolves, or "proto-dogs", needn't look any different from wild ones — so there would be nothing in the fossil record to say they were friendly. This is complicated by the fact that before 14,000 BP people were nomadic, thus the chances of finding good fossil remains proving humans and wolves were friendly is almost zero. Clutton-Brock believes that throughout prehistory women often adopted wild baby animals, but it was only later when the conditions were right for a more permanent situation that unequivocal remains were preserved.

The oldest finds of wolf bones associated with hominid bones date from the middle Pleistocene epoch. These include the site of Zhoukoudian in northern China, dated at 300,000 years BP, the Lazarat site in the south of France dated at 150,000 BP, and the 400,000-year-old site of Boxgrove in Kent, England. All of these sites are beset by difficulties in interpreting whether there was a connection between the species' bones or whether they just happened to end up mixed together over time. But at the very least they show that the activities of the two species frequently overlapped.

These ambiguities, and the fact that the relationship was already very advanced by 12,000 BP, led David Paxton to suggest that the relationship began much earlier.[19] Like Coppinger, Paxton holds with the dog as scavenger model, although he doesn't confine it to the start of village life. Given the similarity of their diet, he believes some groups of wolves may have found it advantageous to simply follow people around on their nomadic journeys. The wolves probably couldn't meet all their nutritional needs in this way, but you wouldn't need more than the occasional feed of scraps from human hunts to make the strategy worthwhile. After all, they would be covering similar territory anyway; basically, both people and wolves went where the food was.

After a time, again under similar selection pressures to those outlined by Coppinger, something interesting would have started to happen. Here, let's go back to Israel, but this time let our guide be David Paxton, with a little additional detail from Dr Colin Groves, anthropologist and specialist in human and primate evolution at the Australian National University.[20] This time, we are visiting a much earlier period, some 80,000 years before now.

The average temperature is rather colder than that of our earlier scenes. The world is still in the grip of one of those recurring Pleistocene ice ages, and although it is getting warmer at a fraction of a degree every century, this literally glacial speed is far too slow for anyone involved to notice.

The countryside is also rather drier. An open, cool semi-desert is the best description of the landscape, which is speckled with greyish little knee-high shrubs a future botanist would name *Artemesia*. Not far away, the highlands are often capped with snow, and the cold winters place quite a demand on the community's best cloak-makers, who prepare the pelts which keep out the winter chill.

The cyclical pattern of the 20-strong community's life is well established. They are fortunate in having access to three excellent cave sites, which provide easily defensible and sheltered home bases, as the group follows the annual movements of the fallow and roe deer which favour these cooler climes. What with the abundant ungulate herds and delicious wild boar, there are very few seasons when they're forced to supplement their diet with dormice.

Of course, at this stage, our community of *sapiens* is not the only hominid species around. Living in the highlands is a group of the "winter people". Occasionally they are spotted in the distance, but generally their paths rarely cross. In another 50,000 years, these creatures with the hairy arms and thick, heavy brows, *Homo neanderthalensis*, would be no more.

The other notable difference from our first scene is this time not the smell, but the noise. Sometimes it's indescribable. A cacophony of yips and barks that wakes up the whole camp; a little like listening to 40 colicky babies screaming in a thunderstorm.

But it does have its uses. Years ago, the tribe was terrorised by a group of cave lions and lost three children in as many seasons; a tragedy from which it took a generation to recover. These days, a cave lion would be lucky to get within a mile of them.

The creatures are good at warning of the approach of human

intruders too. Admittedly, most routine contact with other tribes is welcome; a chance to exchange greetings and sometimes even to add a member to the tribe. But it is not always that way. All in all, there is little doubt the community is better off than before the noisy creatures moved in.

The clue that led Paxton (a self-avowed lateral thinker) to this scenario is that we humans have such a poor sense of smell; in fact you could say it's positively rotten. Our sense of hearing is not particularly good either. These days, it probably doesn't matter much, because being stalked by cave lions is not a common hazard, but what struck Paxton as curious was how we managed when it *did* matter.

For most of *Homo sapiens'* history, we didn't enjoy the ecological ascendancy seen today. When it came to hunting, it was not unlikely that we would be the lunch rather than the lunch-er. And the nightscape in particular must have been a frightening place. With our most acute sense, eyesight, virtually crippled outside the ring of the campsite fire, and our hearing and smell informing us little further, we were "sitting humans" to night-time predators. As Konrad Lorenz himself so vividly conceived in *Man Meets Dog*, for a small band of *sapiens*, the fear would have been particularly acute.

Enter the wolf. The modern dog has over 14 times the olfactory mucous membrane surface area of the modern human. With their acute sense of hearing and fabulous sense of smell, the wolves' awareness covered a radius of kilometres. If the work on modern dogs by Australian animal behaviourist Graham Adams is anything to go by, the animals probably slept as a group in out-of-phase cycles, with at least one in the alert mode of light sleep at any given time.[21] Even during the perilous dark, a biotic radar system was on the job.

But given that initially the animals probably lived some distance from the camp, how would this benefit our prehistoric people? Wolves don't bark!

Wolves don't, but semi-tame wolves, or "proto-dogs", might. The retention of juvenile characteristics into adulthood, known as neotenisation, has long been hailed as the key to the evolution of the dog; of the human too, for that matter. In order to produce "tameness", that is, the reduction in flight distance referred to earlier, those wolves who chose to be camp followers would already have undergone a degree of neotenisation. "Friendliness", or a tendency to be more positive and less discriminating in social encounters, is a classic mammalian characteristic of youth. Another classic characteristic of wolf youth is a tendency to vocalise, or bark.

It is not hard to see how human groups infested with canids would have had a selective advantage over those that were not. With time, those communities would gradually discover they had grown a new set of "artificial ears". There is no need to invoke shared intentions or even affection to see that mixed-species communities were much less likely to fall victim to predators than those that retained the apartheid. More importantly, they were more likely to prevail in the human competition for good water and hunting grounds. Pity the mischief-bound rival tribe hoping to take their "dog-ged" competitors by surprise!

Proto-dogs, of course, would have gained similar protection from predators by being associated with a large group, as well as easy food and shelter. Eventually, too, they would have been able to utilise human brains and technology as they began to team up in the hunt. Over time, those camp-following dogs that abandoned some of their aggression and survival skills in order to fit in (which essentially just means the more dangerous ones were driven off by humans or killed) would have become less and less able to survive without their human partners. In a similar manner to that described by Coppinger, they would have gradually entered our homes and, as Ein Mallaha shows us, our hearts.

Support for the notion that the success of the canid–hominid symbiosis was originally based on this literally extrasensory perception is not hard to find. It is interesting that even today, if you survey human communities around the world you can see the full gamut of relations between the species. But what is universally valued is the bark — and the role of watchdog. As I write this, further outbreaks of violence and sectarian hostility have flared in Papua New Guinea and car loads of big dogs are being trucked into the expatriate residential area to set up guard for the night. On the Gaza Strip, one of the most volatile borders in the world, a 1995 newspaper reported that the locals weren't relying on their state-of-the-art detector systems but had set up a line of alarm dogs. Just yesterday, my mother, unaware of what I was writing, came in to tell me how pleased she was that her new, five-month-old lapdogs (which had been bought primarily for companionship) had learned how to bark. They are barking right now. It is police policy to advise enquirers that one of the best deterrents to house crime is a dog. And one of the things that amused me while I was collecting the interviews for this book, was that time after time my chief technical problem while recording was being interrupted by the sound of barking dogs!

As for the timing of Paxton's proposed partnership, a much earlier link-up than 14,000 BP is not unrealistic. And if so, it starts to place the wolf or dog into some very interesting periods in the development of our own species. We know that wolves and hominids have lived proximately for at least 500,000 years. *Homo sapiens* didn't evolve from the precursor hominid until 100,000 to 200,000 BP. Anthropologist Colin Groves, expert on the evolution of humans, thinks the idea that *Homo sapiens* first started associating with wolves even as early as 100,000 years ago quite reasonable.[22] Indeed, new and exciting evidence of a much earlier association is now emerging. And this time scientists have shifted focus, looking not at the bones but inside living DNA.

A group of scientists, including Carles Vila and Robert Wayne, based in the biology department of UCLA, collected over 300 samples from dogs, wolves and coyotes. Concentrating on a gene in the mitochondrial DNA (a favourite site for this sort of analysis since mtDNA can only be inherited from the mother, thus removing the complication of genetic shuffling), they first calculated the number of mtDNA variations found between wolves and coyotes. Based on the assumption that wolves and coyotes branched on the evolutionary tree around 1 million years ago, they were then able to work out a baseline rate: the average number of diversions in the mtDNA accumulated over time. When they then turned to examine dog DNA, they found there was far more divergence than could possibly have occurred in just 14,000 years. In fact, based on their calculations, dogs may have existed as a separate species for at least 100,000 years.[23]

This type of analysis is not without controversy. Some scientists don't believe the "molecular clock" method is reliable because they are not sure that DNA variations necessarily occur at a constant rate. However, the UCLA team has gone to great lengths to verify their calibrations and are convinced that, even if their calculations involve a large margin of error, there is far too much divergence for the dog to be only 14,000 years old. And if the figures do stack up, then the timing has great significance. Dogs may have been around when humans were going through an important transformation — into creators of cultural artefacts, when scientists believe humans acquired language. And as we shall see in Chapter 3, David Paxton has developed some quite startling and radical theories as to what this might have meant; not only to us, but to that unfortunate evolutionary "also ran", the Neanderthal.

Regardless of when it occurred, though, such domestication would have been without any conscious act or realisation that the unwanted, scavenging canids were becoming extensions of our ancestors' ears and noses; and the human group, an extension of the ancestral dog's brain. We began to rely on our furry auditory prosthesis, and they to rely on us.

These, then, were the terms of Paxton's "genetic contract". We traded an ecological niche, including rights to share our technology, in return for their superb senses of hearing and smell.

WHO'S GOT IT RIGHT?

So which of these origin theories is right? Was the first dog a pet, an insinkerator or an efficient detector system and alarm?

Well, really, that's a trick question, because in a sense they all are. I have chosen to present the theories as mutually exclusive scenarios because they're easier to grasp that way, but actually that's an artifice.

All these processes were probably taking place simultaneously, and perhaps occurred as slightly different variants in many places and at many times. Although the old dilemma of the origin of the dog has now been resolved in favour of the wolf, the jury is still out on whether dog domestication had a single origin which radiated out, or was the result of many domestication events across the world under a similar congruence of circumstance. Perhaps it was that there were many experiments along these lines. Whether many or only one succeeded it's hard to know — but either way, the central reasoning remains the same.

There are a couple of apparent conflicts between the theories. Firstly, the question of whether early hominids had a concept of "pets". On balance, I feel that Coppinger's dismissal of this as simply placing modern values on early hominid behaviour is unfair. We have ample evidence today of hunter-gatherer communities showing this behaviour — a behaviour which is a direct expression of the strength of the human nurturing instinct. There is no doubt that by the time we have focused on, generalised nurturing was already irrevocably entrenched in the *Homo sapiens* genotype. Pet keeping probably happened from time to time, much as it does today. Whether that was enough on its own, though, to produce the stable breeding populations necessary for true symbiosis with humans is less certain. Probably not. And it is likely that more regular pet-keeping occurred after dogs were already loosely associating with human camps.

The dates themselves are a moot point. If we rely only on archaeological evidence, then we are stuck with the dates at which humans started to establish villages, around 14,000 BP. If we accept the mitochondrial DNA analysis, then we really start moving backward into key events in human evolution. This question is unlikely to be resolved for some time.

However, what can be said is that the irrevocable coming together of human and dog to form mixed-species communities could not have happened before the niche of human home bases, whether mobile or not, evolved. It's a question of proximity. Large numbers of the animals had to be living close enough to us for tameness to become a generalised species trait. Natural selection cannot occur without genetic diversity; there has to be sufficient choice to select from.

As scavengers, living off the detritus of human community life, the earliest wolf–dogs were in a relationship biologists describe as commensal, a relationship still commonly seen today, as the descriptions of Italian wolves and unowned dogs, by researchers such as Boitano, clearly illustrate. As the two species — hominid and canid — moved physically closer, not only were the opportunities for nurturing and pet keeping dramatically increased, but it opened the way for a new biological relationship: that of symbionts.

It was presumably these symbiotic or mixed-species communities that were the units on which natural selection was operating. In times of intense competition for resources, which must have occurred periodically, the combined unit would be slightly more likely to prevail than either wolf or human community alone. When it comes to the crunch, humans can be pretty ruthless eradicators of competitors; witness the plight of the modern wolf. Those canines which slipped under the veil of human otherness were no longer vulnerable to their most serious threat. And if it came to strong competition between human groups, those that didn't have the advantage of an early warning system were slightly more likely to succumb to guerrilla-style hostility. Or if they didn't, perhaps they adopted the practice from neighbouring groups pretty quick smart. By pooling senses and resources, mixed-species communities gained the competitive edge. It is little wonder that around 12,000 BP, when bands of *Homo sapiens* migrated from the old world to the new, the dogs went too.

Was the "contract" a good one? Well, on population grounds alone you have to say it was. Humans cover the world and, as we shall see in Chapter 3, dogs and the other domestic animals that followed have played a key part in that conquest. As for the dog, you only have to look around. Today in the United States there are 55 *million* dogs. There are only 20,000 wolves. The modern wolf population has a fraction of the genetic diversity of the dog. If I were a "selfish gene" intent on replication, I'd sooner be hosted by a dog's body than a wolf's.

Call it a symbiosis, call it a bargain, call it a "genetic contract" if you will. None of these descriptions is perfect; each will attract its quibbles and critics. But the fact remains that there is something unique and special about our relationship with the dog.

At some stage in our prehistory, a "choice" was made by two very different, yet similar species. A choice to cooperate rather than to compete. And in that cooperation, birth was given to the ultimate competitor.

CHAPTER 2

EVOLVING TOGETHER: THE DOG

HAVING established the basis of the prehistoric "genetic contract", we now turn to look at what happened next to the two species. In the dog, the changes are obvious. Take a walk in the local park and our impact on their evolution is immediately apparent. You'll see a grab bag of breeds, a dog of almost any shape, colour or size — anyone would have difficulty convincing visiting space aliens they weren't all members of totally different species. They have been described as the most plastic of all animals, their physical malleability a delight to dog breeders. And it is probably this apparent ease of transformation which has helped convince us that we actually created dogs.

What is less immediately obvious is the effect *they* have had on *us*. After all, our appearance hasn't changed as a result (although, as we will discover, David Paxton has a startling proposal that they *may* even have influenced the shape of our face). Yet by any measure, the impact of the human–dog association has been profound. In Chapter 3, we will see how it is possible to pinpoint key loci on a chart of human evolution where, if we had not already formed a relationship with dogs, humanity may have veered off in another direction entirely. But what I want to explore in this chapter is what it meant for the dog. How did one species produce such diverse grandchildren? And, more importantly, how much did the association cost the dog?

RETARDED WOLVES

With diminished brains and congenital defects, these abducted and enslaved forms are the mindless drabs of the sheep flock, the udder-dragging hypertrophied cow, the psychopathic racehorse, and the infantilised dog who will age into a blasé touch-me-bear, padding through the hospital ward until he has a breakdown and bites the next hand.[1]

What have we done?

Anthropologist Paul Shepard, in his disturbing condemnation of the domestication process published in the 1993 book of essays, *The Biophilia Hypothesis*, pulls no punches. He likens the transformation from wolf to dog to the infliction of slavery on the African people. Worse — because at least the human slaves could be freed by political and social action, whereas these "goofies, congenitally damaged, cannot. If freed, they die in the streets or become feral liabilities".[2]

It's a pretty grim picture: that the development of the dog has, in the end, proved a very one-sided affair, with the clear beneficiary being humans, not the canid. It's a view which, while perhaps not always put quite as starkly as this, has been forwarded by a number of reputable scientists and philosophers.

Unfortunately, some of the facts could be seen to support it. Both the fossil record and contemporary comparisons of dogs and wolves show that the transition from wolf to domestic dog meant a reduction in sensory perception. And, more worrying, in brain size. The brain of a modern dog is 20 per cent smaller than that of the equivalent-sized wolf. It's a process that has been described by zoologist Helmut Hemmer as the suppression of the animal's *Merkwelt*; its "perceptual world".[3]

The reason for the suppression of *Merkwelt* is not hard to understand. While alertness and a quick response to stress are obvious survival traits in the wild animal, the opposite is required of an animal that lives with people. From an adaptive point of view, it is hopeless if a wolf-dog reacts to the approach of humans with fear and aggression; the life of such an animal within a human community will be short. Even if it simply runs away, it's at a disadvantage compared with its less sensitive brethren, as unnecessary energy will be spent in the exertion. Docility and tolerance of change and stress are the best behavioural bet, and Hemmer has argued in his 1990 book *Domestication: The Decline of Environmental Appreciation* that reducing the animal's sense of its environment was essential to domestication.

What this means is that the acuity of the senses has been dulled. It's an easy concept to grasp intellectually, but difficult to deal with emotionally. I try to imagine watching a colour television, and then slowly turning the colour down so that it doesn't quite reach black and white, but slightly dulls the vibrant colours. I know this isn't quite fair, because obviously such a process occurred over many generations rather than within one individual. But still, it is undeniable that in this way, the modern dog experiences something less than its wild ancestor.

What's more, Shepard, with his charge of "infantilised dog", has highlighted a process that also clearly occurred to produce the modern dog. Neotenisation is the technical name, and what it means is that the characteristics of a juvenile are retained into adulthood. Put simply, features of the puppy remain in the sexually mature dog. Either that, or you could say that sexual maturity is brought forward to an earlier developmental stage. The Chihuahua shows an extreme case of this. With its domed head and large eyes, it actually resembles the wolf foetus even more than the cub. More than one vet has commented that there doesn't seem much room left in the adult male Chihuahua for anything other than testicles and testosterone.

It was Stephen Jay Gould who drew attention to the appeal of the baby animal, famously tracking the neotenisation of Mickey Mouse in his book *The Panda's Thumb*. If you look at the earliest Disney cartoons, the leggy creature dancing on a steamboat is barely recognisable as the big-headed, squashed bodied character of today. Mr Mouse's head to body ratio increased substantially over 30 years, eventually approaching a ratio more like that of a baby than of an adult.[4]

The modern Mickey Mouse acts as something called a "supranormal stimulus" in which those features that would normally elicit care-giving responses from humans, such as big eyes and a large head, have been exaggerated. The husband's dread of being "cuckolded" owes its labelling to another example of supranormal stimuli, exhibited in the classic textbook behaviour of the cuckoo. This bird lays its eggs in the nests of other hapless birds then leaves; once hatched, the cuckoo chicks have bigger mouths than the other hatchlings, and so induce a frenzy of feeding from the surrogate parents who eventually neglect their own natural offspring. I'm not suggesting we'd throw out a child for a puppy, but the human cuteness factor has meant designing cartoons or Cavalier King Charles Spaniels that are even more baby-like than a human baby.

So is this what has happened? Is this what we've done? Have humans, in some kind of bizarre but self-inflicted mimicry of the cuckoo, simply created a monstrous child substitute, complete with the supranormal stimulus of unconditional love and permanent dependency to replace our wayward and often uncontrollable children? And in the process, have we warped the noble wolf, diminished its brain and its sensory appreciation of this world, and doomed it to a life of intellectually compromised indefinite childhood?

The images *are* disturbing. Not least because of their plausibility. But, while not in any way condoning some of the worst excesses of animal "exploitation", I believe such interpretations are wrong. And this is based not on the instinctive emotional rejection that most people feel when hearing their loved ones described as congenitally retarded slaves, but on a belief that it misses the point. What it fails to take into account is the biological basis of domestication.

TURNING WOLVES INTO DOGS

In trying to understand the transition from wolf to dog, the first question that springs to mind is this: how do you turn a wolf into a West Highland White? Or a Newfoundland or a Chihuahua?

The answer is you can't — deliberately, that is. What would have been selected for by humans — and that not intentionally, at least to start with — is behaviours. And as in any evolutionary adaptation, the remarkable changes in form were the result.

Deliberate human selection for appearance rather than for behaviour is mostly recent. The fact is, despite what many people believe of the ancient lineage of their favourite breeds, many dog breeds have only been developed in the last 150 years. The rise of "dog fancy" was a Victorian phenomenon, and coincided with the new understanding of heredity made possible by Charles Darwin's publication of *On the Origin of Species* in 1859. The first dog show was not held by the Kennel Council in England until 1887, and it marked the beginning of the formalised breed standards which have driven canine evolution ever since. The replacement of performance with championship ribbons as the key determinant of "fitness" — that is, determining which animal gets to pass down its genes — is for the most part new.

But the process by which dogs evolved for probably many thousands of years, nevertheless, had everything to do with humans. Not the obvious interference of humans determining which animals would breed, but something far more subtle. It was the often delicate, sometimes crass, influence of adapting to life in and around the habitations and social structures of another species. The result has been, without it being, I believe, in any way a negative thing, that dogs' lives have become so closely entwined with our own that they do not exist without us.

How that change occurred is fascinating and in exploring it, we can perhaps begin to answer some of the more strident criticisms of animal domestication. And the place we will start is with the mechanism which probably played the biggest part in dog evolution — neotenisation. Because it is from this process that most of the concerns arise.

PERMANENT CHILDREN?

The charge of "monstrous child substitute" is unsettling. It certainly contains elements of truth. Watching my mother's young Tibetan Spaniels, it is obvious that a human projection of "cuteness" played a big role in their breed's development. I'm certainly not immune to it. They *are* cute and I subconsciously refer to them as "the kids" — but to say that they are a degenerate or retarded version of the wolf is misleading. And this issue encapsulates one of the most common misconceptions about neotenisation. It implies that it is a backward step. But rather than being a degenerate process, neotenisation is an excellent way to evolve.

If you think about it, chance mutations, the building blocks of natural selection, are a pretty risky business. In a complex organism, reliant on the cohesive interaction of mind-bogglingly large numbers of parts, any disruption is more likely to be harmful than beneficial. A mutation which impedes the development of eyes, for example, is going to prove a disadvantage — unless, of course, your species happens to live in the dark. More importantly, the mutation which results in no eyes, perhaps due to a change in the genetic code for one particular protein, may well wreak havoc on other organs. Our proteins are inherently thrifty; a particular protein will have many different functions in different systems of the body. However it does mean that if you mess with one system, you risk an effect on many.

But there is a way of reducing the risk. If the mutation simply alters the *rate* at which parts of the system develop, the odds of still producing a functional creature in the end are tremendously increased. In this case it is the timing of a developmental event that is modified slightly, rather than it being an all-or-nothing change. And this is essentially what happens with neotenisation. All in all, it's a relatively safe way forward.

Many species are believed to have evolved this way. The salamander is one. A wonderful-looking creature, the salamander resembles a rejected extra from *Aliens* with its stumpy legs and fluttering gills. Neither fish nor frog, it has been a popular aquarium pet and essential biology example since our earliest infatuation with amphibians. Its popularity is not surprising. Along with great looks comes its ability to live either in water or on land. In order to achieve this remarkable versatility, the salamander's development has been arrested not at the juvenile stage, but right back at the larval stage. It's a fairly gruesome thought, but the salamander's neotenisation is like humans becoming sexually mature as over-large foetuses.

Other species to take the neotenisation route include our own *Homo sapiens* — although not, fortunately, to the foetal stage. Our willingness to learn, our sociability, even our flattened faces, all are thought to be a result of this process.

Not only is it a mistake to think that neotenisation must be a "backward" step, but it also overlooks a very important point about maturation. And this is something that annoys American biologist Raymond Coppinger. It is very easy to think that development is aimed towards "growing up". As Coppinger points out, everyone is always saying to you "grow up" as if adulthood were the Holy Grail of the developmental process.[5] What he is getting at is that at each stage of the life cycle, the organism is superbly adapted for its current niche. The foetus, for example, uses the placenta to extract oxygen from its environment, whereas the newborn baby switches rapidly to a completely different set of organs, the lungs. The tongue of a newborn mammal is a highly specialised organ, equipped with an exquisite sense of touch for teat location, extraordinary dexterity, and a specially devoted part of the brain which eventually atrophies. Later, the infant switches to another means of obtaining nutrients: chewing. And what is interesting is that the two means are not directly related. Just as the lung and placenta are separate organs, so chewing and sucking are discrete motor patterns. Rather than a sudden switch, as is seen to the lung, one behaviour is gradually replaced by another, with a period in the juvenile stage during which both actions may be seen. The adult tongue has lost many of the abilities it once had — as generations of parents will have discovered trying to copy the tongue curls of their smug young children ("Can you do this, Mum?").

Coppinger sums this up in a chapter on the evolution of working dogs in *The Domestic Dog: Its Evolution, Behaviour and Interactions with People*: "Growing up is not a matter of growing bigger but rather remodelling, or metamorphosing ... Behaviour patterns appear, overlap, and disappear as the organism leaves one ontogenetic [developmental] stage and enters another."[6] In other words, just because an animal is at a certain developmental stage, it doesn't mean that it is any more or less adapted to its environment than at the stage before or after. (The environment at the dependent stage includes, of course, the care given by the adult mother, so although the infant may be "perfectly adapted" to the dependent state, it has to continue to later developmental stages in order for the species to reproduce.) As the environment changes, the attributes of an earlier life stage may be better suited to the new situation. For example, when wolf-dogs linked up with humans, they didn't need the usual adult sense of caution in novel situations to be as highly developed — but they *did* need the generalised sociability of their juvenile state.

MAKING BABIES?

This leads us to the other problem of thinking that neotenisation was about creating monstrous child substitutes. It implies that we did it *to* them. That it occurred because humans were consciously selecting for animals that *looked* like babies. But, as I mentioned earlier, the appearance was a side effect; early in the domestication process, what was actually being selected for, and that unintentionally, was behaviour. In the beginning, it was a clear case of form following function.

As we touched on in Chapter 1, young mammals and even birds have a number of important attributes. They are highly social, approaching others with curiosity and openness and showing obvious signs of distress in the absence of companions. Just as importantly, they are also strongly motivated to solicit care from others, parent or otherwise. This has its benefits. Who, for example, can resist the cry of a lonely puppy? Not many, and no doubt this has something to do with the fact that surveys show 41 per cent of people allow their pets to sleep on their beds![7]

There is another feature of juveniles that is critically significant to domestication, and this is their capacity to cross the species barrier. Most adult animals have a strong sense of species recognition, a "people like us" factor, and are wary of others. It's a survival trait; except where there is a clearly beneficial symbiosis, other animals may be competitors or even predators and keeping a distance is generally the wisest option. But many young mammals have no such compunction and, if allowed by their mothers, will frolic with whatever happens to be around.

The explanation of this lies in what is termed the socialisation period. This is the critical time of youth when a young animal learns how to interact with others — how to recognise members of its own species or group, how to communicate, and how not to bite its siblings too hard — or risk an ear-splitting squawk. All essential skills for operating in an adult social group. The socialisation period occurs quite early. In the modern dog it peaks between six and 16 weeks of age, and as some rather unfortunate experiments have shown, animals that miss out on appropriate interactions at this age never quite make up for it; they are doomed to a life as social misfits.

What's relevant about the socialisation period here is that it also provides an opportunity to learn to relate to other species. In fact, if certain young animals spend time with other species during such a critical phase, they can almost come to view them as members of their own species.

A simplistic version of this is demonstrated by young ducks. It's long been known that if newly hatched ducklings are confronted with a human in the first 24 hours of life, that's who they will imprint on; trailing after that person as if he or she were their own mother. The comparison isn't quite right because the imprinting of 24-hour-old ducks isn't strictly analogous to the more subtle interactions involved in complex social rules (the difference between "it's shaped like this therefore I will follow it" and "this is obviously an entity I can communicate with and if I bite like this, it reacts like that, and if I wag my tail thus it responds with a pat"). But the meaning of the illustration is fairly clear.

A more complex example can be seen in many households. Take the relationship between the cat and the dog — long a popular subject for artists and satirists and, most importantly, cartoonists. (It's hard to know how Garfield would manage to get up in the morning — or afternoon as is more usually the case — if he didn't have the slobbering Odie to put through hell.) But as every dog–cat-combination owner knows, cats and dogs can actually become inseparable friends, particularly if they are managed in the right way. And this means introducing them when they are young. It's an awful lot easier to present a kitten to a dog than it is to introduce it to a fully grown cat — a lot safer for the human involved as well, as anyone who's come between a feline in full hiss, spit, scratch mode and the nearest exit would know.

The socialisation period has tremendous significance for an animal's ability to bond with humans. In one substantial study conducted by Freedman and associates in the early 1960s, a number of bitches gave birth in a field away from human contact. The puppies were removed from the field at varying ages, stroked, played with, and made to generally socialise with people for a time, and then returned with their mothers to the field. At 14 weeks the puppies were all tested for their level of attraction to a human handler. The pups that had been socialised at two to three weeks of age scored low on the attraction test. Maximal attraction and friendliness to humans was seen in the group that was socialised at five weeks. By nine weeks sociability was already tapering off, with this group showing a tendency to avoid rather than approach the handler. By 14 weeks of age the reaction was extreme. These pups, that had had no contact with humans at all, were very fearful, tending to cower at some distance, and despite further gentle handling, they proved to be basically untrainable.[8]

So, if you were trying to produce an animal which would remain friendly and outgoing to humans throughout life, what you would need to do is manipulate and extend the socialisation period. And this is exactly what is thought unintentionally to have happened to produce the dog.

It is interesting to note that if modern wolf cubs are put through a socialisation procedure similar to the family dog, they are still far more wary of humans and unpredictable as adults than dogs are. It has been widely suggested by scientists such as Dr John Bradshaw at the Anthrozoology Institute that one of the fundamental differences between cats and dogs and most other mammals is their ability to be simultaneously socialised to their own species and to people.

Let's put ourselves back now to where we left off in Chapter 1, with humans and semi-tame wolves — or dogs — living loosely together. Of course, Pleistocene humans did not deliberately "manipulate" the socialisation period. But if in the early stages there was no conscious selection by humans for canine traits, how was the process of neotenisation and extending the socialisation period achieved? This is where one of the most fascinating and outstanding experiments in the whole area of developmental ethology (the study of animal behaviour) comes in.

FRIENDLY FOXES

On the edges of a town in western Siberia, and surrounded by high wire fences, is a very unusual farming operation. Inside are rows and rows of pens and cages, each about 100 centimetres by 80 centimetres. They contain over 2000 animals and, surprisingly, they are not chickens or mink, but foxes.

There is something else a little unexpected about the situation. They seem extremely friendly for foxes. Many of them jump up at the front of the cage, whining and panting as if begging for a pat. Their faces are somehow softer and more appealing than you would expect, and a couple cock their heads, showing soft, floppy ears. Some of them are strange colours too. The majority are a uniform silver grey, but a couple show quite striking patterns of piebald black and white. One has four white socks on its feet, a white ruff around its neck, and an attractive white star extending from between the eyes to spread and cover the muzzle. It looks like a Border Collie. In fact, that's exactly what all these strange foxes would remind you of: dogs.

This farm is the site of one of the most substantial and celebrated experiments in animal domestication. I am relying for this description on Anatoli Ruvinsky, Russian scientist and now lecturer in genetics at the school of animal science in the University of New England, New South Wales, who spent ten years involved with the project, which has been running for more than 40 years. I was very fortunate to meet Ruvinski, because although I'd read some reports on the experiments, I was now able to hear a first-hand account.[9]

It is quite an extraordinary tale. In the mid 1950s, a fox farm was established with around 200 inhabitants. Such farms weren't uncommon in this part of the world, as the silver fox was beginning to be bred for its coat. This one was different, however, because its designers were not interested in producing the perfect pelt, but in exploring the process of canine domestication. In particular, they were keen to discover how it was that processes which had virtually no variation in the wild population, such as the breeding cycle, could be so dramatically altered in domestic animals. In short, the scientists decided to try to domesticate the fox. In order to do this, they chose to select on the basis of one characteristic only: behaviour. So, within their original population of several hundred animals, only those that were the least fearful and the most relaxed around humans were allowed to reproduce. Essentially, that meant the "tamest" ones.

What amazed even the most optimistic of them was that within five generations — only seven years — they were starting to see dramatic changes. The first noticeable change, perhaps not surprisingly, was behaviour. The animals were much friendlier to humans, actively approaching them rather than cowering at the back of the cage or remaining neutral. And it was non-specific — they were just as welcoming of a newcomer as they were of their regular handlers. They started to show tail wagging; they began lying down at the approach of human visitors. In later generations, some even showed protective behaviour — growling and acting aggressively if a strange person approached someone they perceived as their "master".

Within ten years, the population of the farm numbered in the thousands. Many of the new foxes were sourced from outside, ensuring continued genetic variability and allowing the researchers to be very stringent in selecting breeding stock because the pool was so large.

Ten to 15 years after the start, widespread morphological changes were apparent. New colour variations were appearing. Some all white, some all black; commonly, the patched black-and-white pattern I described at the beginning. Not only that, but a number of foxes had blue eyes. What fascinated the researchers was that in a wild population, the odds against finding such a mutation were tremendous — one in millions, perhaps. Yet it was appearing here commonly.

The shape of the face was starting to show some variation too. Floppy ears and shorter faces — "smashed muzzles", as Ruvinski so aptly describes them. Much like the bulldog and other chondrodystrophoid breeds (those with short faces or limbs) seen in the dog world today. All this, while the researchers were still simply selecting on behaviour.

Perhaps the most surprising results were the physiological changes. First, the animals started to moult at odd times, not just in spring. But more intriguing were the changes to the oestrus cycle. Silver foxes, and wolves for that matter, breed only once a year. Given the climatic extremes they are subjected to in Siberia, it's not hard to understand why. Bringing pups into the world when it's 40°C below freezing outside is no guarantee of child-rearing success. Yet within 15 years, some of the experimental foxes were coming into season twice a year. There is only one other canid which has this oestrus cycle. The domestic dog.

These dramatic developments were reflected in the fox's biochemistry.[10] After twelve generations, the level of blood corticosteroids—the "stress" hormone—halved, and after thirty generations halved again. Brain serotonin shot up. Major variations in hormone and neurotransmitters were creating the cascade of unexpected physical side effects.

And perhaps most impressive of all were the radical alterations to the rate of maturation. The domesticated female fox reached her first oestrus a full month earlier than her wild relatives. The young fox's socialisation period was lengthened by three whole weeks. A transformation uncannily close to that of wolf to dog.

Eventually a house was built inside the farm, complete with backyards for the foxes to play in. The experimenters spent much of the day in and around the houses, with the foxes living in the yards. There, they interacted like a typical family with dogs. According to Ruvinsky, visitors were overwhelmed by the experience of meeting these "wild" animals, wagging their tails and greeting them with every expression of affection and joy.

The project has surpassed all expectations, amazing everyone involved with the power and simplicity of the domestication process, and more strikingly, the speed. To the Russian researchers, the experience has been like watching hundreds, if not thousands, of years of dog domestication speeded up to the blink of an eye.

The lessons for reconstructing the earliest canine domestication process are clear. The only thing that needed to be selected for, and that certainly did not need to happen consciously, was tameness. Neotenisation, the mechanism by which sociability (or tameness) of canids is increased, then takes over. And neotenisation, by tampering with the levels of major hormonal and neural control systems, can contribute to a host of seemingly unrelated changes.

All that was needed was for the less friendly wolves to be removed from the breeding pool, and the rest would follow. Changes in coat colour, increased sociability, an extended socialisation period, barking, and even a dioestrus breeding cycle — all can be generated by the simple expedient of selecting for friendliness to humans.

SENSORY DEPRIVATION

With a better understanding of the biology of domestication, any concerns about humans creating "monstrous child substitutes" should be allayed. Clearly, in the early transition from wolf to dog, humans did not deliberately select for animals that looked to us like children. It was "natural selection" in its truest sense. Only the tamest animals could take advantage of the niche human settlements provided and, within that group, the tamest again were more likely to survive and reproduce. And the tamest ones were those that had the most childlike appearance.

Nor was it necessarily a backward step. Juveniles are less stereotyped in their behaviours and therefore more open to new experiences — a very useful trait for living in mixed-species communities. It also means that the animal's capacity for learning may be enhanced throughout life. However, there are a couple of concerns I have more trouble answering.

Hemmer's contention that dogs have lost part of their sensory perception of the world as a result of domestication seems fairly damning. Their hearing reduced in range, their sense of smell became less acute; their worlds perhaps dimmer than those of wolves. A life, maybe, of olfactory and auditory "myopia".

I know that their world is no longer what it was, but what I cannot decide is whether it means anything. Humans have also lost the acuity of many senses; the olfactory being one. We, too, have been "domesticated" — and I'm not the first to suggest this. Yet I don't feel any sense of loss. I can't imagine what my world would be like if I still inhabited the scentscape of my ancestors; nor, for that matter, can I imagine the living experience of my dogs, whose perceptual world is still in many ways more vibrant than my own. It's like trying to imagine what it would be like to see infrared at the same time as visible light, or feel the clicking feedback of sonar. A fascinating intellectual exercise, but how could it be something that I *miss*?

Of all the accusations against the dog, the hardest to address is that of "diminished brains". It is undeniable that the canid brain has been reduced proportionally in size during the transition from wolf to dog. However, whether that is telling us that somehow dogs are "less intelligent" than wolves is hard to know. How would you measure it? And would the results have any meaning? Certainly, if the test were sensory perception and rapidity of response, the wolf would be the winner. Those parts of the brain determining alertness and awareness of the environment are atrophied in the dog. But in its current environment it doesn't need them. What if the criteria were trainability? The dog here is the clear winner. Some people may see it as a sign of extreme stupidity to willingly learn the bidding of another, and I guess that's a matter of opinion. But the point is that it is a completely appropriate skill for living with humans. In some ways intelligence is a matter of matching behaviour to environment. To compare intelligence in creatures that have evolved in different niches is a bit like deciding which has hit upon the best mode of travel: the dolphin or the horse.

A BREED FOR EVERY NEED

All this is only the first part of the story: the "unconscious" phase. It is highly likely that in the early stages of the association, the appearance of the wolf-dog remained relatively unchanged, perhaps even for many thousands of years. Not until the animals started regularly breeding within human settlements would there have been any chance of deliberate interference by humans and, even then, for a long time the influence would have been subtle. The interference, such as it was, would have consisted more of killing the ones that bit children or giving extra food to the good hunters than anything organised.

We can see this sort of selection working even today. David Paxton points to the treatment by locals of Papua New Guinea of their top hunting dogs. Unlike the other dogs in the community, these ones are often the picture of health, with gleaming coats and well-developed physiques, clearly showing they get the best cuts of meat. But pity the hunter that's injured in the line of duty. A former favourite can quickly find itself at the bottom of the social ladder. With its food withheld, it must scrounge for scraps, and is often cruelly teased by its former partners in a way that is utterly unfathomable to Western eyes.

By at least 12,000 years ago, we can surmise from the fossil record, many, perhaps most, human villages were populated by small-headed, small-toothed tame dogs. With some degree of variation, the population, compared with today, would have been a fairly uniform lot.

What happened next? At some stage, the subtle influence on canid development exerted by the mere presence of humans changed into something more deliberate. Apart from anything, our ancestors would have been faced with a new problem: puppies — and lots of them.

Reproduction in a stable wolf pack is very limited. Wolves come into season and breed only once a year. And the pack operates under strict hierarchical rules. In most years, only the alpha male and the alpha female produce a litter; breeding in the rest of the group is suppressed by the dominant pair. (Often violently — if one of the dominant pair notices a subordinate attempting to mate, they will physically intervene to stop it. If a subordinate bitch does manage to mate and produce young, the puppies are killed within a couple of days.)

Dogs, however, come into season not once, but twice, a year. With traditional wolf social structures disrupted by neotenisation and the move towards multi-species living, suppression of breeding would no longer have been the norm. Just about any female could have a litter — and no doubt did. The result can only be imagined. While the image of Neolithic villages overrun by cute bundles of fluff is very appealing, the situation would never have been allowed to get to that stage. Despite these dogs having a shorter lifespan than the modern pet, at some point the over-population problem would have had to be resolved.

Without recourse to modern desexing techniques, the only

available tool for controlling the population was death. It is interesting to see today how cultures around the world that do not practise desexing approach the issue. A Japanese student I asked remembered his grandmother putting a litter of puppies in a bag and drowning them in the local creek. A Mexican student had a twist to the familiar tale. She recalled visiting a tiny village some distance from Mexico City where, in the community of 70 people, there were 120 dogs. And all of them were male! Clearly the locals approached the population dilemma by killing all the females. These examples are probably exactly the kind of population control practised by most cultures for millennia.

Of course, other cultures still have regarded this fecundity as a bounty. In communities which are starved of other protein sources, the easily caught and abundant canid provides a mobile larder, and one which doesn't have to be penned or otherwise confined. And dogs as food source probably played a role in the colonisation by humans of several parts of the world, particularly by the island-hopping Polynesians.

Once humans are playing an active role in deciding who dies, the opportunity for deliberate selection is created, whether for function, which in itself affects form (choosing dogs capable of chasing gazelles might produce a long-limbed, streamlined variety), or for the simple love of a form itself. Thus are the seeds planted for an obsession that has bloomed ever since: breeding the "perfect" animal. Despite its critics, the fascination with breeding and competition remains strong. It will no doubt continue into the next millennium, as we grapple with the science and the ethics of genetic manipulation.

We can't say when exactly these nudges, both subtle and otherwise, started to give rise to distinctive breed types — part of the problem being that bones don't tell us much about the length and colour of a coat. But we do know that the process was well under way by at least 4000 BP.[11] The Egyptians of the Middle Kingdom already had many of the basic dog types, including the graceful and speedy sight hounds for hunting, the more heavily built mastiff or guarding dogs, and short-legged dogs, which were perhaps used for hunting rodents. We know this because Egyptian frescoes of the time feature dogs recognisably similar to modern greyhounds, Bullmastiffs and terriers. By the time of the Romans, the list of types includes herding dogs and the decorative lapdogs. Given the remarkable capacity of the canine phenotype to withstand all sorts of developmental mutations, it probably didn't take many generations for local variants to spring up all over the place. Clearly, deliberate selection by humans for distinctive shapes was by this stage also taking place; a classic example being the Pekingese, which is thought to be around 2000 years old, and was bred during the time of the Han dynasty to resemble as closely as possible the lion revered in Chinese mythology. By the time the Victorians started fiddling around with what is called "line breeding" (that is, breeding animals back to their close relatives), there was already a veritable doggy supermarket from which to choose their fancy.

One of the earliest traits selected for by humans may have been coat colour. This would have allowed humans to more easily distinguish dogs from wild wolves — when there are sheep to protect from marauders, it's important not to spear your dog by mistake. But there is another possibility. Studies have shown that the genes for the pigment melanin (which would make a dog black) also affect other compounds produced in the body by the same tyrosine pathway. These include hormones such as adrenalin, and neurotransmitters (which pass messages in the brain) such as dopamine. Both of these compounds affect behaviour, and it has been suggested by Juliet Clutton-Brock and Helmut Hemmer among others, that light-coloured dogs might have had a more amenable temperament than darker wolf-like individuals.[12] This idea, that the earliest dogs may have been a light, tawny yellow, gains some support from the fact that this is exactly the colour of the modern dingo and the Southeast Asian pariah dog.

The clear delineation of major dog types seen by the time of the Egyptians 3000 to 4000 BP indicates humans had already formed some concept of heredity, and perhaps they had got to the point of favouring certain sires, so that when a bitch was ready to mate, she was kept confined with the "appropriate" dog. A dog that was an excellent hunter might be favoured, or one that was an outstanding watchdog.

By Roman times the concept that you could breed for behaviour and appearance was obviously understood. Clutton-Brock points to the advice of Columella, written in the first century AD:

As guardian of the farm a dog should be chosen which is of ample bulk with a loud and sonorous bark in order that it may terrify the malefactor, first because he hears it and then because he sees it; indeed, sometimes without being even seen it puts to flight the crafty plotter merely by the terror which its growling inspires. It should be the same colour all over, white being the colour which should rather be chosen for a sheep-dog and black for a farmyard dog; for a dog of varied colouring is not to be recommended for either purpose. The shepherd prefers a white dog because it is unlike a wild beast, and sometimes a plain means of distinction is required in the dogs when one is driving off wolves in the obscurity of early morning or even dusk, lest one strike a dog instead of a wild beast. The farmyard dog, which is pitted against the wicked wiles of men, if the thief approaches in the clear light of day, has a more alarming appearance if it is black.

Sound advice, no doubt — and advice that has obviously been followed to this day, judging by the forbidding colour scheme of the Rottweiler or the Doberman.

The next known explosion of dog breeds occurred in Europe in the Middle Ages. The aristocracy of the time placed great stock in the hunt, which developed into a highly formulaic ritual. A different style of dog was required for each choice of prey, so deer hounds were developed for hunting deer, otter hounds for otter, and so on. Not satisfied with this degree of demarcation, dogs were bred for different stages of the hunt; sight hounds for spotting and chasing game, scent hounds for tracking it. It is doubtful whether one all-purpose animal couldn't have done the job, but it was all part of the art of the hunt.

The establishment of breed standards at the end of the nineteenth century marked the next leap in canine diversity. Today there are more than 170 dog breeds registered in Australia alone, grouped by breeders into the following major classes: working dogs, terriers, toy dogs, sporting dogs, gun dogs, hounds, utility and non-sporting dogs.

THE BUILDING BLOCKS OF DIVERSITY

As we have already mentioned, to generate all these types there was no need to select for things one at a time. No one would have sat down and thought "All right, well this year I'll go for nice short legs for getting down rabbit holes, and once that's established, I think a slimmer, more upright tail would be nice". Or if they did, they were doomed to disappointment. We now know that genes rarely act in isolation. As we saw with the example of the foxes selected simply on behaviour, genes tend not to affect just a single aspect of the phenotype (how the genes are physically expressed), but rather a whole package of appearance and behaviour. Even without understanding the mechanics, Darwin himself noted that "if man goes on selecting, and thus augmenting any peculiarity, he will almost certainly modify unintentionally other parts of the structure, owing to the mysterious laws of correlation".[13] So even selection for, say, tracking ability might lead to a host of unexpected changes in the dog's appearance.

The sources of variation are many. The most important is, of course, different degrees of neoteny, and certainly some dogs appear more puppy-like than others. But variation is not quite that simple, and this is probably a good point to clarify another common misconception about neoteny's role in breed development.

Neoteny seems to imply that at one end of the scale you have an animal that is most like an adult wolf, such as the husky, and at the other end, an animal most like a wolf cub, such as my mother's Tibetan Spaniels, as if this were a linear arrangement, with development being "stopped" once it reaches a certain stage. This notion has been reinforced by our understanding of the hunting sequence. It is popularly supposed that dog development has been "stopped" at various points along the hunting development path. Thus the sheepdog generally goes no further than the circling phase, whereas the cattle dog goes the next step to nip at the heels; hopefully neither completes the sequence to the kill — an unfortunate and messy possibility, reduced by good training.

But rather than stopping development at some point in a pre-determined sequence, what neotenisation (more accurately in this instance described as heterochrony) actually does is throws all behaviours into the melting pot. Just as the juvenile shows both suckling and chewing motions, so too does it display both adult and neonatal behaviour patterns — not necessarily ordered into any functional sequence. This raises the exciting possibility of organising these "bits" of behaviour into brand new sequences.

And this is definitely what has happened in the dog. If not obviously useful, we call the outcome "play". But if it is, this is the basis for a whole new functional behaviour; a behaviour which can be exploited by a delighted or, more likely, selfishly expectant human partner.

The classic example is the Border Collie. Apart from its stunning colouring (and the popularity of the "Footrot Flats" dog), the breed is chiefly known for its "eye stalk" behaviour. This is where the dog drops into a half-crouched position, muzzle pointed directly forward, and "eyeballs" the animal — usually a sheep. This may be followed by the forward moving, slow stalk, then back to the "eye". The point is that "giving eye", this distinctive, stereotyped behaviour, is not even seen in the wolf. According to Raymond Coppinger, it's really a new motor sequence, and one that is so strongly present in the breed, they will literally eye anything that moves; human children included. More than one Border Collie owner has looked up from their book to find the kids have been neatly rounded up!

Other mutations aren't part of the neotenisation package, but have obviously been a source of great joy to breed fanciers. The best known is chondrodystrophy. This is where bone development is disrupted so that the growth plates at the end of long bones (these are the bits of cartilage which allow bones in the young to grow) close up early. The results range from the weird and wonderful to the catastrophic. The short, bowed legs of the pug are due to chondrodystrophy, as is its squashed face. An extreme version of it is seen in the Pekingese, whose face is so flat you could stand a drink on it. Not that I recommend trying — I'm told Pekes don't bear indignity lightly.

A further source of variation is the ancestral wolf itself. All appearances to the contrary, the genetic codes of the dog and the wolf still remain very close. Wolves can mate with a dog and produce fertile young. So can coyotes, for that matter, although DNA analysis reveals there is no evidence that this has ever happened. While it's not known at this stage to what extent this kind of "back breeding" has taken place over the millennia, it has probably occurred from time to time.

THE COLLIE-DINGO

This brings us to another interesting question about the origins of the dog; a question that has intriguing parallels in the human sphere.

One of the hottest debates in the study of human evolution has been the altercation between those who propose a single origin and those who propose a multiple origin of *Homo sapiens*. It's partly a result of confusion over how to interpret the fact that earlier species of *Homo* turned up in Africa and also China 500,000 years ago. (The multiple origin people say this means *H. sapiens* may have evolved independently in different parts of the world. The single origin people, who say *H. sapiens* only came out of Africa around 200,000 years ago, believe the Chinese findings mark a dead-end road; that *H. erectus* became extinct before *H. sapiens* arrived.) At this point, the single origin theorists are clearly winning. There aren't many scientists left who'll even admit at a dinner party to favouring the multi-origin view.

In a rough parallel to this, although without the same intensity, has been the discussion over a multiple versus a single origin of the dog. (Did wolves spontaneously strike up a pact with humans in many different parts of the world? Or did only one subgroup of wolves move into human home camps and evolve into dogs, and from there spread to other human groups?) And in contrast to the argument about humans, at this stage it seems the multi-origin theorists are winning.

Robert Wayne, a biology professor and pivotal member of the UCLA team that is examining the mtDNA (mitochondrial DNA) of the dog, first started researching dog DNA while studying for his PhD.[14] Since that time, as he and his colleagues have collected more and more samples on their way to extraordinary findings about the ancient nature of the dog, he has been first in one camp, then the other. In the first round of mtDNA analyses several years ago, he felt that the genetic variability was so great that it must mean there are more than one origin of the dog. His sympathy was firmly with the multi-originists. Then, many more computations and analyses later, in 1996 it looked as though it must be the other way round. All this variability could have come from just one subpopulation of wolves. Time to shift to the single origins camp. But then in 1997, with the analyses of over 150 dogs and 150 wolves under the team's belt, the evidence had shifted back: multi-origin.[15]

But it's not quite that simple. Professor Wayne found that all the dog sequences could be sorted into four groups or clades. The two major clades showed that most dogs arose from two distinct wolf ancestors. One of the groups was special. It not only contained around 75 per cent of today's dog breeds, it hosted all of the most ancient dog types such as the New Guinea Singing Dog and the greyhound. So even though a second domestication event occurred (probably much later), the evidence suggests that it was one unusual event—an ancient coming together of one subpopulation of wolves with one subpopulation of humans—that gave rise to most of the dogs we know today.

And if the dog *has* come primarily from the one ancestral group, with periodic incursions of genes from other populations of wolves, then perhaps the pariah dog tells us what that original dog would have been like. Menzel and Menzel,[16] amongst others, have suggested that the pariah dog of southern India is the "basic dog"; that every kind of dog we see could be bred from pariah dog stock. Others have suggested the converse: that if you allowed all the dogs in the world to interbreed and live loosely associated with humans, you'd eventually end up with something resembling the pariah dog.

David Paxton has a variation on the theme. Again he looks to the local dogs of Papua New Guinea. Similar to the pariah dog and known locally as dingoes, Paxton has seen in them just about every phenotypic variation imaginable. He and his companion have turned dingo spotting into a bit of a game. "Oh look", they say, "there goes a Dachshund Dingo, that one's an Old English Dingo, and over there, the famous Collie Dingo."

A CO-EVOLUTION

We started out this chapter contending that *Canis familiaris* evolved with *Homo sapiens*. But perhaps the extent to which they have co-evolved is best highlighted not by looking at the dogs that live closest with humans, but those that live farthest away.

The best and longest running studies of free-living, or feral, dogs have been conducted in Italy. Boitano has already been mentioned, but working in the same area, in some cases on the same group of dogs, has been another team headed by an English zoologist, David MacDonald.[17]

Both groups have studied the free-living dogs in and around the villages in the Abruzzo region of central Italy. In some cases the animals occupy similar territories to wolf populations, in others they seem to have moved into niches left vacant by wolf eradication. Their ecology may be similar, but in important ways the lives of the two groups of canids have been found to differ.

First of all, although they form packs, the dogs do not show any cooperative care of the young. Any bitch can have pups, but once she does, she tends to move away from the pack and lead a semi-detached lifestyle for several months. This lack of paternal care is unique to dogs in the canid world. Nor do these wild dogs show cooperative hunting behaviour. In fact, the subjects of the study were rarely observed to hunt. Virtually their entire nutrition is based on scavenging human refuse — larger packs forming in areas with a concentrated food supply, such as the village dumps.

Furthermore, rather than being stable units, the pack structure is fluid with a continual flow to and from the "owned" dog population. One of the significant sources of pup loss identified by the researchers was humans raiding the feral litters, either for pets or to kill them. (Keep the boys and kill the girls, it seems — a male sex bias is apparent in feral dog populations around the world.) Part of this fluidity is artefact, because it is clear death by human intervention was a major contributor to the flux. Perhaps if the groups were independent of human interference, more stable kinship bonds would form. But this presupposes that dogs *can* live independently of humans. The evidence would suggest that they cannot.

The point is that even these so-called free-living dogs do not live independently of humans. Their food is indirectly provided by humans, their reproduction and mortality influenced by them. With the possible exception of the dingo, which has been in Australia for at least 4000 years (and even in this case it is uncertain whether they ever lived entirely independently or moved in and out of Aboriginal camps), nowhere in the world is there a stable dog population living independently of people — unlike other animals which have "gone feral" after introduction to this continent. Their niche is human settlements. Where there are dogs, there are people.

Dogs don't survive without them.

CHAPTER 3

Evolving Together: humans

THE impact of *Homo sapiens* on canine evolution was incalculable; without humans, dogs simply would not exist. But what about us. Was *our* path also diverted? To what extent would our lives have turned out differently if we hadn't linked up with dogs?

Would we look different? Probably not, although as we shall see later in this chapter, David Paxton's radical theory involves the dog giving us our face. Would our communities be different? Our technology? Our culture? Undoubtedly. There are key points in human development, in our "rise to civilisation", where, if we hadn't already formed a symbiotic partnership with dogs, the next step may not have been possible.[1]

Until very recently, our technology rode on the animal's back. Without domestic animals, it has been suggested by scientists such as Jared Diamond that our technology would never have got beyond flint and stone. Animals *were* the power source that drove our ploughs, clothed communities, and decided wars.

Killing from a distance

Let's start with a familiar date, our first set of coordinates on this chart of human development: 14,000 years Before Present. The time when the fossil record shows us that at least in middle Asia and western Europe, the wolf skull had changed in shape and size to become the dog. (As we have seen, this may have been a considerable period after the earliest dogs became associated with humans, but the skeletal changes could mark a more developed stage of the relationship — such that, by this time, dogs were living entirely within human camps.)

Juliet Clutton-Brock has singled out this particular point in our history, and has done so because of something she thinks must be more than mere coincidence.[2] What intrigues her about this time is that it was not only the wolf that was undergoing a metamorphosis. Culturally, humans were changing significantly as well. They were starting to gather in more permanent settlements, and to build their own artificial caves in the form of little huts of stone. They were also starting to take out insurance against hard times by storing caches of wild grain. But more than this, something was happening to their technology.

In the hypothetical Natufian village scene described in Chapter 1, we can assume all the men would have been handy with big stone axes. After all, hand axes and, later, hafted axes had dominated hominid hunting strategies for the previous 1.5 million years. The hunters would also have had a pretty good handle on the spear, and the merits of netting.

These weren't always the best ways to hunt, however. Delivering the final death blow with a stone axe is a fairly hazardous business. You have to get right in, close enough for a fatal strike, without being smashed yourself by a powerfully driven hoof or tusk. No doubt many a brave hunter suffered more than a bruised ego from a well-aimed kick. Even spears, which can be thrown from a distance, can only be thrown once. Then you've got to grab another spear or go and collect the first one. What if you miss?

But the people of our Natufian village would have been coming to grips with an exciting new development. Because it was between 14,000 and 12,000 BP that small, long-distance projectiles—arrows armed with tiny stone blades called microliths—came into use throughout Europe.

The difference these weapons made must have been incredible. Not only could you kill from a distance, reducing risk to life and limb, but if at first you didn't succeed, many more arrows could be fired at once. More importantly, the bow and arrow was a better prospect entirely for small prey animals—at the time an increasingly significant consideration.

With the retreat of the polar ice caps, the balance of available game species was changing dramatically. Large mammals had both an altered climate, and an expanding population of ever more technologically advanced humans to contend with. The result was a fairly sorry one for much of the megafauna.

Extinctions included the woolly mammoth and the cave bear. Many more species were forced to retreat north and were limited in range. The elk and reindeer once extended as far south as Spain. Even the rhinoceros was once a European inhabitant. The wild ancestor of the horse was very nearly wiped out in Europe and entirely killed off in North America. (Fossil records show that horses were abundant in America before the arrival of humans 10,000 to 20,000 years ago, but then were rapidly exterminated. Some millennia later, descendants of the Amerindians stood little chance against mounted Spanish invaders.)

To return to Ein Mallaha for the moment, the Natufian villagers tied to their new stone dwellings would have noticed that large game was becoming harder to find. The invention of bow and arrow presumably allowed far more efficient hunting of small-to medium-sized animals, and was a welcome boon to the hunting of large beasts. But the method had one disadvantage. And it is this disadvantage that led Juliet Clutton-Brock to suggest that the fundamental development in hunting technology may never have taken place if we hadn't been associated with dogs.

Arrows wound, but rarely kill. The intention is to drain the life and energy of an animal sufficiently to make the job of getting in close enough to kill less hazardous. Or, for smaller game adept at hiding in thick bushes, more practical. But to hunt successfully this way, the initial shot is simply not enough; wounded animals need to be tracked, often for some distance, and then forced to stand still long enough for the fatal strike to be delivered.

As any modern hunter will tell you, the masters of tracking and bringing to bay wounded animals are dogs. This aspect is such a critical component of the bow-and-arrow hunting strategy that Clutton-Brock believes that unless humans had already formed some sort of alliance with wolves or dogs, they would never have been able to hunt successfully this way, and perhaps would never even have thought of it. (I should note that there is some controversy about the dates of microlith hunting, but even if it were much earlier, the reasoning still holds.)

Even if the question of whether the bow and arrow could have been invented in the absence of dogs is debatable, clearly dogs have contributed to our effectiveness across all hunting strategies. Dogs run faster than humans; they can drive and worry game. Their sense of smell is better. In some pitch ranges they hear better. Across a range of cultures today dogs are almost ubiquitous members of the hunting party. Given the retreat of the megafauna coincided with the spread of dogs within human communities 12,000 to 14,000 years ago, Clutton-Brock thinks it reasonable to suspect that dogs contributed to their demise.

It was this partnership with dogs, then, which proved the winning, literally the killing combination: a hunting unit with no parallel. If there had been a Holocene Hunting Olympics, *sapiens* and *lupus* were the gold-medal team.

DOMESTICATION

Let's move a little further along our chart now. Coordinate two takes us forward a few thousand years. The date is around 10,000 BP. This is one of the most important points in our history for it marks the development of agriculture and the domestication of livestock animals.

For an Australian, farming is an ambiguous enterprise. I grew up in Western Australia, a beautiful but desiccated place — one of the driest stretches of land in the world. Except in the far north and a strip in the south, the colours of the state are blue for the intense sky and the brittle sea; white for the beach sand; and red for the great tracts of ferrous earth. Even the vegetation is blue — the green-grey blue of the sclerophyll plants, the only ones that can survive there — not the soft greens and golds of fertility.

One of my strongest childhood memories is of a drought that lasted five years. Some grass grew in winter, but it dried out and disappeared down hungry mouths in spring. In summer the ground cracked, exposing the ungenerous dirt beneath the thin layer of powdery superphosphated soil. For more than six months of each year, the stock were handfed bails of hay. In those years, the white of Western Australia was of drying bones.

Agriculture remains the cornerstone of the Australian economy. Yet every few years, the whole thing collapses. This is the pattern of the Australian climate: droughts lasting not one year, but several. Evidence from coral bands in Queensland suggests that droughts of up to 16 years have not been uncommon. Drought is normal and inevitable, and Western Australia is not alone. There are other parts of Australia as dry and drought prone as the west, and there are other parts of the world just as susceptible to the vagaries of the weather. In Australia, crop failure does not mean the people go hungry.

Elsewhere it means famine, and people die. The point is that even with all the technology of an exceptionally innovative CSIRO, agriculture is still a risky business. So why did humanity give up the relatively easy hunter-gatherer lifestyle to take up the drudgery and the lottery of tending crops? In the process, humans lost abundant leisure time and 17 centimetres in height, were plagued by dental caries, and succumbed to waves of diseases brought about by overcrowding and malnutrition. In the absence of any better explanation, the general conclusion is that they must have been forced to.[3]

Ten thousand years ago, in and around the little village of Ein Mallaha in Israel, life was getting harder. Much of the game was gone, wiped out by the efficient dog–human–arrow combination. The climate was also getting drier. Still not so arid as those parts of the world are today, but certainly the comparatively lush growth of the post-Pleistocene era, when food plants and animals were plentiful and within a short walk of camp, was long past.

The so-called "fertile crescent", which stretches roughly from northern Israel, up through Lebanon and Syria and round into southern Turkey, really wasn't so fertile after all. Looking at it today, it's hard to know how it ever attracted that name. But unlike much of the surrounding country, the oasis of Jericho deserves its fertile title, and it's not hard to see why it is the longest continually habitated site known in the world.

Archaeological excavation of the Tell of Jericho — a tell being the mound of clay created by the successive building and erasing of mudbrick houses — yields a story of nearly 9000 years of people living and dying within the famous Jericho walls. (Yes, even then the city was walled.) Early on, of course, you would hardly call it a city, more a large village, home to around 2000 people. But the dwellings were built of sturdy mudbrick, and the village surrounded by a low wall of stone. Clearly, the locals had no intention of letting other less hardworking people in to steal the fruits of their toil.

At the time Jericho was established — presumably earlier than 9000 BP, but that is the date our archaeological record gives us — the surrounding countryside was already fairly dry, and water was no longer as easy to find as it had been. Reliable springs must have become as sought after and fought over as gold was later. But situated on a permanent source of water, the conditions in Jericho were just right for the development of agriculture.

Cultivation of plants occurred not because the land was universally fertile, but because parts of it were not. It was on such marginal land, which lay on the edges of the really inhospitable tracts, that the effort of deliberately sowing grain presumably began to seem worthwhile. After all, if you lived farther north in Europe, where the pickings were good and water not hard to find, why would you bother? Ten thousand years ago or more, unwilling to leave their only reliable source of water, the people of areas such as Jericho were finding that the lands around them no longer of themselves produced enough to eat.

On top of this there were more mouths to feed. Permanent settlements are a two-edged sword — they allow the fabrication of better dwellings and the accumulation of "things", since no longer do "things" need to be carried around. And these "things" include children. As the UCLA zoologist Jared Diamond has pointed out in *The Rise and Fall of the Third Chimpanzee*, without beasts of burden, nomadic groups must carry their children from place to place. If anyone has been on piggyback duty at a kindergarten, they'll know there are only so many youngsters a person can carry. Hence the numbers of children under the age of four was limited — probably, as some modern hunter-gatherer groups show us, by infanticide. Without this pressure, in settled communities many more children presumably survived. And as the population grew, the demand on the local food supply increased. Therein lies the dilemma in times of hardship. Even if the people wanted to leave — who would carry the children?

There was another reason agriculture started here in the unfertile crescent. Growing wild all around the human and dog communities were many species of grass — species which produced large seed-filled heads, easy to grind, cook and consume. They included what we now know as wheat and barley, cereals that still provide a substantial percentage of the kilojoules consumed in the world today. These wild grains had already been collected for many thousands of years, however not all the seeds would have reached hungry mouths. Some would have dropped in and around the settlement, there to take root and provide handy pickings for the next season. It would not take much more than the pressure of a few poor seasons for people to start doing this deliberately.

By 10,000 BP the cultivation of plants had begun in earnest. Cereals from that time show the beginnings of the characteristic changes of domestication: primarily, an increase in the size of the seed head and a more easily removable seed covering. How these characteristics would have evolved is not hard to follow. All it would take is for people to choose to harvest the easiest plants; those that gave the biggest result for the smallest amount of effort. Who wants to work harder than they have to?

All this may seem a bit of a digression because, of course, what we're really interested in here is not the plants, but the animals. But we have to start with crops, because without the plants, the rest of the animals wouldn't have come.

The dogs were already there, so much a part of life that people would barely have noticed the canine sensory wall which extended far past their stone barriers and provided the first line of defence against invaders. The other domesticated animals were yet to arrive, and — like the dog — rather than us choosing to invite them in, they may have come and "chosen" us. They probably started out as pests.

Picture the scene: lovely golden heads of wheat, waving enticingly with every flutter of breeze. A smorgasbord, a banquet, beckoning any grain-loving creature within pitter-pattering, flapping or trotting distance to wander over and partake. So they did: the birds, the rats and the mice, and along with them the sheep and the goats.

They must have been a real nuisance. Thieving rodents and birds would have been annoying enough, but at least they didn't trample everything as they stole. The hard ovine hoofs, which have wreaked havoc on the thin Australian soil, would have had an equally destructive impact on ancient Middle Eastern crops. Rather than ineffectively warning them off, in the end, it must have been easier to fence the animals off.

Animal behaviourist Frederick Zeuner, back in 1963, was the first to suggest the "crop robber" theory of domestication.[4] His theory goes like this. Just as the establishment of human camps and refuse dumps provided a new resource, so too did crops introduce a new concentrated energy source into the ecological system — particularly as primitive irrigation increased the bearing capacity of the relatively parched land. Certain animals were able to exploit it. They were not so flighty as the gazelle — which despite being a major human food source at the time was never domesticated — and they were not so particular in their eating habits as some species of deer. The raiders may have come at night, sneaking through the fields when their human harassers were safely asleep. As with the dog, those animals most able to tolerate close proximity to human settlements were best placed to use the resource. Selection for "tameness", or a reduced flight distance, would have occurred naturally. By the time some bright human thought to put a collar on a young animal, humans were already living near a subgroup of pretty docile creatures.

Of course, at the same time, sources of "wild" meat were running out. The early inhabitants of Jericho were definitely still hunters. Gazelle were their preferred option, and, it has been suggested, were hunted systematically by driving them (no doubt with canine assistance) into enclosed areas like ravines and slaughtering as many as they could. But they also had a choice of wild ox, boar, sheep, goat, ass, hare and red deer. Surprisingly, the fox made a significant contribution to the diet as well.

As supply became more erratic, the storage of meat would also have increased in importance. Every time there was a large haul of gazelle, there must have been a frantic race on to dry as much meat as possible before it all went bad. Obviously, at some point, it was decided there had to be a better way.

Short of refrigeration, by far the best way to store fresh meat is "on the hoof". With semi-tame goats and sheep nearby, and wild animals increasingly harder to find, someone must have thought to capture a few young nuisance ungulates, feed them up, and keep them as a mobile larder. What's more, there was a clear model of domestication in front of them. Dogs had been living willingly and productively in and around human settlements for millennia, and perhaps by this stage there was already some direct influence by humans on their breeding. So somewhere along the line, this is what the people did.

From around 9000 BP, the domestication of sheep and goats began. Animal remains of this period from Jericho show the tell-tale morphological signs of domestication: reduction in size, the shortened faces, the compacted teeth. Perhaps cattle and pigs were also kept, but there is no fossil evidence for it this early. For that matter, plants — and even sheep and goats — may have been domesticated long before; all we can go on is what the fossil record shows. Nevertheless, we know that by 9000 years ago, domestic goats and sheep were the principal source of meat for the region.

OF BULLS AND GODS

The domestication of cattle may have followed a slightly different path. For one thing, a wild bull is bloody dangerous. The rather nauseating spectacle (at least to me) of the bull run or the bull fight is a poor mimicry of the original contest. For an ancient citizen of Jericho, crossing the path of the male wild aurochs, *Bos primigenius*, was a dicey prospect indeed. These forebears of the modern bull possessed huge, scimitar-like horns. They were big, heavy and fast. Provoked to a charge, their sound would have been exactly like the rumbling roll of thunder — and no doubt they had a temperament to match. Even the modern docile version is treated with caution by farmers, and we still use the ancient practices of castration and nose ringing to ensure control of the "savage beast".

The people of ancient civilisations clearly had some notion of spirituality. They had explanations for why things were the way they were. Why the sun rose, why the seasons changed, why the stars were so. The models for these explanations came from what they could see; what was familiar. The aurochs were a mighty presence, to say the least, and they made great symbols. As veterinary epidemiologist and historian Calvin Schwabe points out, "wild bulls, possibly the largest, strongest, bravest and most successfully libidinous animals with which the founding people of most ancient civilisations were familiar, became their pre-eminent models both for male power *and* fertility, especially as applied to their chiefs or incipient kings".[5]

Bulls populated the skies as bovine constellations, they pranced between heaven and earth as gods, they sat on the thrones of power as kings. They were linked with the most powerful agent of nature, the sun. In several ancient civilisations, the kings *were* bulls — at least, the bull's were the attributes the king was perceived to hold. The pharaoh of ancient Egypt held the title "mighty bull", and his people were "the cattle of Ra" — the supreme sun god who himself was often represented as a bull.

This diversion into the cultural life of ancient civilisation is relevant to cattle domestication. Unlike sheep and goats which we can presume more or less wandered in by themselves, Schwabe suggests cattle were domesticated later and more intentionally — and the driving force was religion.

All animals had some role in the spiritual life of ancient civilisations. But in some parts of the world, the bull seems to have been extraordinarily influential. So-called "cattle cults" were not uncommon. The best evidence of cattle being domesticated for religious purposes comes from Anatolia in southeastern Turkey. At the famed site of Çatalhüyük, countless altars have been found filled with long cattle horns and other bovine paraphernalia.[6] While the evidence for such practices in other parts of the Middle East is not as strong, it seems reasonable to suspect similar processes were at work. And certainly by 8000 BP, fossil cattle remains from Jericho show the classic reduction in size indicating that domestication had occurred.[7]

However it happened, once brought into the human sphere, the power of the bovine was immense. Reverence did not preclude recognising the animals' utility. Castrated, it was tractable — literally. Schwabe even argues that the transition from primitive digging-stick agriculture to more intensive systems would not have been possible without castration and the resulting domestic ox. It could be harnessed to ploughs, wagons and any other conceivable load, magnifying by tenfold the strength of a man. With new improved "engines", the people could develop new, improved technologies, including large wheeled carts and multi-tined ploughs which could dig many furrows at a time. (It is interesting that the earliest depictions of milking and short-horn cattle are dated at around 5000 BP. This is around the same time as the development of the wheel — perhaps the wheel would not have been so important if we hadn't had the beasts to pull the carts!)

Cattle were immensely valuable — as they still are in various pastoral communities. It has even been proposed by anthropologist Richard Lobban that it was the substantial wealth acquired through foreign cattle raids which funded the Egyptians' enormous monuments.[8] He also argues that after the Nile delta was captured by the kings of Upper Egypt, its rapid change to intensive plant cultivation had little to do with feeding the people and more to do with meeting the ravenous appetites of vast herds of cattle.

CATS

Although later incorporated into religious functions, the origin of the domestic cat was decidedly secular. Like sheep and goats, cats came to humans because of the crops. Only this time, it wasn't the grain that beckoned, but the animals that fed on the grain: the rats and the mice. The crop fields and grain stores were rodent heaven — unlimited food, a sheltered habitat and few threats. Too small and fast to be killed easily by humans, rodents were certainly not amenable to being tethered for food. Bumper crops must have been a mixed blessing, because along with them came the rodent hordes. And following its food source, therefore, came *Felis libyca*, the ancestor of the domestic cat, into the human communities.

In many ways, of all the domesticates, it's easiest to understand how cats came to be there. They are perfect rodent predators, and immensely adaptable, able to thrive in a wide range of environments. This feline adaptability extends to social situations. They can live the solitary lives of their purported ancestors or the highly social life of the cat colony. In the Holocene Middle East, there were other rodent predators around which on the surface seem as suitable candidates for domestication as the cat — such as the genet or the mongoose — yet none of them were tamed. As we shall consider further in Chapter 5, it was the unique social abilities of the cat — an animal which has for a long time been unfairly labelled as antisocial — which ensured that they alone came to share our hearths.

Human settlement was just one more niche for cats to occupy. The humans, in response, were unlikely to be disturbed by the invasion of an animal that preyed on one of their major pests, and didn't seem to do too much else wrong. Cats didn't hunt in packs or attack small children; they didn't even smell bad. Apart from the occasional raid on the equivalent of the Sunday roast, there was probably little to be annoyed about. It is not unreasonable to assume they were tolerated and eventually encouraged. And like many of the animals which "chose" us, it was probably not easy to get rid of them. How much success has anyone ever had in trying to keep away an unwanted tom?

The date of feline domestication is as difficult to determine as that of the dog — perhaps more so. The common understanding of cat domestication is that it occurred in Egypt around 4000 years ago, and that so highly valued were these animals that various religious cults sprang up around them. This is what most of the cat books tell us. They also often mention the fact that killing a cat was punishable by death, and that Egyptians shaved their eyebrows at the death of a house cat (how widespread this practice was is up for conjecture, but the source is pretty reliable, coming as it does from the scripts of Herodotus, who was writing as far back as 450 BC). And they tell us that cats were mummified in their thousands. All this is true. But, as with the dog, it is difficult if not impossible to distinguish wild and tame cats by their skeletons. The association between cat and human may have occurred much earlier. The reason for giving the ancient Egyptians credit for cat domestication is that yet again, for a definitive date, we are forced to rely on cultural evidence.

The earliest depictions of cats in Egyptian tomb art date back to around 4500 years ago. However, it is not until the tomb of Baket — c. 3950 BP — that researchers can be sure the animal wasn't a semi-wild visitor. Here the cat is depicted facing to the right with its tail partly curled up. This is the hieroglyphic form, the stylised pictograph which formed part of the ancient Egyptian written language. In the tomb picture, the cat is sizing up a rat; on the cat's left is a man holding a baton, indicating to scholars that he was a house attendant whose duties would have included looking after the pets. As Dr Jaromir Malek, of the Ashmolean Museum in Oxford, notes in his book *The Cat in Ancient Egypt*, this animal could be nothing other than a welcome member of the household.[9]

Another piece of cultural evidence dates from just a century or so later, around 1800 BC. In a small tomb in the famous burial ground of Abydos, in Upper Egypt, archaeologists found a small chapel containing the skeletons of 17 cats. Nearby was a neat row of offering pots. Did these perhaps contain jewels, gold, or holy relics? Well, no. The excavator, Flinders Petrie, obviously drawing on his vast knowledge of cat husbandry, decided they were put there to contain milk!

The central importance of cats in Egyptian religion is also true. But the same was the case for most animals found there at the time. In Egypt, all animals were deified. If anything, cats were rather late-comers to deification, well behind other contenders, such as baboons. The peak of cat idolatry was not until as late as around 500 BC. To further complicate matters, the "worship" of animals, such as cats, was not direct. Cats were seen to represent various gods — but it was a pretty fluid process. A single god could at times be represented by a whole range of different animals. Even the supreme sun god, Ra, often pranced around as a bull, and had a few spells as a cat. It's simply not enough proof to say that because the cat was sacred to the Egyptians, that they were "responsible" for the cat's domestication.

Just like the dog, you get into trouble trying to define something that was essentially a slow biological event in terms of an identifiable cultural one. Given the biological processes going on, it's hard to believe that the cats didn't turn up as soon as the crops with their mice did. *Felis lybica*, the African wild cat which was probably the major ancestor of the domestic cat, had a range extending throughout northern Africa and the Middle East. Its area overlapped with the burgeoning agricultural regions, and it seems most unlikely that this champion exploiter would fail to plunder such rich pickings. A tooth of a cat has indeed been found in Jericho and dated at 9000 BP, right back in the Neolithic period.[10] Actually, cat remains turn up quite commonly in Neolithic excavations — but we can't be sure whether they were welcome companions, or just killed for their pelts. In Mostagedda, located in Middle Egypt, a fascinating burial site reminiscent of the Ein Mallaha find has been dated at 6000 BP — well before the time of the Egyptian pharaohs. A man — to judge by his tools a craftsman — was buried with two animals at his feet. The first was a gazelle, presumably placed there so the man could have a snack during his journey through the spirit world. The second was a cat. Perhaps the cat was seen as healthy spirit food too, or perhaps the man was inordinately scared of rats. But it seems more likely the animal was simply a pet.

During the 1980s, an intriguing twist was added to the puzzle of the origin of the domestic cat. At the excavation of a Neolithic village in Cyprus, researchers, to their surprise, identified the remains of a cat. The thing is that there are no wild cats native to Cyprus. Cyprus is a small island, some 100 kilometres from the mainland and 500 kilometres from the supposed origin of the domestic cat, Egypt. Yet these remains were dated at 7000 BP. There was no way the cats could have got to Cyprus *unless* humans brought them. Archaeologist Colin Groves puts it quite bluntly. It seems all this time the ancient Egyptians may have been getting undue credit. They were not responsible for domesticating the cat. In fact, he believes, the Egyptians, who were by all accounts lousy nutritionists and hopeless at keeping their captured animal menageries alive, weren't capable of domesticating anything.[11] Cats must have been tamed thousands of years before.

The idea of a human–animal symbiosis is easiest to comprehend in the case of the cat. Cats were in and around human settlements, valued because of what they could catch, rather than what they could do. Some scientists have suggested that domestication was completed when the walls went up around the Neolithic villages; the cats were figuratively walled in too. Yet like the dog, there was something that distinguished them from other similar opportunist predators. It had to do with their social character. Unlike their non-feline predatory contemporaries, when kittens were born near humans, they could learn to socialise with humans too.

But did the cat influence the course of human history? The domestication process is interesting, but it's the influence on *our* development which is the main theme of this discussion. There simply isn't anything very clear cut. As far as we can tell, cats didn't contribute to dramatic changes in human technology, nor did they effectively meld with us to form part of our sensory system. The cat *did* play a part in protecting the livelihood of those ancient civilisations which were so dependent on grain. And its presence or absence certainly had a role in determining the course of certain outbreaks of rat-borne diseases. I'm not sure that you could say, however, that our history would have turned out very differently if cats had not been with us. What's intriguing, nevertheless, is that they have been so singularly successful in integrating themselves into human communities. There doesn't seem to be a *rational* explanation. What there does seem to be is an *emotional* one. And as we shall see later in this book, it is this ability to connect with us *emotionally* that may very well mean that their greatest impact on human development is yet to come.

HORSES

The complete reverse is true of the horse. If anything, their day is gone. Obviously they still bring immense pleasure to horse-lovers around the world, but the logistics and cost of keeping them while living in a city preclude ownership to all but the richest or most dedicated. This change in status has been a rapid one. For millennia, right up until less than one hundred years ago, horses were an essential part of daily life — the smell of horse manure an undercurrent of every human odourscape. Some societies would have collapsed without them, providing, as they did, the only means of high-speed travel and long-distance communication. These roles they play no more.

The domestication of the horse occurred rather late, probably some time around 6000 BP. Better late than never from the horse's point of view though, because prior to this the ancestral *Equus ferus* was well on its way to extinction. Indeed, as we have noted, such was its fate in North America where, until the arrival of the Europeans, it had not existed for at least 8000 years.

The horse was a child of the Pleistocene. Adapted to the vast open plains of temperate Europe, Asia and northern Africa, it was ill-equipped to cope with the encroaching postglacial forests which choked out grasslands in Europe and Asia and hampered its most effective defence against predators: speed. Horses were even less well equipped to resist the human–canid hunting unit, by this time the horse's major predator. If it weren't for domestication, the horse may well have been extinct as early as 4000 years ago.[12]

Even by 10,000 BP, only scattered populations of wild horses remained in western and northern Europe. Gradually, the horse was being forced east, away from the still fertile grasslands of Europe into the semi-desert plains of central Asia. We know the habitat was not ideal for the ancestral horse, because its only surviving wild descendant, the Przwalski horse of Mongolia, appears to have shrunk in size as a result of the poor nutrition available there. The Przwalski is a very small horse and, in a process ironically analogous to that seen in every animal which has been domesticated *except* the horse, it has overly large cheek teeth and mandible, indicating that the skull was once much bigger.

Interestingly, the Przwalski horse provides a modern-day parable of the barely avoided fate of the pre-domesticant equid. Surviving in an isolated area of Mongolia, aided no doubt by the fact that once harnessed, the horse became an object of reverence and hunting them or their like taboo, the "P horse" (as it is affectionately known in modern zoos) disappeared only after World War II. They are now extinct in the wild; the last remaining herds eaten by humans during the famines and cultural upheaval which followed the Sino–Japanese wars and the arrival of communism in Mongolia. Their survival today is due only to preservation of stock in zoos around the world, including the Western Plains Zoo in Dubbo, New South Wales, and it is surely one of the most gratifying events in zoo conservation to watch the current reintroduction of the "P horse" to the plains of Mongolia. Their close relative, the Tarpan, was not so lucky. Also a true wild horse surviving in Ukraine, it was wiped out at the end of last century.

By 6000 BP, if someone were searching for horses, there was only one area in which to look. This was the plains of eastern Europe, stretching from Ukraine to Turkestan. Researchers believe it was here and at this time that the earliest domestication of the horse took place. And what a momentous event it proved to be. It not only made conquerors of "inferior barbarians", determined the course of wars, and held together vast empires, but it seems the horse may have given us the basis of our modern language as well.

Proto-Indo-European, otherwise known as PIE, is the reconstructed parent language of around half the people living in the world today. Its modern descendants include English; most other European languages except Basque, Finnish, Hungarian, Estonian and Lapp; and the Asian languages extending as far east as India. The search for the "homeland" of PIE has been something of a quest, occupying scholars for at least 100 years. And in that time, suggestions have ranged almost right across the globe — as one wag of an archaeologist has it, the question isn't where scholars locate the PIE homeland, but where they locate it *now*.

Jared Diamond, the American zoologist, in his book *The Rise and Fall of the Third Chimpanzee*, writes beautifully about the problem, and of the methods used by linguists to determine the home of the original speakers of our ancestral tongue. It would be pointless to attempt an inferior version of it here, and I refer readers to his work. What are important to relay, however, are the conclusions.[13]

Diamond's *now* lies between 5000 and 7000 BP; the where-abouts of his *now* is the plains or steppes of southern Russia, north of the Black Sea. You will no doubt anticipate the answer but let's ask the obvious question anyway: how did a small group of relatively unsophisticated herders stamp their language on half the world? How could they make such an impact on the more technologically advanced, populous settlements to the west?

Well, they did have one thing going for them that no other human population had: horses. An animal which could run faster and longer than almost any other, which could hold a man upon its back to raid and retreat before the hapless enemy even realised what had happened. The earliest experience of riding must have been incredible — a sensation as close to flying as any human was to achieve right up until the Wright brothers. Sheer terror of course, but later, freedom. And it was enough to tip the balance, ensuring that the steppe people of southern Russia, and no other, stamped all of Europe, western Asia, and now North America, South America and Australia with the horse brand of their native tongue.

The earliest evidence for equine domestication belongs to the ancient Botai culture, located on the eastern Eurasian steppes in Kazakstan.[14] Here, horse skulls have been found that have been dated at around 6000 BP. What is important this time isn't the shape of the skulls themselves — as we have noted, horses are the only animals *not* to show the reduction in size and tooth compaction typically following domestication — but what has subsequently happened to the skulls. Marks worn into the cheek teeth have been interpreted as evidence of that still essential tool of the modern rider — the "bit". Probably made from nothing more than a simple rope, but a bit nonetheless.

The steppe people used their new-found military advantage to great effect. They lived a fairly austere lifestyle; the constraints of herding livestock across the plains in search of forage keeping their numbers limited and their possessions few. To their west, however, lay great treasures: rich farmland and large villages peppered with stockpiles of precious grain. With their new mobility, village raids provided easy pickings.

This scenario is supported by the archaeological examination of eastern European villages of the period, which were heavily fortified, although to little avail, it seems. As well as this, typical steppe-style graves appear across the fertile lands, as far west as Hungary. Thus began the campaigns of the "Mongolian hordes", culminating in the great rampage of Genghis Kahn in the thirteenth century, whose massacres are now legendary.[15]

This is not to say that a small group of rampaging Mongolians smashed their way to England. Diamond points out, marauding nomadic tribes probably didn't make it as a group much further west than Hungary. However, just as many tribes- people settled and produced children in the new land, so the language they imposed on the vanquished gave birth to numerous descendants. It is these descendant tongues which, through the ebb and flow of humanity during the next few thousand years, came to dominate the linguistic landscape.

The early steppe people made a unique discovery, one that would not be repeated until the arrival of the Europeans in the new world of the Americas more than five millennia later — that a group with horses was easily able to attack a population without them. The results in both cases, in terms of loss of culture and human life, were similarly devastating. And both groups had a tremendous impact on the language of those they conquered.

Why is the horse singled out in this tableau? There *were* other factors. While deficient in some areas, the steppe people certainly had a number of key technologies, including wheeled vehicles. Most importantly, they had developed metallurgy, enabling the production of devastatingly sharp weapons. Nevertheless, so did everyone else. "Of all the innovations that drove the steppe people's steamroller," writes Jared Diamond, "the sole one for which they might get full credit is the domestication of the horse."[16] Horses were the only thing that really set them apart.

Unlike most other domesticated animals, it cannot be argued that the horse in any way "chose" to live in human communities. It did not "choose" to be captured and tethered for meat. Nor did it bend its knee and offer humanity a ride on its back. These are clearly human innovations in the true sense of the word. But again it has to be said that the horse as well as the human did rather well out of it. By 4000 BP horse remains start to crop up across the old world. A 3500-year-old find from Egypt reveals large, slender-limbed horses. The ancient Scythians, who lived just north of Macedonia, were famed for their skill with the horse, and although they were largely illiterate, have left us friezes illustrating their superb abilities. Alexander the Great learned his horse skills from the Scythians, and managed to conquer 2 million square miles of the ancient world with his cavalry. All this, without even the benefit of the stirrup! Stirrups didn't turn up until around 400 AD.[17]

Although I have said their day has past, horses are still doing better than their wild counterparts. There are around 110,000 thoroughbred horses living in Australia alone, according to the Australian Jockey Club. In the whole world, there are only 1300 "P horses". And there are *no* Tarpans.

ANIMAL POWER

The significance of animal domestication has been highlighted in Jared Diamond's book, *Guns, Germs and Steel: The fates of human societies.*[18] The reason he wrote it was to answer one vital and intriguing question: why is it that if you walk out onto the streets of Sydney, for example, the faces you see are mostly white? There *is* another type substantially represented in the largely European crowd, but it is of Asian descent. Also pale. Not black. Not the colour of people who have inhabited this land for the last 60,000 years.

Why? Were they stupider? Clearly not. There is no evidence for a difference in intellect between various human subgroups around the world at all. What was it then? Why didn't it happen the other way round, why didn't *they* develop the technology that would have allowed Australian Aborigines to take over Europe? In addressing these questions, Diamond has devoted no fewer than seven chapters to animal domestication. The answer, he claims, is that it all was an accident of biogeography. Like the Mongols who happened to live in the only part of the world that had horses, the homes of my ancestors happened to be invaded by a series of what turned out to be extremely beneficial biological partners.

Jared Diamond is clear about where he thinks humans would be today if we hadn't linked up with animals. If we had not established the domestication partnership, there would be no modern technology, no modern culture.[19] Humans would still be living as their hunter-gatherer ancestors did 13,000 years ago.

Learning to speak

That just about does it for our chart of human history, but before we leave it there's one more coordinate to go. This time, we zoom right back, past our first stop and the development of projectile hunting, way back to 50,000 to 100,000 BP. This is the one I have been promising: David Paxton's radical hypothesis.[20] Put in question form, it goes like this: did the dog actually have some impact on the most important human development of all, the evolution of human speech?

The period we are talking about is a murky one in human prehistory. Tremendous changes were occurring, albeit slowly, eventually gaining the critical momentum for what is sometimes known as the Great Leap Forward — usually dated at around 50,000 BP. This is when new and varied tools suddenly appear in the archaeological record: fish hooks, awls, needles. Art leaps onto the scene and the walls — leading to the glorious animal frescoes of the French caves at Lascaux of 30,000 years ago. And at some stage in this period from around 100,000 to 50,000 BP, our human forebears evolved the most sophisticated and complex communication system possessed by any creature, ever.

The problem is, we can't tell when. It doesn't show up in the fossil record. Most of the organs responsible for speech, like the larynx or tongue, are soft tissues and consequently not preserved over time. There are ways in which the architecture of the skull tells us about what happened — for example, changes to the skull cavities which house the prefrontal lobes involved in language, or the position of the hyoid bone which suspends the larynx — but even these give no indication of the complexity of vocabulary or grammar. No amount of bone structure can tell us what was being said.

The conclusion drawn by a number of scholars is that the development of human language, with all its syntax and grammatical rules, must have been the impetus for these advances in art and tool-making. This gives us a rough date. There is little else the advances could be attributed to. Humans had been anatomically the same for more than 100,000 years prior to this. Little had been added to the cultural repertoire since the time of *Homo erectus* — we were still using the same simple flaked-stone tools as our smaller-brained predecessors. The appearance, 50,000 to 100,000 years ago, of the whole gamut of capacities we consider to be distinctly human must have had some cause. Language is the obvious candidate, for not only did it allow several people to plan together, but it also allowed the *individual* to frame his or her thoughts in an entirely new way.

There was another consequence of this development. Living near the changing *sapiens* was another group of hominids. These were the heavy-boned, heavy-muscled, heavy-browed Neanderthals. The two species co-existed in the world presumably peaceably, certainly successfully, for at least 100,000 years; the earliest definite *Homo neanderthalensis* remains are 130,000 years old. Yet their demise took place around 25,000 years ago. And whether they succumbed to new tools of war, disease, or were simply out-competed, outsmarted and forced to occupy increasingly inhospitable lands, the culprit seems to be the newly creative and ever more vocal *Homo sapiens*.

So what does Paxton think the dog could have had to do with all of this? To understand Paxton's proposal, we need to look a little more closely at what is involved in developing the apparatus of speech.

No other animal has our verbal flexibility. Cognitive studies of chimpanzees have shown they certainly have the mental capacity for symbolic thought, and can recognise and use up to 600 words in American Sign Language. But their tongues and vocal chords can't make the sounds of recognisable speech.

Our vocal architecture is notably different. The *Homo sapiens* face is foreshortened, the bite rounded, the tongue short and dexterous, able to work efficiently against the palate and teeth to punch out clear, distinct sounds. The roof of the mouth is more concave than any other mammal's, providing a chamber to amplify the sounds produced by resonating vocal chords. The larynx has also dropped, freeing up the whole system to be manipulated by precise facial muscles. All in all, it's a pretty remarkable structure; as any opera fan more than appreciates.

In the process of getting there, some things may have been lost. Our heads became smaller, faces flatter, brows lighter. To a modern observer, we became more graceful — and perhaps this grace was a prerequisite for speech, because heavy musculature of the jaw and throat would hamper the flexibility required. David Paxton suggests that, amongst other things, what was lost was most of our remaining sense of smell.

There's a structural limit to how much you can fit in the one head and still be supported by the skeleton. For example, I might decide that in addition to what I already have, I would like my skull to house a sonar system, a few extra eyes, a great sense of smell and perhaps a big horn out of my forehead, just for decoration. The problem is that fitting all this in would probably make my head so heavy it would keep falling forward onto my chest. Either that or I would have to develop a set of thick, inflexible neck muscles and a stronger skeletal frame to support it. Everything is a trade-off — if I still want to be able to sing, dance and move my head lightly, I can't be restricted by all those extras.

So, according to Paxton, to free up the face, a few things had to go. Representations based on the skull shape of hominids like *Homo erectus* and even early *Homo sapiens* reveal a far more prominent lower face. In fact, it probably wouldn't be overstating it to describe the more extreme protruding face of *Homo neanderthalensis* as a muzzle. Now, the thing about a muzzle is that it allows a lot more room for one important sense organ, the olfactory mucous membrane or the lining of the nose. This organ's sensitivity to chemicals is translated by the brain into what we call a smell, and the degree of discrimination of this membrane is proportional to its total surface area. As the "muzzle" receded so, too, perhaps did the total olfactory mucous membrane.

By abandoning a survival skill such as the sense of smell, surely *Homo sapiens* would become more vulnerable to predators? Perhaps their communities were already so tightly organised that it didn't really matter. But it must be remembered that in the early stages, *Homo sapiens* presumably didn't have the language skills to facilitate this organisation. According to Paxton's theory the two occurred together: vocalisations couldn't become more refined until the protruding face, and hence perhaps the sense of smell, was reduced.

What Paxton argues is that for *Homo sapiens*, even during that difficult transitional time, it didn't matter. This wasn't a survival issue. We didn't need to worry about the sense of smell because there was someone else already doing the job for us. We had already begun unconsciously to pool the senses with *Canis lupus*, or the semi-tame wolf. In a war of the genes for different features of the skull, the genes for larger nose and more acute smell, which may have also impeded vocalisation, didn't have much of a chance. They conveyed no advantage, as the dog — or wolf — was already playing the part. Even if it wasn't a "companion", the animal quite probably barked at the approach of predators or led hunters to game, thereby providing just about everything a human could want from a big nose.

This meant one thing less to fit in the skull. It contributed to the refinement and flattening of the face and jaw and hence the apparatuses of speech. And for that, according to Paxton, we owe dogs a very vocal debt.

This theory, wonderful as it is, nevertheless relies on quite a few stretches of the imagination. First of all, it assumes that many human communities had been infested or were accompanied by canids by the time the speech apparatuses were being refined. If we were to rely only on the archaeological evidence, we might think not. (Although, as we have noted, archaeologists such as Juliet Clutton-Brock and Colin Groves have no problems with the idea of a much earlier association.) The mitochondrial DNA evidence for dogs perhaps being up to 100,000 years old, however, definitely puts us in the ball park.

Second, it assumes that the development of human language occurred roughly as has been suggested. The evidence for that is probably as good as it's going to get. No one knows for sure how it came about, and perhaps never will.

The third imaginative leap is much harder to make. Was the sense of smell really of much importance to early *Homo sapiens*, given that they had so much else going for them? And did they, with their more protruding faces, even have a better sense of smell than we do? Chimps appear to; but that isn't conclusive. Most importantly, was the flattening of the face an essential component of the development of speech or could it have happened some other way? I can't answer those questions. Even to me, parts of the theory do seem incredible. Nevertheless, it is a fascinating idea that the association with canids may have been one of the key influences in the maelstrom of our evolutionary history, particularly in such a fundamental development as language.

David Paxton's speculative proposal has as yet only been published as a PhD thesis. It has not been widely reviewed by the larger anthropological community, and is probably destined to remain firmly in the left field of evolutionary theory since by its nature the idea is not easily testable.

So why has it been included here? The first reason is, testability notwithstanding, the theory is so appealing. The second and more important reason is that even if there is criticism, something important may yet be achieved.

The implications of such an early human–dog relationship have not even been considered. By focusing attention on that ancient symbiosis, it may prompt a reappraisal of its nature. At the very least, this theory highlights the possible impact the pooling of biological resources with the canid had on the development of *both* our species.

PIECING THE PUZZLE TOGETHER

The question we started with is, would *we* have turned out differently if we hadn't linked up with dogs? On one level that is impossible to answer. A "what if" question by definition doesn't have an answer. The dog's life has been integrated with humans for so long that trying to tease out what can be directly attributed to it and what cannot is an impossible task.

But we can make inferences. Let's go back over the pieces of the puzzle. The first part was improved hunting prowess and the development of bow and arrow technology. It's highly likely the dog played a role. The result, as it has been in every other part of the world where humans have gained a sudden advantage over their prey, was overhunting. This contributed to the demise of the megafauna in the Middle East, increasing the pressure on the inhabitants to find alternative food sources and develop agriculture.

The next piece is animal domestication itself. The animals domesticated after dogs most definitely shaped our cultural development. Would the wheel have ever been invented if we didn't already have animals to pull wagons?

It would be pushing it to claim that cats, sheep and horses could not have become domesticates without dogs. But I *am* suggesting that their domestication is part of a package for which the dog *did* provide the model. None of the domesticated animals can really be considered in isolation. The process was on the one hand cultural; on the other a biological event. Without all the ingredients, it's hard to know what would have happened.

The last and most important puzzle piece (which was actually probably the first step in the process) is the effect that augmented sensory perceptions had on those earliest communities that were infested by canids. You don't have to believe that it affected our speech to see how our canid companions might have determined which human groups were the most likely to survive.

AN EXTENDED PHENOTYPE?

There is another way of looking at the dog–human partnership. In 1982, evolutionary biologist Richard Dawkins, of *Selfish Gene* fame, jolted the scientific community as well as the public with a new notion — that of the extended phenotype.

Put simply, the phenotype is the scientific term for the way we look. All of us have a distinctive sequence of DNA code which forms genes, and it is these genes that code for the proteins that ultimately go to make up our bodies. What Dawkins has proposed is that there are genes for things that happen outside our bodies as well. When a beaver builds a dam, the shape of that structure is determined by beaver DNA which contains rules for how you build dams. When a bird builds a nest, again it is shaped by codes for nest building in the bird. Dawkins argues that the nest is as much an expression of the genotype as the bird itself. He has termed this the "extended phenotype", and what it means is that the mechanisms by which genes ensure they are replicated can lie outside the host organism. In other words, if I were a bird, the nest I have made will increase my chances of reproducing.

Quite independently, and as I discovered, unbeknownst to the other, two researchers on opposite sides of the world have, in the last year, begun applying this concept to studying the human–dog partnership. Both David Paxton and John Bradshaw, director of the Anthrozoology Institute in Britain (more from him in later chapters), were generous enough to share their notes with me.[21]

Their premise is simple. If the criterion is that something outside our own body is enhancing our capacity to survive, then the dog would seem to fit the bill. The dog has taken over our senses of hearing and smell, providing an extension of our bodies in a literal physical sense. And, likewise, the human could be seen as an extension of the dog: we enhancing their brains and powers of communication and cooperation.

What this raises in terms of the idea of our having evolved together is fascinating. Do dogs have genes for associating with humans?

You would have to say that they do. The dog is so well adapted to living with us that you cannot find a dog community today which does not live with humans. Such communities simply cannot survive. Even so-called feral dogs are not truly independent. They do not form stable communities; members drift in and out of the human sphere from year to year, with a constant fluctuation between full and partial dependency — unlike the cat. Moreover, dogs have many effective behaviours for soliciting food and care for humans.

Do humans have genes for dog ownership? That is more difficult to say. The relative influence of human genes and human culture on behaviour continues to be debated by our best scientists. There's no direct evidence for "dog loving" genes, and indeed many individuals dislike dogs. But certainly, try as I have, I cannot find anyone who knows of a community that does not contain them. Even the Maoris, whom I thought must disprove this thesis because they lacked dogs when Europeans invaded, turn out to have had dogs when they first arrived in New Zealand a thousand years ago, but had eaten them in a nutritional crisis. They have them now. There's also the intriguing fact that humans have a physiological reaction to friendly dogs — a lowering of blood pressure, as we shall see in later chapters.

Assigning some kind of divine or genetic purpose to such connections is always a trap. But it *does* seem as if there is some kind of inbuilt tendency for humans to associate with dogs.

CHAPTER 4

FOR BETTER OR FOR WORSE: THE CHANGING VIEW OF ANIMALS

THIS book began with a puzzle. Why should so much of our social history and so many of our households be filled with animals, especially with dogs? It may seem too obvious a question to bother answering — as plain as the nose on your face — but then, as we've seen, that too may be more subtle than it seems.

In the first three chapters we explored the biological reasons for the presence of dogs in our lives. If, as is contended, our respective species formed a highly co-evolved biological unit, then it makes sense that people didn't — or couldn't — leave them behind.

There is, of course, more to it. Being human, we can't help overlaying everything biological with something else entirely: human culture. For better or for worse, very different societies have had to deal with the animals that live amongst them — and the animals' cultural fortunes under this arrangement have been mixed to say the least.

The current high status of most cats and dogs in Western countries is not a "natural" one, any more than is democracy the "natural" form of government. At different times and in different places, animals have been at the bottom of the heap. Gone, as animal behaviourist Professor James Serpell has described it, from "paragon to pariah".[1] If there is anything in common with the following examples it is this: domestic animals, whether friend or simply food, were never simply *there*. They have become an integral part of our culture. In some societies they are even quasi-human.

CONDEMNED AS A WITCH

> She confessed: That the divell about seven yeeres agoe did appear to her in the shape of a little dog and bid her to forsake God and leane to him: who replied, that she was loath to forsake him. Shee confessed also that shee had a desire to be revenged upon Tomas Letherland and Mary Woodruse now his wife. She further said that the divell promised her, that she should not lacke, and that she had money sometimes brought her she knew not whence, sometimes one shilling, sometimes eight pence, never more at once; shee called her divell by the name of "Bunne".

So opens the confession of the affirmed witch Joane Williford, executed along with her fellows, at Faversham in Kent, for being a witch, on Monday, 29 September 1645. The extract is taken from *The Examination, Confession, Triall, and Execution, of Joane Williford, Joan Cariden and Jane Hott,* published in that year. "Being a true Copy of their evill lives and wicked deeds, taken by the Mayor of Faversham and Jurors for the said Inquest. All attended under the hand of Robert Greenstreet, Mayor of Faversham."[2]

Her crimes were heinous indeed, and clearly her mortal fate deserved — as Williford herself agreed when queried upon this very point by the esteemed Robert Greenstreet. With the aide of her "Divell" and her "fellowe" Elizabeth Harris, she cursed the boat of John Woodcott so that while it went cheerfully out, "it did not come cheerfully home". She confessed "that her retainer Bunne carried Thomas Gardler out of a window, who fell into a backside". She accused Goodwife Argell of cursing Mr Major and also John Mannington, and said that he should not thrive, and so it came to pass.

Furthermore, the devil promised her "that if shee were thrown in water, she should not sink". Indeed, when this was put to the test on her co-accused, "the widdow Jane Hott, the widdow *did* flote upon the water, contrary to her prior claim that if put into the water she should surely sinke". What's more, according to Williford's own confession, "the Divell sucked twice since she came to the prison, he came to her in the forme of a Muse [mouse]".

With only a slight degree of paraphrasing, this is the real thing — taken from the original transcript of the one of the more infamous of England's notorious witch trials. (In addition, I took the liberty of changing all the scripted "f"s back to the more familiar "s", hopefully sparing the reader any discomfort upon discovering how frequently the Divell "sucked" the accused.)

The confessions of Williford and her unfortunate "fellowes" are striking for their sheer absurdity. They are ripe for satire, recalling the bizarre logic of the judge in Monty Python's *The Holy Grail*, who solves his dilemma by comparing the weight of the accused with that of a duck (witches and ducks both float, of course). It's still jolting to read original transcripts though — and appreciate that this sort of thing actually happened.

More relevant here is the name of the devil: "Bunne". Bunny is a funny name for a messenger of Satan and purveyor of all things foul, loathsome and evil. But a perfectly good name for a sweet little dog — which is clearly what this denizen of hell really was.

Many of us are vaguely aware of the role of witches' "familiars", that is their animal associates, in consigning their owners to the funeral pyre. To appreciate what it really meant, however, we turn to the Associate Professor of Humane Ethics and Animal Welfare at the University of Pennsylvania, James Serpell.

James Serpell's recently revived classic, *In the Company of Animals*[3] is a seminal work on pet-keeping and human–animal interactions. In attempting to trace the history, prevalence and cultural context of pet keeping, Serpell has searched for evidence of the keeping of animals for emotional reasons. It's not always easy to find — largely because in the past, animals were often written about in terms of their utility rather than their value as companions. If you can't rely on the dominant writings of the period, then where do you look? Especially when examining, say, the Middle Ages — a period apparently dominated by a fairly nasty utilitarian view of animals. As Serpell has discovered, evidence of the emotional bond between humans and animals is sometimes hidden in the cracks of history. And this is why he was drawn to witches.

Serpell has been studying a series of witch trial proceedings. What caught his attention are the names of these servants of the devil: "Bunne", "Rutterkin", "Pretty" "Tiffin" and "Pusse". They are all pet names. Clearly, the devil's cohorts were all simply pets.

The "true confessions" go through elaborate contortions to deny this; the wording implicitly warning the reader not to be fooled — ignore their disarming appearance for these creatures are truly agents of the devil. One spirit appeared "in the likeness of a little white Dogge", another "in the likenesse of a Kittin". A "thing" came to visit "the widdow Jane Hott" and lie upon her breast, and when she struck it off with her hand, "it was soft as a cat". (What a clever disguise.) The evil imp Rutterkin sealed the fate of his mistress, Margaret Flower, in 1618 by being observed to "leape upon her shoulder, and sucke her necke". It's distressing to read how frequently such a friendly gesture damned its recipient.

When Serpell decided to score how frequently different species of devil were cited in the trials, as well as the expected cats, dogs and toads, he was surprised to discover that flies ranked high on his list. How so? Well, according to popular wisdom, a witch's familiar must feed from the blood of its mistress at regular intervals or die. Following accusation, the women were stripped down and searched for signs of a "witch's teat" — the source of this nourishment. Not hard to find; any odd lump would do. The women were often then incarcerated in dank prisons, while expectant adjudicators waited for the familiars to turn up and prove the witch's guilt. Lo and behold, they always did! Sometimes in the shape of a mouse, sometimes a fly or an insect. It was an excellent test for devilry — guaranteed to give results.

The unfortunate women were invariably poor and often lived alone — widows without the powerful protection of a husband to ward off the accusations of malicious neighbours. The sad thing is, as Serpell points out, it shows that just like today, lonely, isolated people often turned to animal companionship to supplement or replace meagre social networks.[4] And it was for this — to all appearances a natural human tendency — that they were vilified.

DOMINION OVER ALL THE ANIMALS

The involvement of animal familiars in witch trials was apparently a peculiarly English thing — not featured in continental witch trials. Why this difference is not quite clear. However, what *is* certain is that it was a manifestation of the traditional Judaeo–Christian hostility to viewing animals as anything other than objects put upon the earth by God for our use. How this view came about has been well documented by a number of scholars, but it is worth running through briefly here.

Fittingly enough, it all starts with Genesis. In the first chapter, God creates humans in his own image. Helpfully, He then creates lots of other useful creatures and awards His new people dominion over every living thing "that moveth upon the earth". With that single line, the theological tone is set for millennia to come. It's a wonderfully liberating philosophy — as animal rights philosophers have pointed out, anything can be justified. Someone thinks it would be a good idea to tie a few animals to a turnstile and make them go round to power a small mill? Fine. That's what they were made for. Hunting deer seems like a fun thing to do? Excellent — God says that's their destiny.

This is not to say that the Christian church has not at times strongly advocated the humane treatment of animals and a sense of duty of care. Indeed, Saint Francis of Assisi, who gave birth to the nature-loving order of the Franciscan monks in the twelfth century, is still widely revered today. Yet, ironically, it was not long after Assisi's death that this benevolent approach changed. Something was added to the theological scene which would ultimately mark the Middle Ages as one of the more shameful periods in the history of human–animal relations.

In the thirteenth century, a Dominican friar, Thomas Aquinas, took it upon himself to translate the works of the ancient Greeks, including Aristotle and Plato. Subsequently, certain aspects of classical philosophy were incorporated into Christian theology, in particular Aristotle's ladder of life. Constructed on the basis of the ability to reason, it put Greek men at the top (naturally), women and other free people somewhat lower down, and slaves and barbarians a step lower again. Animals slotted into the next few rungs, and plants further down again. The great thing about this plan was that each level of the intellectual ladder was destined to serve the one above — wonderful if you happened to be a Greek male. Or, as it was loosely translated, a white Christian male — preferably a member of the clergy.

The utilitarian and profoundly anthropocentric approach reached its heights (or depths) in the seventeenth century when René Descartes, of "I think therefore I am" fame, spelled out his ultimate objectifying ideology. Animals are just "things" — machines, like those marvels of human ingenuity, clocks. Lacking reason, they lack sensibility or an ability to suffer.

This harsh anthropocentrism was not unique to Christianity. Sophia Menache, Professor of Mediaeval History at the University of Haifa, Israel, and herself Israeli-born, has been studying the phenomenon across different religions — Christianity, Judaism, and Islam. What she has concluded is that such a view is common to all monotheistic religions.[5]

Dogs are mentioned in the Bible 32 times — always in a pejorative sense. They are considered impure, and a strict orthodox Jew to this day will not keep a dog — all right for Gentiles, but not to be suffered by believers of the true faith. In Revelation 22:15, Saint John states that only whores, dogs and criminals will not be allowed to enter the heavenly kingdom of Jerusalem. Menache finds it telling that alone of all the animal world, dogs are singled out (alongside "fallen" humans) and explicitly barred.

Just as the Bible contains little to commend dogs to humans, so the Koran is at times openly hostile. Muhammad advised that all dogs should be killed, in particular the black ones as they harbour the devil. In Damascus in the fourteenth century, it is recorded that thousands of dogs were expelled from the city, watched by the inhabitants as they hung hopefully around the outskirts; they died before long of thirst.

It can still make dog ownership tricky today. At an international veterinary conference I attended last year, I met a Pakistani veterinarian called Ramsee Guranathan, who explained to me why it was that although pet keeping is becoming more popular in his predominately Islamic country, there are a couple of drawbacks. The faithful are required to pray in a mosque five times a day. To enter the sacred area, they must be neat and completely clean. If, while on their way to the mosque, they are touched by a dog, they have to go home, change their clothes and clean themselves again. At a rate of five trips a day, the extra travel time might begin to be a bit annoying — not to mention the risk of running out of things to wear!

So why this need for religions to objectify animals? Why, in the case of dogs in particular, an open hostility to the point of it being explicitly dictated within fundamental religious texts? There are many answers, but the first we will deal with here is the most obvious — the singular human drive for self-preservation.

If we look at where the world's monotheistic religions originated, it takes us back to a familiar location — the Middle East and the Levant and, ironically, the very place where we find some of the earliest evidence of dogs being kept as pets. This environment has for a long time provided favourable conditions for one of humanity's most feared diseases: rabies. And although a vast range of mammalian species can contract rabies, the primary mode of infection to humans, accounting for 99 per cent of human rabies deaths today, is the bite of a rabid dog.[6]

Rabies is an invariably fatal encephalitis — or infection of the brain. Apart from the inevitability of the outcome, it strikes terror into the hearts of observers for the violent madness which precedes death — and ensures the disease is spread, as sufferers will often bite any victim foolish enough to get close. The disease is carried by saliva, so although the bite of an animal is the most likely source, it can be transmitted if infected saliva comes into contact with an open wound. Like so many former scourges, a modern vaccination for rabies has removed much of its power. However, there are still many parts of the world where rabies maintains its fearful presence. And its cultural resonance has remained strong. Even in Australia, which has never had rabies, we baulk at the suggestion of "mad dogs", and accuse our more intemperate politicians of being "rabid". In those parts of the world where dogs are regarded as pariahs, such as India and Southeast Asia, the original reason may have been rabies. Certainly, I have noticed many mothers of Asian origin fearfully ushering their Australian-born children away from the neighbours' beloved pet. Ramsee Guranathan pointed out to me that Islam regards a wet dog as the ultimate in uncleanliness — and he believes this can probably be attributed to a link with saliva on the coat of the dog.

While rabies is certainly adaptable to almost any climate and maintains cycles in most parts of the world, in the close confines of the ancient cities of the Levant, with many unowned scavenging dogs eking out their living in fairly squalid conditions, rabies outbreaks must have periodically run rife within the city walls.

Fear of rabies (and by extension other zoonoses, or diseases which can be transmitted between humans and dogs) gives us one possible reason for religious antagonism to dogs, but clearly it's only a small part of the answer. It doesn't explain the wider issues of why monotheistic religions felt it necessary to codify human domination over *all* animals. Or why the Christian church of the Middle Ages was so down on pets.

Let's start here — why the medieval church didn't like pets. The problem with pet keeping is that it challenged their carefully constructed world view: God first, man next, everything else created specifically to serve man. Sophia Menache suggests that this helps explain why vilification of the types of animals often kept as pets is a particular feature of monotheistic religions, but not polytheistic ones; faiths which sport many gods often take a far more reverent approach to the non-human. She feels this may be linked to the importance of maintaining control. Religions adhering to the concept of an all-powerful, omniscient single god, rely on a strict hierarchy to keep everyone in their place. Perhaps, suggests Menache, when humans form a relationship with another species, it breaks this "natural" chain of command, undermines the authority of the clergy, and makes the lay community far less subservient.[7]

Another and possibly more sustainable argument is that pet keeping considerably strained the Christian church's determined efforts to separate man from beast. As we have seen, this obsession came from a number of sources — including the intellectual traditions of the Greeks, and the attitudes inherited from a Middle Eastern community justifiably concerned with disease. (I focused on rabies as it is the most striking example, but other zoonoses would also have been prevalent, such as hydatids, common in sheep-growing regions.) A third reason was also related to control. The polytheistic pagan religions, widespread throughout Europe before the blitzkrieg of Christianity, were strongly centred within the "natural world". From the thirteenth century on, the drive to obliterate all traces of pagan belief involved stamping out anything with even the slightest whiff of animal worship.

Whatever its origin, the human/rest of creation divide was, by medieval times, a fundamental tenet of the Christian faith — with the clergy committed to upholding it. And how was this chasm maintained? By the simple expedient of asserting that humans have "reason" and "souls" — and the rest of the animal world does not.

Hence the problem with pet keeping. How could someone live closely with an animal as empathetic as a cat or dog and not believe they were sentient? If they believed in souls, how could people grieve for the death of a beloved companion and take comfort in a faith that said the essence of their pet was not with

God in heaven? As Serpell has suggested, pet keeping subtly elevated the status of animals to that of "semi-human".[8] It was not something to be tolerated by the church with its clearly mapped hierarchy and, as we have seen with the witch trials in which the church was often involved, it was at times quite ruthless in its condemnation.

The ultimate expression of this obsession over the human–animal distinction was seen in the issue of bestiality. To paraphrase Serpell, if pet keeping turned animals into people, then bestiality turned people into beasts.[9] The response of the judiciary and the church (often one and the same) to such a crime was immediate and violent. Death was automatically the sentence — for both parties. Ayrault, the seventeenth-century author of *Ordre Judiciaire*, wrote that he had seen animals put to death many times for the offence of bestiality. A later writer recorded that in 1662, a 60-year-old man by the name of Potter was taken to the gallows — but not before witnessing the execution of his fellow sinners and lovers: one cow, two heifers, three sheep and two sows. Obviously a veritable farmyard Lothario — despite being a "pious member of the church" for 20 years.

Mind you, there was one donkey that got off. In the town of Vanvres, France, in 1750, one Jacques Ferron was caught in the act of coition with an ass, and both were taken into custody. When it came to trial, the man was duly sentenced to death. The local priest, however, spoke up on behalf of the donkey, arguing that she was the unwilling victim of her master's violence. In a signed statement, he and several other commune members attested that in the four years they had know the she-ass, she had always shown herself to be virtuous and well behaved, both at home and abroad. They were willing to vouch for her good character and, if shown clemency, were sure that she would never sin in that way again.[10]

The anti-pet line was an impossible one for the Christian church to maintain. Even its own members were disposed to living with animals. In a famous example, a group of nuns at Romsey Abbey in the thirteenth century were discovered by a (male) clergy member to be keeping pets. So distraught was he by this affront that he immediately dispatched a letter, warning the nuns to desist at once or imperil their mortal souls.

The illuminated texts of the Middle Ages, so lovingly and lavishly decorated by the educated clergy, are littered with cats, dogs and other creatures; climbing up margins, eyeing off rats on the opposite page, and entwining themselves in and out of the elaborate lettering. And frequently, the portrayal is sympathetic — these animals were clearly not despised satanic agents, but objects of affection. Animals even found their way into the most holy of religious scenes — in one picture of the crucifixion, a little dog sits at the feet of Jesus.

Other writings betray the care and pride taken in animal husbandry. In the fourteenth century, the French Comte de Foix, Gaston Phoebus, published an exquisitely illustrated book, *Le Livre de la Chasse* — the book of the hunt. In it, he catalogues the various tasks which must be undertaken to ensure healthy and happy dogs. He advises that dogs must be taken for a walk two to three times a day, and that the straw or hay used to line a dog's kennel must be replaced daily. Another section shows figures carefully examining the teeth or legs of their charges, and applying bandages and medicants to treat various common canine illnesses. Early veterinary medicine — and obviously quite advanced by medieval times. Rather humbling for a modern vet, actually.

Esther Cohen, a senior lecturer in medieval history at Israel's Ben Gurion University, lists a series of examples where the clergy faced a losing battle — or were even won over to the other side.[11] In Germany, the priests were annoyed by the peasants' seemingly incurable habit of showing holy relics to their horses whenever they were sick. A "mass for horses" was held throughout parts of Europe — and was particularly common in Bavaria. There are other examples of animal feast days, in which the clergy were obviously willing participants, but the most celebrated case of Church endorsement is that of the dog that became a saint. Legend has it that a knight, upon returning home to find his dog covered in blood near his child's cradle, turned on the hound which he thought guilty of murder and killed him. When he later discovered that the dog had, in fact, saved the still-sleeping child from the bite of a snake, he was filled with remorse, burying the dog carefully in a well, and planting a stand of commemorative trees. The site became a destination of pilgrims, with the local peasantry attributing great healing powers to the dog, which was made a saint — Saint Guinefort. A thirteenth-century Dominican clergy-man, Etienne de Bourbon, did his utmost to eradicate the cult which grew up around the dog — yet remnants of it could still be detected as late as the nineteenth century.

Although seemingly less confused in their approach, even the more overtly hostile religions such as Islam are suffused with contradictions. Just as in European art and story-telling, and in what we know of ancient Greek and Roman cultures, even in apparently antagonistic cultures the dog could symbolise faith-fulness and loyalty. The Koran tells of an incident where a group of the faithful are running in fear for their lives from persecution. A dog approaches to stand guard. Obviously not appreciating the dog's higher motives, the men throw stones at the unfortunate canine and break three of its legs. At this point, the mouth of the dog, Kitmal, opens and says, "I too am the creature of God. As I love him as my creator, and loving God, I love thee also who love God. Sleep masters and I will keep watch over you." Allah, impressed with the dog's faithfulness to its tormentors, gives the dog the power of speech, and rewards it with a free trip to heaven.

My acquaintance, Ramsee Guranathan from Pakistan, told me another illustrative story. An Islamic man who worked in a nearby government department once called on Ramsee and begged him to come quickly, for he'd just found an injured stray dog. The dog, to use a technical Australian veterinary term, was cactus. It had internal injuries, and a spinal blow meant it was a quadriplegic. When this was explained, the man agreed reluctantly to have the dog put down but not before, visibly upset, he pleaded with Ramsee to be gentle and kind when he did it.

The final story in this litany comes from David Paxton. Unlike the previous examples, it does not concern any of the monotheistic religions, but comes from a region where the dominant culture is Hindu.

While he was working for some months in India, Paxton became involved with a local shelter which looks after people and animals. Despite the discussion earlier about the relative benevolence of polytheistic religions, life for an animal in India is frequently far from idyllic. Reverence for life often leads to benign neglect — to Western eyes, the height of cruelty. And the Indian pariah dog must be one of the sorriest-looking canines around.

While Paxton was visiting the shelter one day, a group of shopkeepers brought in a rather decrepit and clearly sick dog. Obviously, the animal was one of the street dogs that hung around the market area. Yet over the month the dog was being treated, one or other of the shopkeepers visited every day. They were never observed to pat the animal; they would just sit quietly at a distance. But every day, they brought the dog a tomato. Why, Paxton asked. "It likes tomatoes", one of the shopkeepers replied simply. After the dog recovered, the shopkeepers took it back to live on the street.

Such is the profound nature of the relationship between humans and dogs that even in cultures where dogs are despised, there is still a great reluctance to kill them. The exception, of course, is where dogs are dinner.

DOGS AS DINNER

Visitors to a Southeast Asian market are often dealt a nasty shock. Even though you expect it, it's difficult for a Westerner to look at the rows of skinned dogs and cats swinging from their meat hooks with any degree of equanimity. And to be offered dog or cat as dinner is a formidable test for even the most willing multi-culturalist.

A friend of mine, biologist Dr Amanda Vincent, recently spent some time in the Philippines studying her great love, sea horses. The house in which she was staying was in a small village and had a dog. This dog kept getting pregnant, so Amanda decided it should be spayed and started to make inquiries. The first problem was making herself understood by the villagers. Once that hurdle was crossed, she was met with total bewilderment and consternation. Why would she want to do such a thing? "But," she responded in desperation, "what will we do with all the puppies? What if we can't find homes for them all?" That totally stunned them. Then they started to laugh. They assured her that, really, she shouldn't worry because there wasn't a problem. Amanda says it was one of the few times she felt totally silly and Western.

Dog eating has obviously been shocking Europeans for centuries. James Serpell relates the story of the nineteenth-century North American explorer George Caitlin, who was incredibly impressed by the devotion the Sioux Indians displayed towards their dogs.[12] They hunted together, shared their beds, and remained in close, affectionate proximity at all times. Only, shortly after

Caitlin arrived and started thinking his lyrical thoughts, the Indians slaughtered several of their faithful companions and served them up as stew. Despite having to endure probably one of the more queasy meals of his life, Caitlin understood the incredible honour he was being shown. This was the ultimate sacrifice for the ultimate pact of friendship; and was performed with all the solemnity befitting a sacred religious rite. The Sioux also had the good grace to shed the odd tear.

Dogs and cats are regarded as food items in quite a few parts of the world — Southeast Asia, Indochina, the Pacific islands, North and South America and parts of Africa. The practice of eating dogs may even have been widespread throughout Neolithic and Bronze Age Europe.

Its origins are probably quite simple — lack of other suitable protein sources. Dog and cat eating is commonly found in island communities, where a shortage of indigenous mammals or domesticated herbivores has meant that at various stages during the colonisation of these areas the scavenging cats and dogs were fair game — the only readily obtainable source of meat around. (Amanda Vincent points out that dog eating was never done lightly — only if the fishing harvest failed, or in association with some special ceremony.) It's no coincidence that dog eating is often practised in the same areas as cannibalism. Both are thought to have originated from protein shortages. From there, the practice of eating dogs was overlaid with human culture — so much so that I've been told that some Asian students today are encouraged by their families to eat dog before an important exam — apparently it's good brain food.

But eating dogs still poses some dreadful dilemmas for the communities in which it is practised. It's very hard to empathise with a being, let it into your home, perhaps even, as happens in various Polynesian islands, suckle a puppy on the breast alongside your own children, and then cook it up for dinner. How is it managed?

In answer: all sorts of justifications are resorted to. First of all, there is commonly a clear distinction between those dogs which are pets and those which are food. In Polynesia, closer examination by anthropologists revealed that those animals which were suckled by humans were never eaten. This was justified by asserting that the animal which was thus fed took on some of the essence of the human and was therefore exempt.

Food animals are further distinguished by virtue of naming. A lottery, but if an animal manages to get named, it's a bit like holding a "get out of the pot free" card. The same naming principle works on Australian farms. Sunday roast is still a treat in many parts of the country, and any anonymous lamb frolicking in the fields has a chance of being taken for lunch. But not Betsy or Lambkin or Molly who were bottle-reared by the farmer's children. They will be wandering around the paddocks, untroubled and unmolested until the day they die of natural causes.

In South America, the journey along this demarcation path has gone even further, with a distinct breed of dog developed purely for eating. It has no hair and looks quite un-doglike. So the separation is clear: over here are the dogs that are human's best friend; over there is food with a tail.

There's one more way to ease the guilt. It helps, of course, if being eaten by humans is *good* for the animal. Then you don't need to feel bad at all. If the animals are "sacrificed" in a spiritual, ritualistic way, then we nice humans are actually doing them a favour, assisting them on their way to paradise, or some such wonderful place.

Of course, these kinds of contortions and obvious absurdities are not confined to dog eating. We see them with all forms of animal use or exploitation. Part of the unique problem which faces our species and no other is that at a visceral level we identify other animals as fellow sentient beings like ourselves, while still wanting to take whatever we can from them. James Serpell has summed up the central moral dilemma thus: a human being is a "killer with a conscience". And we cope with our conscience by denial. And this brings us to a deeper explanation for the Church's condemnation of pet keeping in the Middle Ages.

The reason was rampant self-interest. Humans use animals — as we noted in the previous chapter, if they hadn't, we probably wouldn't have got where we are now. No cars, no computers, no little lights which cheerfully pop on when we open the fridge door. It is difficult (although not impossible) to use friends — particularly if that use involves a fair degree of hardship for the friend used. The more barriers we place between ourselves and those familiar others, the easier it is to exploit them. The Church says animals were created for our use; other philosophers help out by saying they don't have any feelings; and presto — we are absolved of all guilt. The thirteenth century in Europe marked the beginning of a period of substantial animal exploitation. The aristocracy intensified its hunting, shooting and fishing activities, and the economy increasingly relied on expanding agriculture. Humans were pitted against the "natural world"; and were determined to tame it and win. The Church did its bit — and pet keeping was an unfortunate casualty of a larger ideological war.

The ultimate "use" is, of course, to eat another being. Because our imagination gives us such an incredible ability to empathise, to eat our flocks and herds we humans need as much help as we can get — God letting us know it's okay isn't enough. James Serpell groups the methods employed into four categories: detachment, concealment, misrepresentation and shifting the blame.[13] We detach ourselves from those we eat by giving names to some of our animals but not others. We conceal the killing process by having it done for us by someone else — in Australia by highly automated slaughterhouses, and then using euphemisms such as "pork" for the "product" we consume. We misrepresent the killing of animals that don't suit our purposes by declaring them to be "vermin". And we shift the blame by separating out the killing process so that one person rears the animal, another transports it, another kills it, another packages it; and no one is directly responsible.

The Cambridge anthropologist and Amazonian expert Stephen Hugh-Jones has compared the "civilised" approach taken in France to meat eating with that of the "primitive" Amerindian tribes he has spent so much time living among.[14] Looking beyond the superficial differences, what struck Hugh-Jones was how similar they are. The operations of the French abattoirs are suffused with symbolic separations. Chief of these is that the killing process is, in effect, performed by two people. One person stuns the animal, which is then passed on to the next person, who slits the animal's throat. No one actually "kills" it. What is interesting is that this self-deception is strongly reinforced in the abattoir design; the two parties are prevented from actually seeing each other.

Faced with the same problems of guilt associated with killing, the Amerindians must take a different approach. With their hunter-gatherer lifestyles, they don't have the luxury of divorcing themselves from the killing process, and are further hampered by their spiritual beliefs that animals are persons and all possess souls. In their myths they make no distinction between animals and people — all creatures talk and interact. Hugh-Jones had it explained to him by an Amerindian friend thus: *"Animals are like people"*.[15]

Hunting is therefore a very complicated business. It has to be planned correctly, the shaman consulted, and appropriate gifts given to the spirit animal masters, otherwise dire consequences might ensue. At worst, a person's soul could be captured by the spirit tapirs to stock up on the animal souls, so instead of coming back as a human, they come back as an agouti!

ANIMALS AS PETS

So far we've looked at several different cultural views — animal as devil, object, pariah and dinner. But what about the most familiar category of all? Animal as pet.

Throughout this book, the term "pet" has been used fairly loosely to mean an animal with which people have an affectionate relationship. Here, the term is used quite specifically to mean an animal that is kept for *no other purpose*.

The Amerindians are the quintessential pet-keepers. They keep no animals to eat, but their communities are absolutely full of animals. And they are all pets. These are not animals that have been bred within the villages, but babies which the hunters have gone out of their way to find and bring home. Especially macaws. Once there, the animals more or less have the run of the place — living out their lives in the village, or leaving when it's time to breed. Stephen Hugh-Jones suggests that to some extent this may be some form of atonement to the creature's parents. As if to say "I'm sorry I killed you but look what a wonderful job I'm doing with your children". But he also thinks there's a much easier explanation. Like us, the Amerindians are delighted by the antics of their pets.

(Incidentally, it's fascinating that the only animals with names "like people have names" are dogs. A macaw is called "Macaw Macaw"; an agouti, "Agouti Agouti". Dogs get *real* names. Like "Ohari", meaning "ashy" — a name a bit like our "Spot". Or the good hunters might get a noble name like "Toopari", which means "great warrior" — much like our "Caesar". Dogs are the only animals which breed within Amerindian communities. It's one more insight into the unique relationship of dogs to humans.)

In Europe, the rise of pet keeping from the eighteenth century onwards paralleled a steady shift in views of animals — from opportunism towards empathy. And the two movements were related.

Harriet Ritvo is a historian whose book *The Animal Estate* closely examines these changes in eighteenth- and nineteenth-century Britain.[16] Importantly, she traces the emergence of the RSPCA. Among other issues, Ritvo has looked at why it was that the RSPCA was founded in England. And she has found it was not, as popularly supposed, because England was a nation of "animal lovers".

In the late eighteenth century, at the time of the first uneasy stirrings towards animal protection, and for reasons we have already outlined, treatment of animals in Britain was probably at its worst. Far from being outstanding proponents of animal welfare, the British were known throughout Europe for their cruelty. In fact, England was referred to on the continent as "the hell of horses". The streets were full of abused animals — they were beaten, starved, driven beyond exhaustion until their feet bled, baited for sport, and forced to fight to the death for the amusement of their human masters. It was probably partly because treatment of animals was *so* bad, that the revolution occurred.

When the first — limited — animal protection Bill was introduced to the English parliament early in the nineteenth century, it was laughed out of the House. "But, these are the things that make the British what we are!" Members of parliament claimed cruel sports like bull baiting were character building — food for the fighting spirit, training arenas for the military might which underpinned Our Great Empire.

But the voice of compassion was consistent. In 1820, the first

Act to prevent animal cruelty was passed. It was restricted to livestock and draught animals and excluded dogs and cats and bulls — bull baiting and running, of course, being popular with the villagers, and essential for toughening the national character. It was truly the thin end of the wedge though, and in the 1830s legislation was passed to protect bulls, and later the comprehensive prevention of cruelty to animals Acts were introduced, which characterise the Western legislative frameworks of today. So, for example, in Sydney recently a man was prosecuted after he went to his office leaving his dogs in his car, returning half an hour later to find that of the three dogs he had left there, one was dead, another dying, and the third was able to be revived.

The Society for the Prevention of Cruelty to Animals (SPCA) was founded in 1800 by — ironically, given the Church's more recent history on this score — an Anglican priest. It hit a profound chord with the public and rapidly became *the* charity for, as it was sometimes patronisingly put, "little old ladies to remember in their wills". The society was exceptionally good at marketing (a strength, by the way, which continues today). With royal patronage bestowed by Queen Victoria in 1840, the group has never looked back.

Why was the time ripe for such a philosophical reversal? I have already mentioned a kind of "backlash" effect after the revolting excesses of rampant utilitarianism. But there were of course other reasons. One of the most important was the feeling that the war against nature had been won. No longer was the world that wild and fearful place which had to be subjugated and tamed at all costs. Humans had proven they were all-powerful — their civilisation could turn untidy wilderness into manicured gardens, their burgeoning science would solve all conceivable problems. In addition, the growing middle class was removed from direct dependency on animals for their livelihood, so could step back and view them in ways other than as a means to an end.

Other humanitarian movements were emerging as well. The anti-slavery lobby slightly preceded animal welfare, and calls for the prevention of cruelty to children emerged slightly after. In fact, the child protection movement actually began as an offshoot from the SPCA. Incidentally, this link between the treatment of animals and people is remarkably consistent. Studies have shown that cruel and violent behaviours towards people in adult life is correlated with cruelty to animals in childhood; the one often prefaced by the other. Social workers are aware that children who kick dogs while out and about may be giving a clue to violent parental behaviour at home.[17] Around the world, animal protection legislation frequently appears to parallel the growth of belief in human rights. Ghandi famously said that the measure of the maturity of a civilisation is in how it treats its animals.

The final reason was undoubtedly an increase in the practice of pet keeping. The population had shifted to the city — home to the new and powerful middle class. In looking for things to do with their new-found wealth, they copied as far as possible the lives of the aristocracy — the only group who regularly kept pets for *no other purpose* than companionship. The middle class started keeping pets. This *was* new — a large proportion of the population keeping animals purely for their company. And it certainly wasn't just fashion. It also had something to do with the fact that most people no longer had much more association with the countryside than that of a tourist. The link between the rise of pet keeping and the rise of the SPCA is not hard to fathom. A pet becomes an honorary person and, if you believe your dog is a person it's easy to be horrified at the ill treatment of other dog-persons. And then to extend that to other animals. And then to join a widespread movement to improve the welfare of animals.

One curious outcome of the animal welfare movements which soon extended to mainland Europe concerned the French habit of eating horses. Far from being the ancient pagan ritual many assume, the practice, which so revolts Australian visitors, started only last century and, according to historian Harriet Ritvo, for mainly humanitarian reasons. At the time, the exhausted, half-starved ancient cab horse was an all too familiar sight. Someone had the bright idea that if people could be encouraged to eat horse, not only would it be a cheap source of protein, but the drivers might be inclined to keep their animals in better health, knowing they could be sold for food rather than glue. Exotic "hippophagic feasts" were staged, where the great and good sat down to sample a hundred and one ways to cook a "bellerophon" steak. It caught on in France, but not in Britain — it was all too much, it seems, for a people who eat sausages made of blood, and stuffed sheep's stomachs full of ground-up organs!

To finish, we return once more to the Europe of the Middle Ages. We started this brief tour of the cultural contexts of living with animals with a witch trial. We will close it with another trial. This time, on trial are not the people but the animals.

Animals on trial

The judge declared:

> We, in detestation and horror of the said crime, and to the end that an example may be made and justice maintained, have said, judged, sentenced, pronounced and appointed, that the said porker, now detained as a prisoner and confined in the said abbey, shall be by the master of high works hanged and strangled on a gibbet of wood near and adjoinant to the gallows and high place of execution belonging to the said monks, being contiguous to their fee-farm of Avin.

Witness accounts attest to the gravity of the crime:

> On the morning of Easter Day, as the father was guarding cattle and his wife Gillon was absent in the village of Dizy, the infant being left alone in its cradle, the said pig entered during the said time the said house and disfigured and ate the face and neck of the said child, which, in consequence of the bites and defacements inflicted by the said pig, departed this life.

The year was 1494; the place, a French monastery. Readers will be gratified to learn that this reprehensible (and apparently all too common) act of infanticide was punished in a fitting manner; but only after due consideration in a court of law. It was presided over by the respected "Jehan Levoisier, licenciate in law, the grand mayor of the church and monastery of Saint Martin de Laon of the order of Premonstrants and the alderman of the same place".

It's all in a remarkable book, called the *Criminal Prosecution and Capital Punishment of Animals*.[18] First published in Britain in 1906, the book outlines in great detail (and some humour) the extraordinary practice of putting animals on trial. This was common throughout the Middle Ages, and surprisingly did not cease until the early part of this century. In 1906 in Switzerland, a man was killed and robbed by Scherrer and his son, "with the fierce and effective cooperation of their dog". All three murderers stood trial. The two men received lifelong prison sentences, but the dog, "as the chief culprit, without whose complicity the crime could not have been committed, was condemned to death".

Child-killing swine were apparently a regular medieval hazard; there are umpteen accounts of pigs being strung up at the gallows as a deterrent to potential wrongdoers. What is so strange is not that the animals were put to death — after all, there was the public good to protect — but that the people went through the elaborate farce of a full trial beforehand. Animals were afforded exactly the same rights under the law as humans. In prison awaiting trial, they were entitled to the same allowance of the king's bread. Jailers charged the same fee for their board. At trial, they were entitled to legal representation. One sixteenth-century jurist is said to have made his reputation at the bar defending the province's rats. These irascible rodents had apparently had the hide feloniously to eat and destroy the local barley crop. Clearly this was not to be tolerated, and justice demanded they be tried for their crimes. Bartholemew Chassenee, appointed to represent the rats, was an unexpectedly enthusiastic champion, conducting his defence with great creativity and flair. He firstly obtained a stay by claiming that a single summons was not sufficient to notify all his clients, given that their homes were scattered in various villages around the countryside. Later, when the accused failed to appear for their revised assignation, Chassenee argued passionately that his clients could not be expected to attend court as it required placing themselves in great personal danger. The journey was not only lengthy, but involved the serious risk of confrontation with their fearsome and mortal enemy, the cat. With such a defence, it is no wonder they got off.

The farce went further, with the animals often dressed in human clothing for their public appearances, and ordered to be tortured before death. One sow was found guilty of killing a five-year-old boy, and was sentenced to be hanged by the hind feet. Her six piglets, who had been discovered stained with blood, were indicted as accomplices. Fortunately, they were acquitted because there was no direct evidence linking them with the murder. But three weeks later the piglets were brought back to court, as the owner refused to vouch for their future good conduct!

All this cost time, effort and money. Just to give some idea, the following bill was presented for the internment and execution of a sow in 1403:

> Cost of keeping her in jail, six sols parisis. Item, to the master of high works, who came from Paris to Meullant to perform the said execution by command and authority of the said bailiff, our master, and of the procurator of the king, fifty-four sols parisis. Item, for a carriage to take her to justice, six sols parisis. Item, for cords to bind and hale her, two sols eight deniers parisis. Item, for gloves, two deniers parisis.

Not to mention the legal fees for prosecution and defence counsel, and the time spent in court.

What was going on? Why go to such complicated lengths to rid the town of what essentially was a minor menace? And how, when the Church said that animals have no reason and no soul, could animals be held morally culpable in a court of law?

The Church, as it turned out, could not deal with this. They *ran* the trials — for much of the period under discussion, courts were essentially ecclesiastical. What's more, judging from the transcripts, it was frequently members of their clergy who actually brought in the complaints. But by their own definitions, an animal could not stand trial. Stymied.

There was a way around this, though. The culprit *could* be brought to justice if it wasn't an animal — if the animal were possessed by satanic influences. Therefore, if an animal had committed an evil act, it must, by definition, have been under the direction of the devil. In which case what was being prosecuted was not the soulless animal, but its ethereal inhabitant. Problem solved by a backflip with triple pike.

But was this the *people's* reason for bringing the animals before the law? Did *they* believe that what they were doing was ridding the world of devilish influences?

In the foreword to the recent reprint of the 1906 criminal trials book, three reasons for people bringing animals to trial were given. First, it was noted that by killing a known "rogue" animal, a social danger was eliminated. But why go to such elaborate lengths when all you have to do is get out the axe? Second, was the idea that the whole process served as a warning — as if to say, "Look, even a pig is not immune to the attention of the law; be ever watchful lest you transgress". The third reason (and here the author mentions the amazing fact that in ancient Greece even *statues* were prosecuted for falling on people) is based on the premise that it is almost impossible for us today to understand the real helplessness those of the pre-industrial age must have felt when faced with the apparent lawlessness and chaos of the world around them. The author feels that this is the heart of the matter. That the people, by subjecting such apparently random acts to the due process of their human-constructed law, were in some way able to feel they had a modicum of control. They were not totally hostage to the vagaries of a poorly understood, and frightening nature.

While I basically agree with this analysis, I believe there is a fourth reason. It comes back to the same simple, fundamental battlefield. The clash between the need to separate ourselves from others in order to allow their exploitation and the recognition of similarities, which leads unerringly to empathy. Despite the teachings of the Church, in living closely with animals which behaved in so many ways like them, the medieval mind could not but fail to think they had purpose. Sentience. Enraged at the brutal and senseless murder of a beloved child, betrayed by the sow they had sheltered, fed and raised, what the grieving parents called for was revenge. Her guilt was clear; the perpetrator had to pay. Whether she was possessed by the devil or not was completely irrelevant.

Like the Amerindians, they recognised a commonality. Unlike them, they were forbidden explicitly to express it. The animal trials represent an overflow from a subconscious pool of belief: *they thought animals were like people.*

CHAPTER 5

CULTURAL EXCHANGE: TALKING WITH THE ANIMALS

THE other day I was in a park. With me were my mother's two Tibetan Spaniels. As we wandered along, enjoying the sunshine and the abundant new speckles of pink and white and yellow of the spring garden, Joss, then Chloe, spotted a figure over by a bush. Tails wagged, ears pricked up, and I had no choice but to follow the dogs running across to the rose garden. I could see Chloe hang back a little shyly as she usually does, but Joss was confidently engaging a rather larger German Shepherd. They were nose to nose at first; then the canine waltz began, each pursuing the rear end of the other in a stately, circling dance. Before long, the pas de deux broke and Joss was standing quite still, allowing the larger dog to sniff delicately around the base of his tail. All this happened very quickly — in the minute it took me to stride the extra few metres to join the group. By that time a young woman whom I didn't know was already bending down to offer her hand to Joss and say hello. A laugh and a half-uttered greeting from me was interrupted as her dog put his nose under my hand and demanded I acknowledge him first. I bent down, patted him, told him how handsome he was, and only then looked up to say hello to the young woman.

All the while, parallel conversations were taking place — me with the young woman, each of us with the other's dogs, and the three dogs exchanging greetings, credentials and engaging in a bit of a play. This took about five minutes. When the stranger and I accepted some mutual, unspoken signal to continue on our different paths, we parted and called the dogs to us, who eventually broke off their game and trotted forward with the correct human, ready for the next adventure.

What I had just been part of was a *cultural exchange*. Two people, three animals; each participant with their slightly different ways of communicating, yet with sufficient mutual understanding to ensure the exchange was an amiable one.

This chapter looks at animals and culture in a rather different way. It looks at how animals have insinuated themselves into our higher cultural expression — our art, our literature — but it also examines the more interesting question of whether this has been a two-way street. Just as they have affected our culture, have we altered theirs? Do animals even have a culture? And, most provocatively, over the millennia of our cohabitation, has a new language evolved to help us talk with the animals?

DOGGED BY ANIMALS

In 1996, an unusual Australian film took the world by storm and was tipped to win an Oscar. The film was unusual not because it was Australian and did well overseas, but because the human actors took such a backseat role — the star was a talking pig. Memorable players included a wise Border Collie, who supported Babe in his quest to become a sheep-pig, and a sheep called Ma, who explained that all Babe, the little pig, had to do to get the other animals to oblige was to ask politely. More than one grown-up needed a tissue when Babe won the sheep trials.

The success of *Babe* isn't surprising — it's just that it's been a few years since we've had quite such a prominent animal hero. Skippy was an international phenomenon, and Lassie was single-handedly responsible for convincing the world that Rough Collies can understand human speech.

Animals have featured heavily in human cultural expression since the beginning. You'd think, being the self-important species we are, that our earliest attempts at art would be about ourselves. They weren't; the first cave paintings were almost always of animals. The oldest recognisable figures, at Lascaux and similar sites, are of prey animals — horses, deer, buffalo. (Interestingly, zoologist Desmond Morris suggests in his autobiography, the position of the hoofs in these paintings indicates that the artists used animal corpses to help get the fine detail right — the hoofs are curled over in a way you don't see in life.[1]) Once the domestication process was well under way, the more familiar cohabitants crop up in the artwork repeatedly.

Greek, Roman and Egyptian artefacts are covered in animals. They cavort around amphorae and frolic across frescoes — which is useful for historians, because this is the sort of information that tells us so much about our ancestors' relations with animals. How, for example, dog breeds have changed over time.

As we noted in Chapter 4, even medieval Christianity couldn't keep animals out of art. And a grand tour of the British National Gallery shows how intrinsic to European art cats and dogs were.[2] They leap across canvasses — from van Eyck, to Stubbs, to Gainsborough, to Constable, to Hogarth. And in the main, the dogs are not only nobly portrayed, they are groomed.

Dogs were essential to wedding pictures; proof of the loyalty and devotion of the happy couple. They were also very useful to fill in foregrounds. And, most importantly, dogs are pointy. Many famous artists have used this accident of anatomy to great advantage. In one lovely wedding portrait by Gainsborough, the dog's triangular nose points to an important spot on the bride's hand — the site of her wedding ring. In another picture by George Stubbs, the noses of two dogs on either side direct the eye up across the composition in an arc shape. Dogs are, in fact, pointed at both ends, so in the famous Constable painting "Hay Wain", the dog in the foreground acts as a fulcrum, with the tail drawing the eye up into the left of the painting, and the nose taking you up to the right. Perhaps the relative scarcity of cat pictures had little to do with their being less common in society, and more to do with a decided lack of pointiness!

Representing, as they often did, the moral standing of their owners, animals didn't always assume such noble positions. A cautionary tableau by Jan Steen shows a slatternly looking child feeding a kitten some of her pie, while a woman offers a parrot wine from a glass, and another woman sleeps near an empty jug — all "The Effects of Intemperance". A series by Hogarth shows the descent of a marriage into hell. In the first picture, a nice pair of dogs accompany the well-presented couple. In the next few frames, things deteriorate. By the final scene, there are dead bodies lying everywhere and the dog looks positively skeletal, glaring about it like some ghoulish fiend.

Using animals to represent human characteristics in this way has an ancient pedigree, and this should not surprise us. When our species first started to develop the capacity for symbolism and abstract thought, naturally they turned to what was around them. As we have seen, the worlds of hunter-gatherers are suffused with animal "persons" — living and ethereal. The totemism of some cultures (which links a person with a spiritual animal partner) is mirrored by the metaphor and allegory of our own. We tend to endow animals with certain traits — deserved or not — and then apply them to our fellows. So a thief is "as sly as a fox"; a recalcitrant "as stubborn as an ox"; a battle hero "as brave as a lion" (a particularly unfair accolade, given that it's the lionesses that do all the hunting, while the males just stand around looking good and roaring). Every culture uses animal symbols as tribal or clan markers.

And although most animals are treated with some consistency across cultures (the bull and lion are universally admired; the rat shunned), the symbolic fortunes of the dog seem to fluctuate. At times, and often simultaneously, dogs are used to symbolise both the highest and the lowest of human characters.

In ancient Greece and Rome, dogs did pretty well. The most famous classical poem, the *Odyssey*, describes how dogs often escorted their owners to social and political functions, and were given special tidbits by their masters. When the hero returns home from his epic voyage, quite a point is made of the fact the only one to recognise Ulysses is his ancient dog Argus, a model of fidelity.

The Spartans used words for the male and female puppy as nicknames, and ancient writers consistently emphasised the dog's loyalty, affection, faithfulness — with humans usually the poorer for the comparison. There is a story recorded by the Greek writer Plutarch about the evacuation of Athens during the Persian invasion in 480 BC. Apparently, as their masters boarded their boats, the dogs they were leaving behind ran alongside with yearning cries of increasing distress. One dog, owned by the father of Pericles, could not bear the abandonment, finally leaping into the sea and swimming across the strait to the side of his master's boat. He was pulled from the water, only to faint and die immediately. The site of his "tomb" is still pointed out as a tourist attraction.

The Roman writer Pliny related the tale of a dog belonging to a dead slave. When the unfortunate man's body was thrown out onto some steps, the dog stood by the corpse and howled. When someone threw food to the dog, he took it to the mouth of his dead master. When the body was thrown into the Tiber, the dog leaped into the water and tried to keep it afloat. All the onlookers were very impressed.

Yet, at other times, dogs have represented gluttony and debasement, their lewd and shameless behaviour on the streets an affront to any upstanding citizen. In England, the divide often ran along class lines, so that while the hounds of the aristocracy were nobility itself, the behaviour of the lawless curs and mongrels of the lower classes was proof of their owners' moral inferiority.

Then again, such reactions may just have had to do with one peculiarly canine habit. When dogs mate, the male twists around, restricting the venous drainage from the penis back through the body, at the same time as a muscle in the female dog's vagina clamps shut. It's called the "copulatory tie", and the two animals can remain locked together for up to an hour. This rather public and prolonged display has been known to upset a few sensibilities in more prudish times. But although it may have offended folk of the Victorian period, it hasn't worried the Lisu tribe of Thailand, who have come up with a good explanation for the phenomenon. Apparently, humans were once stuck with the copulatory tie. As you can imagine, this was extremely inconvenient, and sometimes made it very difficult to get much work done. So humans went to God, asking for some help. God obviously agreed it was a bit of a handicap, and generously decided to swap human genitals with those of dogs. What a relief! Now it is only dogs that have to put up with being stuck together for hours at a time; but that doesn't matter, because dogs don't do any work anyway!

Myths are invariably populated by animals: from the cautionary tales of Aesop to an African tribe's explanation for death. One such legend has it that when death first appeared, the people sent a cat and dog up to heaven to plead to God for help. Unfortunately, the dog became distracted by a large pile of bones, and it was all up to the cat to carry on with the message. Only the cat, being stupid as cats are, got the instructions mixed up. Now, everyone dies and stays dead. Of course, the Beng don't blame the cat because that is what you expect of a cat. They blame the dog for being greedy![3]

In poetry, however, the cat comes into its own. Whether it's because cats are intrinsically more "lyrical" than dogs, or a result of the clichéd "cats are the companions of women and artists", they feature heavily in verse. From Chaucer to Ogden Nash to T. S. Eliot, cats saunter across stanzas and dance through ditties. And many poets are under no illusions as to who's the boss.

> Listen Kitten,
> Get this clear;
> This is my chair.
> I sit here.
> Okay, Kitty,
> We can share;
> When I'm not home,
> It's your chair.
> Listen Tom Cat,
> How about
> If I use it
> While you're out?
> Richard Shaw[4]

In today's advertising and film, the cat usually represents family values and contentment. The surreptitious addition of a sleeping cat to a scene selling lounge room furniture tells us that this is a place where we can curl up and feel at home. For example, a Natural Gas ad doesn't have any people in it: a cat and a dog sit comfortably together, gazing into the glowing gas fire. You can feel the warmth emanating from the magazine page. There is another side to the coin, however: cats are absolutely essential to the horror film. Nothing is quite as startling as the "Rrreeoow" of a frightened cat!

Modern Western imagery now seems to have spurned the negative connotations of the dog. Advertisers use dogs as shorthand for faithfulness and friendship. In the United States, they are frequently used to sell beer. Spud Mackenzie is *the* party animal: if you drink like him you'll be really popular and have plenty of buddies. In Australia, patriotic shoppers go out to buy the completely Korean Daewoo car because it must be all-Australian, like that clever cattle dog in the ad. And a remarkable series of photographs shows the American presidents relaxing with their dogs. Nixon had a Labrador; Ford, a Golden Retriever; Reagan, a dog that was apparently uncontrollable. Clinton had no dog when he entered the Oval Office but, under pressure, acquired one before leaving it. Politicians know the value of image — dogs spell trustworthiness.[5]

These are just the briefest of examples of how our animal companions — cats and dogs — have entered our poetry, art and advertising. Our culture has indeed been invaded; the evidence is on my television, hanging from my walls, staring at me from my bookshelf. Let's turn now to the most important sphere of influence. Our conversations.

ANIMAL CHATTER

"I've been working like a dog, I'm dog tired, and basically I think my life has gone to the dogs."
"Why, what's bugging you?"
"He's a complete and utter pig."
"You don't think you're being a bit catty?"

"No, I've just found out he's been sniffing round that bitch in dispatch."

"Ahh; someone let the cat out of the bag. If I were you, I'd forget him. Move on and let sleeping dogs lie."

It doesn't take much imagination to work out that this is a hypothetical conversation between two women. Excessive, but an opportunity to cram as many animal clichés as possible into one short paragraph. (By the way, the origin of the term "letting the cat out of the bag" dates from at least the fourteenth century, when all supplies were purchased at weekly farmers' markets. A prized item was a young suckling pig for feast days or special occasions. The piglets were sold in bags, and occasionally unscrupulous farmers substituted a cat that weighed about the same. Unless the purchaser checked, she'd get home and find a worthless cat in her bag.[6] I dread to think how they stopped the "piglet" miaowing!)

Think of all the conversations in a day, a week, a month. Then, take a note of how many times you use a description of an animal. You probably haven't even noticed, such is their subtle pervasion of our language. Yet there's rarely a day when we don't use some faunal phrase. Even if it's just the half-conscious early morning thought after a heavy night out: "God, I feel sick as a dog".

Recently in Australia, we were inflicted with the politics of the "underdog". Following an election result in Queensland where the popular incumbent was overturned after a skilful appeal for the protest vote, every party started heading for the doghouse. This was the prize position. In a complete reversal of traditional politicking, the underdog status was fought for as bitterly as dogs over a bone. Before the 1996 federal election, even clear winners in the polls were quick to point to their own mangy status compared with the fat cats on the other side. It's a dog-eat-dog world in politics, as they say.

Political arenas are not known for their civility, so it's not surprising that dogs occasionally feature heavily. It's intriguing how often dog terms are used to denigrate opponents. Even in cultures that hold dogs in high esteem, to be likened to a dog is invariably a term of abuse. A man is quite happy to be called an ox or a stallion, even — if pushed — a cat (especially if it's a tom), but no one wants to be known as a dog. To be called a dog, or to be told you live "like a dog" is always an insult. Even their much applauded loyalty translates into a weakness; to be accused of "fawning like a dog" is a great slight on a person's character.

Why? Again, it has to do with the sorts of issues raised in the last chapter. The dog is singled out for this rocky ride because it is simply too close to us. As James Serpell, scholar of the pet-keeping phenomenon, states, the dog lives in the uneasy space between human and non-human. Symbolically, "an interstitial creature, neither person nor beast, forever oscillating uncomfortably between the roles of high-status animal and low-status human".[7]

The frequency with which familiar animals are used in abusive language is telling in itself. In 1964, a ground-breaking paper was published by anthropologist Edmund Leach. It was entitled *Anthropological Aspects of Language: Animal categories and verbal abuse.*[8] In it, Leach explores the invocation of animal terms, linking it with taboo, edibility and the language of obscenity. Of chief interest here is his conclusion that humans only have three forms of verbal abuse: obscenity (to do with bodily functions), profanity (to do with religion) and animal terms. It is a complex paper, and one that has stimulated discussion and debate ever since. The reason I raise it is not so much for what's in it, but because of a comment made to me *about* the paper. Professor Andrew Rowan was one of the founders of the relatively new science of anthro-zoology, the study of human–animal interaction. He helped establish the multi-disciplinary journal on the subject, *Anthrozoos,* of which he is now editor. (And it was in this journal that Leach's paper was reprinted in the late 1980s.) When I asked Andrew Rowan why he had chosen his life-long study, he replied, "Whenever one of my colleagues asks me that, I tell them about the Leach paper. I then tell them *I* have chosen the only subject which is as important to humans as sex and religion."

Animal chatter isn't all unfavourable, however. While sex, religion *and* politics for that matter are all topics we are told should not be raised at dinner parties, it seems the one topic that's not only permissible but almost obligatory is that of pets.

Try this next time you visit a small group of friends for a delicious meal, Chardonnay in the right hand, bread stick in the left. Tell one story about a pet, just one. Then sit back (if you can resist the overwhelming urge to join in) and watch it happen. Each guest will compete for the chance to tell their favourite pet story — tumbling over each other in their eagerness, two sometimes talking at the same time, the loudest declared the winner. As one friend put it: pet stories propagate. These tales, however, fulfil an important function. There are so few topics common to all, and the art of storytelling is limited nowadays by lack of practice and opportunity. Yet everyone can tell a tale of a pet. We can also talk about children this way, but these days we don't all have kids. A study by social researcher Maree MacCallum shows just how important pets have become as a conversation topic. It claims "pet stories are an abundant source of folklore, legends and stereotypes which amuse and deeply satisfy pet owners".[9]

And books for young children are just teeming with animal characters. Brer Rabbit, Peter Rabbit, Winnie the Pooh, the Muddle-headed Wombat and Blinky Bill. Children's cartoons rarely feature a human at all; and when they do, it's invariably as a foil. In "Tom and Jerry", we never even see the face of the human characters — only bodies and legs. This combination of animals and children is so obvious that psychiatrist Aaron Katcher decided to analyse the phenomenon, eventually reporting the extraordinary finding that 94 per cent of books used to teach young American children language use animals.[10]

It's an amazingly high percentage, and is yet another reminder of how deeply the fortunes of our two species are intertwined. We use animals to teach our children language. What are the words a child learns soon after Ma and Da? Dog, cat or cow. One friend expressed her chagrin that her baby learned the words for Da and dog before she learnt Ma. (Although she did hastily mention that babies find the "d" sound easier to pronounce than the "m" sound. Still it's a tough one to explain to your friends.) And this brings us back to the central motif of this discussion, and one which we will explore in greater depth now: how we talk with our animal companions.

TALKING WITH THE ANIMALS

When I was a small child, my cat was my constant companion. She'd be waiting for me when I got home from school, she slept on my pillow at night. I have to confess, she even had her kittens on my bed.

I talked to my companions all the time. You see, I was convinced I could speak fluent Cat. My parents aided and abetted me in this delusion. Whenever one of the cats miaowed, Mum or Dad would ask me seriously what they were saying, and I would miaow a few notes myself, and cock my head as I listened to the reply. I'd then explain that Jo Jo was hungry, or she had been busy today and was a bit tired. Wherever I went, it seemed to me cats would seek me out for a chat.

Other animal languages I didn't find quite so easy, though I was rather good at Crow. At my grandparents' farm, when we heard the "Aaah, Aaah, Aaa-ii-eoww", which announced the crow had arrived in the nearby gum tree, lunch would stop, and my grandfather would open the window so I could exchange a few squawks. I didn't know what I was saying, but I did know that I was having a conversation. I was sure the crow understood.

I can't remember when I lost that — when the crow stopped visiting; when the miaows of cats no longer had specific meaning. By the time I reached veterinary school, it was well and truly gone. I didn't miaow any more. Animals had behaviours instead of meanings, and I accepted that although I might understand a lot about their motivations, real communication was for people. Since then, I've changed my mind again. I had it right as a child; I really *can* speak Cat. Only not in the way I thought I could.

A FANTASY?

When you think about it, it's remarkable how much we talk to our pets. We chat, point things out to them, and ask their opinions. It's a defining feature of the relationship, and one which once threatened to disrupt the research plans of Professor Aaron Katcher. Katcher, of whom we'll hear much more in the next chapters, was one of the founders of the field of studying human–animal interactions. More than a decade ago, when he was setting up an experiment to measure human blood pressure in the presence of a pet, a graduate student came and said the experiment wouldn't work. "What do you mean, it won't work?" asked the professor. Well, said the graduate, your design requires the subjects to sit silently with their pets, and no one can sit with a pet without talking to it!

The design of the experiment was duly changed, and Katcher later went on to study the phenomenon of human conversations with animals. Not only are we unable to resist talking to them, we even leave pauses to allow them time to "reply".[11]

This sort of conversation, though, is clearly one-sided. Much as the humans enjoy it, the animal surely has little idea of what is happening. It can hardly be called real communication when only one partner gets to contribute. So what *is* going on? When we talk to our pets, are we really communicating, or is it just fantasy on our part?

To find the answer to that question, we begin by taking a quick look inside the heads of our animal companions. How do we know whether they even have the bases for real communication with us? In fact, can we be sure they're conscious?

DO ANIMALS THINK?

The issue of animal consciousness has been a hot topic of debate among ethologists for some years. Many believe the concept can't be studied by reductive science, and should therefore be left to the philosophers. Others, that this is a "cop out", and that consciousness can and should be studied. And one of the foremost members of that growing camp is Marion Stamp Dawkins.

Marion Stamp Dawkins lectures in animal behaviour at the University of Oxford. For her doctorate in the early 1970s, she collaborated with one of the founders of the science of ethology, Nobel laureate Niko Tinbergen. She has also worked extensively with Donald Griffin, who has been stirring the pot on animal consciousness since the early 1980s. In 1992, Stamp Dawkins confronted the issue head on herself, with the release of a book called *Through Our Eyes Only?: The search for animal consciousness.*[12]

The crux of Stamp Dawkins' argument is that consciousness must make a difference to an organism. Otherwise, why would it have evolved? And if it makes a difference, then surely that difference can be studied.

She starts with the question of whether animals have intellect because this is relatively easy to test. Do animals think ahead or do they simply respond to a series of coded rules which say "if x is fed in, then y comes out", just like a computer (although it *is* extremely easy to believe your computer crashes deliberately). To think ahead, animals must have models in their minds which can be manipulated imaginatively. They have to "work things out" and choose the best option, rather than go through the time-consuming process of testing every alternative through trial and error.

This has been tested by scientists in many ways. One method is to see whether an animal can anticipate, based on a previous trajectory, where something is going to reappear once it goes out of sight. Pigeons are surprisingly adept at this, and cats can also track an object even if it disappears from view (for example, behind a tree) for part of the time. Mental maps are another testable concept. There's plenty of evidence of animals keeping maps in their heads, of which the most famous is the case of the honeybees, who were shown by Karl von Frisch to do a particular waggle dance to indicate the exact location of food. Certain animals — including rats — have been shown in experiments to have some notion of counting. In one experiment, rats were trained to enter a tunnel, but only if they passed a certain number of identical tunnels first — something they proved quite good at. This reminds me of my childhood belief that my cat, Jo Jo, could only count to four. Over several years, Jo Jo had four litters; on two occasions she had a litter of four, on the other occasions a litter of five. Each time after a kitten had been taken to its new home, Jo Jo would begin a frantic calling and searching phase, obviously quite distressed. Except she only did that when the number of kittens left was below four. When she had a litter of five, she never seemed to notice when the first one went.

Probably the most tantalising clue can be found in the question of whether animals can lie — the so-called "Machiavellian intelligence". Contrary to the popular perception that animals are "innocents" incapable of "sin", they do indeed lie, sometimes in quite convoluted ways. A classic example is the case of Belle and Rock, two chimpanzees. Their experimenters were investigating what happened when they hid food, but they only ever let one of the chimps in their study group know the location. Whenever Belle was chosen, she immediately led the group straight to the food. But then Rock, a dominant male, started to steal the food from her. So she tried sitting on the food — but he'd knock her off. Her next tactic was to go in the approximate direction of the food rather then straight to it, but Rock soon cottoned on and started keeping a closer watch. Eventually it got to the point where Belle would start by leading the group in completely the opposite direction, then quickly run back once they were busy. Eventually Rock started to keep a constant watch on Belle and she was thoroughly stymied!

While nowhere near as sophisticated, many dog owners have observed similar shenanigans in their own pets. Archaeologist Juliet Clutton-Brock, whom we met in Chapter 1, tells a story about her own dogs. Her two wiry crossbreds, mother and son, love to bark. No one can pass the front door without everyone knowing about it. One day, Juliet was watching the pair eat, and mother was taking all the food. Suddenly the son raced to the front door and started to bark. Sure enough, mother quickly joined him, whereupon he raced back and polished off the food. Juliet says he doesn't do it often, but every now and then will revel in his "marvellous trick".

Some animals, then, would seem to have a rudimentary capacity to count, have mental images of the world which they can manipulate, and can solve certain problems by "working things out". It points to an "intellect" of sorts — although of course there is still the killjoy rejoinder that a computer can do all these things by means of complex programs, and no one claims *they* have an awareness. More convincingly, a number of animals at least act in ways designed to "fool" others. For scientists such as Marian Stamp Dawkins, this implies they are "thinking ahead" and are aware of what they are doing.

DOES MY CAT LOVE ME? (THE DANGERS OF ANTHROPOMORPHISM)

So animals think. The next question is do they feel? Few scientists would doubt these days that animals have feelings of sorts. But whether these can be tested or whether they can be called "emotions" like those humans have is still open to discussion. Of course, what pet owners really want to know is does my cat love me or does she just "love" the cupboard?

Investigating animal emotions suffers from the same problems of methodology as investigating animal intellect, only more so. It's impossible to train a bird to peck a key if it is "happy". And when there's no simple test to gauge another human's feelings other than by asking them, can you ever really know what an animal feels?

The conundrum has flummoxed animal behaviourists for years, and it is evident in the technical literature. Mothers don't "love" but have maternal behaviours; fighting dogs don't show "anger" but aggression; animals don't have emotions but motivations. The worst insult you can hurl at a scientific colleague is to accuse them of anthropomorphism.

Anthropomorphism is almost impossible to prevent, however. Asking a human to stop seeing the world anthropomorphically is like asking them to stop eating or exploring or imagining. A tendency to perceive agency in all that surrounds is deeply ingrained. The ancient Greeks prosecuted statues, the office-bound consultant sees wilfulness in her computer. And there is a reason for it. Anthropomorphism had survival value. Our capacity to succeed is dependent on our skills of judgment; at "reading" a situation and choosing the most fruitful option. For our early ancestors, believing that others had minds helped them to make advantageous choices about their environment. So a hunter might think, "If I were a Macaw, where would I live?", or a farmer might think, "I must water these plants because they like to keep their feet wet". Some scientists have referred to this sort of reasoning as "applied anthropomorphism".

Plenty of theorists now hold the view that it was our need to interact socially that applied the strongest evolutionary pressure on our species for the development of intelligence and speech. We evolved social intelligence to deal with our companions, but the same intelligence proved useful for dealing with the world. Aaron Katcher sums this up beautifully in *The Biophilia Hypothesis*: "When living things are thought to be purposefully signalling to us, then all of the environment becomes a social environment."[13] Such a notion calls up a miraculous image of partaking in the life of a living, feeling universe — shades of Gaia.

But if you're a scientist trying to make objective sense of what you see, this natural tendency to imbue humanness must be fought — lest, horror of horrors, you fall into the "Clever Hans Trap". Clever Hans was hailed, at the beginning of this century, as the horse who could do sums. His owner was so convinced of his charge's abilities, he agreed to testing by the sceptics — only to find that what the animal was doing was reading subtle body language cues to stop tapping his hoof when he reached the right answer. What a disappointment. To this day, Clever Hans is used as a cautionary tale for every budding ethologist.

There is, of course, another potential danger from anthropomorphism. That is: of under-using it. In the fear of too loosely applying human emotions to animals, we may deny them emotional experience. This is certainly the tack taken by psychoanalyst Jeffrey Masson and biologist Susan McCarthy in their controversial book *When Elephants Weep: The emotional lives of animals*.[14] And it does seem rather unreasonable to assume that, despite mammals having similar hormones and brain structures to humans, they don't feel. Just as it seems illogical to believe that something as complicated as emotion could appear spontaneously in its full complexity in only one species — humans.

Many scientists, Marion Stamp Dawkins included, now believe animals *do* have emotions and, what's more, they can be studied — because emotions have a function.[15] Emotions make things *matter*. So an animal that feels something very strongly is much more likely to pursue a behaviour. If the pain is acute, to do anything to get away; if the "love" for offspring is intense, to go to insane lengths to protect the "loved" one. Such actions can be measured. And while we can't ask animals directly what they think and feel, we *can* design experiments that show us what they want. We can teach them to paw at a key if they would like a pat or run through water to find a particularly tasty piece of food. (Stamp Dawkins quotes one researcher who discovered much about the feelings of mice towards cigarette smoke by accident. He was trying to measure the effects of a constant stream of smoke, only the mice kept gumming up with their own excrement the tube that let in the smoke. A clear case of voting with your faeces!)

And if we're trying to discover whether animals "care" deeply about one another, it is significant that scientists have indeed shown that for many species, the desire for social interaction is a powerfully motivating force. Some years ago, I experienced a striking example of this kind of motivation in a cat — a species not generally known for being particularly discriminating in its attachments. After I had been away for almost four years, my old cat Jo Jo made no obvious greeting when I returned. Yet before I had even slept on my bed, she moved into her customary position in the childhood bedroom which, I was told, she had not entered since the day I left home. What is more, this one-eyed 15-year-old cat, who had never been the best of hunters and who had not caught a single animal in eight years, on the fourth day of my visit brought a bird to my room. She never did it again after I left. She was clearly "feeling" something.

This is certainly not to say that animals have the *same* feelings as us. Apart from anything, a dog can't feel the same because it can't think in the same way. Humans think in words — it makes our minds irrevocably different from all other animals. Whether, therefore, we can even use the same *words* to describe what animals are feeling as we do to describe what a human feels is still a subject of debate. But, all in all, when a dog comes running up to us, wagging its tail and licking us as though our coming home was the best thing that had happened to it all day, it seems fair to call it "love". It's probably as valid as when we use the same word for walking, yet they do it with four legs and we do it with two.

But does this actually mean animals are conscious? Well, as with emotions, it seems unreasonable to assume consciousness suddenly sprang up in one species. The philosopher of science, Karl Popper pointed out how much more practical it is to think all the options through, rather than go out and try each one and risk being eaten. Consciousness, it has been suggested, arose progressively through evolution because it gave its possessors an advantage. So a familiar thing such as driving a car might best be done "unconsciously", whereas in a completely novel situation — such as learning to drive — conscious thought helps. Another modern philosopher and cognitive scientist, Daniel Dennett, has looked at whether there is any definable property which sets apart one organism from another; some definable sentience.[16] He can't find one. He believes there is no sudden onset of "consciousness", merely increasingly complex minds. And, as we will see later, Dennett also believes that of all other animals — barring the primates — dog minds are the most akin to humans.

To the argument that we can never know the feelings of another creature, Marion Stamp Dawkins has this response: the same could be said of other humans.[17] There is no such thing as telepathy. We can't look inside each other's heads. We deduce what other people feel by observing their behaviour; for, as we know, words may deceive. A "leap of analogy" is made every time we watch another person and impute their feelings based on what we would be feeling if we were doing the same thing. The leap to animals which behave in ways we recognise is not that much further than the little hop to other people. It doesn't require a pole vault.

A NEW LANGUAGE

It probably comes as a surprise to most pet owners that anyone could doubt their animals are conscious. Scientists take more convincing. There are still critics — animal behaviourist John Kennedy's 1992 book, for example, warns against the emergence of *The New Anthropomorphism*[18] — but most now grant cats and dogs conscious experience. It seems a fair basis on which to claim, then, that when we "talk" to our pets it involves a genuine exchange of meaning — even emotion. It's a "real" conversation.

Now let's have a look at that conversation. When I was a child and had long conversations with my cat, she obviously had little idea what the words meant. She was still *engaged* by the conversation though, because underneath the words there was a great deal of communication between us. Yet although all pet owners know it happens, scientists know surprisingly little about the *elements* of that communication. For one simple reason: over the last few decades, a tremendous amount of work has been done on how wolves or dogs or even cats talk to each other, but until recently no one has looked specifically at how dogs or cats communicate with people. The one notable exception is a group of animal behaviourists operating out of the Anthrozoology Institute in Southhampton, England. And their research is turning up some surprising differences.

Dr John Bradshaw, who heads the institute, started with an idea. He suspected that the 12,000 (as is commonly held) years or more of living with humans could not have left dog language unchanged. As useful as wolf language is as a model for dog behaviour, Bradshaw thought it was time to consider dog language separately. So, to test whether there has been a substantial diversion from wolf communication, he and his colleagues looked at whether modern dogs displayed many wolf visual signals or behaviours. And they discovered that with few exceptions, they don't.[19]

Bradshaw and his team selected ten different groups of dogs, each one containing members of a single breed. They were chosen on the basis of a perceived gradient from the most wolf-like (the Siberian Husky) to the least (the Cavalier King Charles Spaniel), and the dogs in the different groups had to have lived together for at least a year.

Each group was then observed interacting in its familiar home environment, first, with no extra stimuli, and then with the addition of a bone or toy or person. Behaviours were recorded and scored against a report card listing fifteen significant wolf signals you might expect to see in a similar situation. When they collated the results, six of the breeds showed fewer than half the wolf signals. One breed, the Cavalier King Charles Spaniel, demonstrated only two out of the possible fifteen. In other words, most breeds of dogs are *not* speaking full wolf language.

So what does this mean? Well, there are several ways of looking at these results. The first theory put forward by the team has to do with neotenisation. Before conducting the experiment, the team hypothesised that they would find a gradient in the use of wolf signals corresponding with the degree of neotenisation of the breed (or, more strictly in this case, paedomorphism: the retention of juvenile body shape into adulthood).

This proved to be the case. With one interesting exception, when the breeds were ranged in appearance from the most wolf-like to the least, the signals dropped out. Clearly enough to be plotted on a line. The exception was the German Shepherd, which, although looking very wolf-like, showed fewer signals than the baby-faced Golden Retriever. This may be because Shepherds were actually developed from a line of classic sheep-herding stock, and then bred back to look more like wolves.

Another possible explanation of these results is that the complexity of body language in dogs has diminished — either because of the failure of some signals to develop in the dogs' highly juvenalised state or, more simply, because the animals have so changed in shape, they can no longer make the physical gestures of their ancestors.

But another rather more appealing explanation for dog owners lies in the radically different social settings of wolves and dogs. To understand this point, we need to look at what the wolf signals are for. In the case of wolves, the language developed with one clear purpose — harmony within the pack. Distribution of limited resources relies on maintaining strict hierarchies — and it's been proposed that much of wolf body language is about preventing the escalation of fights. So the submissive wolf quickly rolls on its back and shows its private parts and the dominant wolf sees there is no need to take the other wolf on. What Bradshaw and his team suggest has happened in the case of the dog is that the cost of signalling has been greatly reduced. In other words, if I were a wolf and tried to put my paws across the shoulders of another more dominant wolf, I'd probably have my head bitten off — literally. If I were a Golden Retriever and pawed another dog, it would all be taken as exuberant play. Goodness, I might even be rewarded for it by my owner. The fact that in the breeds that showed fewer than six of the possible signals it was almost without exception the submissive behaviours that had been lost, gives further support to this idea. Competition for resources needn't be fierce because humans provide all.

It is the third proposal, however, which is really exciting. One of the reasons Bradshaw's group started this kind of work was to issue a challenge. As we've mentioned, traditionally animal behaviourists have been looking for wolf-type behaviours in the dog. This has great merit, and it's helped us learn a lot about dogs. But what the members of the institute are saying is, if over 12,000 years or more of co-evolution dog language has diverged from wolf, does it necessarily mean that their language has diminished? Is it possible something new has emerged? If dogs can't or don't need to use the full range of wolf "language", could new "words" have taken their place?

The first contender is smell. To go back to the meeting between Tibetan Spaniel and Stranger in the park that opened the chapter, the choreography of the dog dance was all about smell. Each was trying to discover as much as he could from the other's nether regions (the area of the highest density of secretory organs), without letting out too much information about himself. The result was the circling motion — trying to get the nose in while moving the tail out. In the park meeting there was little of the body talk you'd expect at a meeting between strange wolves. John

Bradshaw's explanation is that since visual signalling has been compromised, the role of smell, or olfactory communication, has taken on greater significance. In other words, smell talk has taken over small talk.

There is some evidence for this. Wolves, of course, use smell talk, but the pattern which they follow is different from dogs' use. With wolves, only the lowest ranking animals are sufficiently unaggressive to let strangers sniff them, yet dominant animals will confidently present their smell zone to members of their own pack. With dogs, it's on for young and old. They're all trying to get a sniff and all trying to avoid being sniffed— as if simultaneously playing dominant and submissive roles. Dogs also seem to go much further with their urine scent-marking. Queues at the local postbox as each dog waits its turn to cock a leg are a familiar urban scene, and it drives me crazy when I take the Tibetan Spaniels for a walk and they stop at every single tree.

In support of his ideas, Bradshaw points to one of the conundrums which most perplexes humans. How is it that when a Great Dane looks at a Chihuahua, it knows it's dealing with another dog? Yet undoubtedly it does — and Bradshaw believes the key information is encoded in the odour.

Smell talk's all very well between dogs, but the problem is it doesn't work very well with humans. Young Golden Retriever meets nice new lady. Nose straight for the smelly bits — and what's the reply? A slap. So how *do* they talk with us? Because it is undoubtedly true that the complexity of the exchange between dog and human is well beyond that we experience with any other animal. Sure, if an animal is studied for long enough, its ways and "words" become clear. But with the exception of the primates, it's hard to imagine anything as sophisticated as the dog which, on smelling smoke in the kitchen, barks, races up the stairs and pulls at its mistress's nightdress until she wakes and follows it out of the room. The answer is that dogs talk to us with everything *else* they have. Their faces, their eyes, their bodies, their voices.

There are distinct changes that have occurred since our mutual domestication. Wolves don't bark, dogs do — a lot. We've already discussed the evolutionary significance of the bark in terms of early warning systems, but there is one other useful side effect. The bark — short, sharp, discrete — can be used to mimic the words in human speech. Certainly in some exchanges with humans, dogs will interject or "reply" with a bark. This does not mean that they understand human language — but some quickly learn that if they bark in the right places, humans like it. So the bark had the added selective advantage for the dog of helping convince humans that "this is a friendly creature with whom I can talk, so maybe I'll give it an extra bone and let it in the house". And this is the crux of the argument that human–dog "language" has improved and evolved over time. In the tough competition for gaining human favour, those that convinced us of their usefulness or affection, were more likely to be allowed access to breeding partners or resources than those that did not.

Interestingly, cats are far more adept at the actual talking side. Repeatedly, surveys show that one of the things owners love about their cats is that they speak. Cats have a range of vocalisations — from seven to 16 discrete mews or trills, according to whom you read. Some cats talk constantly — and it's one of the things to be aware of when considering a Siamese or a Burmese cat. These breeds can't take a short stroll around the house without giving a running commentary. What's fascinating, though, is that "talking" does not occur in wild cats. Nor do cats miaow nearly as much when they interact with each other — with the possible exception of a mother with her young. It is something that has developed purely for the benefit of communicating with humans. And Bradshaw suggests that they learn it at an early age.

Because humans are so voice-orientated, cats discover that if they want any attention, they need to make a noise. Perhaps a certain miaow results in the fridge being opened — so they use it again next time. Another miaow might get the door opened, or even a cuddle, so they try it some more. Many cat owners will tell you they know exactly what those miaows mean — and they probably do, because between the two of them — human and cat — they have developed a language that works. And what's really interesting is that in the cat's desire to socialise with humans, the miaow, which sounds even more like a word than a bark, is used to take part in a conversation. Cats may not know what the words mean, but they know that if they participate, they get their owners' full attention. This is probably what was happening when, as a small child, I had those long miaowing talks with my cat. She continued to reply because it seemed like a sociable thing to do — and I continued it because I was under the firm delusion she understood. The point is, we both got something socially rewarding out of it. In that sense, it was communication.

If a new "language" of sorts has indeed evolved, then at the core of it is the trend towards greater sociability. Many of us still hold the outdated notion that cats are not social — yet there are now a range of studies which show they are. Early scientists made the mistake of assuming that because cats don't hunt in groups and because many ferals lead solitary lives, they don't have a social drive. Anyone who has lived with one of the more social breeds, such as my Burmese cat, which follows me from room to room around the house, knows that the idea that all cats are motivated by food rather than company is absurd.

As for dogs, their obsession with human company is legendary. Dogs can literally pine to death at the loss of their owner. Even when they have the company of other dogs, human attention is a resource which is competed for. Another study by Bradshaw's group showed that when one dog of a group was being patted, the other dogs all made attempts to attract the patter's attention. That's probably got a lot to do with currying favour with the alpha "dog" — but still, it is remarkable that puppies that continue to have the company of their litter mates and mother, will whine when their human playmates leave.

Essentially, all the communicative signals that scientists have been able to distinguish from those of the ancestral wolf or the ancestral cat are about being friendly.

The tail wag is a classic. Yes, it is seen in wolf pups, but only occasionally in adults — and always as a submissive gesture. Dogs wag their tails all the time. It says, "hello, I'm friendly", and humans read it that way; they don't need a degree in ethology. The smile has a similar origin. Dogs do smile — and although again you can see traces of the smile in the submissive behaviour of the wolf, in dogs it's exaggerated. It may be that mimicry of our gestures has some part. In fact, to humans, dog facial features are the most expressive of any animal. Wolves presumably experience the same range of mental processes, but we humans are less likely to read them because their smaller eyes and long snout just seem to reveal less to us. Dog facial muscles allow tremendous mobility — far more so than the cat, for example. They present a range of expressions which we interpret as emotions — fear, sickness, happiness, depression. Regardless of whether they actually feel what we think they feel, our interpretation is usually close enough and information gets across.

Cats are more limited in their ability to communicate with their faces than dogs (they are physically incapable of smiling, for example), but they are superlative body talkers. And interestingly, they too have evolved a tail talk mechanism. The feline tail-up position is very familiar to us — displayed at dinner time as they weave sinuously around our legs, held high as a banner as they miaow and run toward us when we get home from work. Charlotte Cameron Beaumont, also working with the Anthrozoology Institute, decided to accept a brief to discover whether the same thing was seen in other related felid species.[20] To do this meant spending many hours at a zoo sitting in front of the cages of the Geoffrey's Cat, the Wildcat (*Felis silvestris* — purportedly the ancestor of the domestic cat), the Jungle Cat, and the Caracal — all chosen for their similarity in size and appearance to the domestic cat. The results were gratifying. Although many of the cats were quite friendly, having been raised in zoos, not one showed the tail-up approach. It's a new behaviour — one which has evolved in the domestic cat, driven by the twin needs of adapting to the more communal lifestyle of cats in towns and perhaps, more importantly, of communicating with a new and important co-habitor — humanity. As Bradshaw points out, cats are quite heavily armoured with their claws and teeth, and the raised tail no doubt gave them some advantage to show a clear and obvious signal of their benign intent — a prominent white flag.

There is also a discernible difference between the way cats use their tails with other cats and the way they use them with humans. In another study by the Southampton Anthrozoology group, the approaches cats made to other cats and to humans were recorded and contrasted.[21] Like the tail wag in the dog, the tail up essentially means, "I'm friendly". In cat-to-cat interactions, the tail up was used occasionally — in situations where there was a possibility of a fight. Yet the tail-up position was used in *most* approaches to humans. It has the effect of turning nearly every gesture into a friendly one. Clearly cats *do* distinguish between humans and other cats, and for whatever reason (maybe it's an appeasement gesture because we are so much bigger; maybe cats that seemed friendlier were historically better tolerated), humans are to be treated more amicably than other cats. I find it absolutely fascinating that my own cat greets the arrival of a strange cat with a hiss, a back arch and a fluffing of fur, and a strange human with a miaow, a run, a jump and a purr.

These differences are so exciting — and yet have barely been explored. Animal behaviourists intrinsically take the view that cats see humans as "some other kind of cat" and dogs see humans as "some other kind of dog" (just, I suppose, as we tend to view them as "some other kind of person"). Yet clearly this is not the whole story. Whatever has happened to their "languages" — or communication mechanisms — over the millennia of our cohabitation, it has had to incorporate dealing with more than their own species. And obviously this requires they make mental distinctions. The reactions of a dog to another dog, or a human, are different. What's more — and anyone who has lived with both cat and dog in the same house will have seen this — the systems have had to be flexible enough to embrace not just humans, but other animals which share the same living space. They've become multilingual.

Part of this flexibility lies in something we explored in Chapter 2. Neotenisation has not only opened the way to new forms and functions, but has also enabled the sculpting of new tools of "talk". Many of the signals used commonly between cats or dogs and people, can be found in other contexts in the ancestral young. They may have been recombined in new and meaningful ways — and this is the sort of thing the Southampton group is keen to investigate. The extended socialisation and learning phase that results from neotenisation also allows cats and dogs the time and the *inclination* to learn from others. The wolf can't learn cat talk because it doesn't spend time with cats as a pup — and even if it did, its more limited socialisation period would probably mean it would still not be as amicable as a dog with a cat. An old dog is not only still open to meeting strangers (canine or not), it can learn new tricks. The dog remains receptive to learning throughout life and, as we know, can be taught that a number of sounds or hand signals mean perform this or that action. As can other animals, but it's all a question of degree.

The complex language that develops between an individual dog and its owner contains both genetic and cultural components. Genetically a dog is "programmed", if you like, to be particularly attentive and receptive to the goings on of other animals around it — and of humans in particular. It has also evolved codes for specific social signals which work extremely well with humans, such as the upright tail wag. Culturally, it grows up in a human environment. It learns through trial and error what works to get its meaning across ("If I whine and scratch at the door, someone comes and opens it"), and it concurrently learns that signals from the human mean that it would be a good idea to respond in a certain way — often, for the simple reward of a smile and a pat.

In the late 1940s, scientists E. R. Guthrie and G. P. Horton thought they'd discovered evidence for a cultural ritual in cats. A cat was put in a box, and trained to escape by jostling a rod. Yet once the cat had worked it out, it always went through a prelude of weaving back and forth, rubbing its head against the front of the box and turning in circles, before finally touching the rod. The scientists were surprised, and even suggested it may be some superstitious ceremony along the lines of "the door won't open unless I do this first". In 1979, two other scientists repeated the experiment — except that this time, they discovered that the cat's strange "ceremony" only took place when there were people present. They'd discovered a ritual all right. Only it wasn't some incantation to make the door open. It was a cat saying hello to a person.[22]

At this stage, let's backtrack a bit. None of this means that cats and dogs are simply child prodigies with fur, that they think and feel exactly like us, and that they understand everything we say. Or that when we see a dog looking "embarrassed" or "guilty", we can assume that they know they've done something wrong. Far from it. In fact, the expression which owners commonly interpret as guilt is actually the dog's submissive posturing when it reads something in its owner's body language that says the owner is angry. The grin on the face of the chimpanzee on the cover of *Time* magazine as the chimp landed from its space flight was actually the grimace of total terror. We need continued excellent studies of animal behaviour to keep the ever-present spectre of over anthropomorphism at bay. Animals are not the same as humans.

What I *am* suggesting is that, in the case of cats and dogs, we are all working with a "language of best fit" — a language which has improved through selection over time. Each of us reads the other's messages within our own framework. If humans are anthropomorphic, then so too are dogs cano-morphic and cats felo-morphic. Each of us interprets the other as "what would I mean if *I* had done that" and somehow the message gets across. And it is by far the most advanced with the dog.

It's not a perfect language. Mistakes are made, sometimes with tragic consequences. The dog interprets the eyeballing and stumbling approach of a two-year-old child as aggression and reacts with a bite. The human interprets the trashing of their garden as a wilful act of destruction and sends the dog to the pound. But the point is that while it may not always be the perfect match the "fit" is close enough often enough that it works. Whatever has happened over those millennia, it is true that with no other animal are we so convinced of mutual understanding than the dog. The language that has developed serves us both pretty well — and as John Bradshaw of the Anthrozoology Institute has put it passionately on a number of occasions, it is our challenge now to determine its elements.

CULTURAL EXCHANGE

I have a favourite cartoon by Michael Leunig. In it, two dogs are having a conversation. One says, "I liked the statement that Rex made on the lamp post." The other replies, "Yes, but I think his installation on the footpath was bolder and more memorable." The caption reads, "The art of dogs receives very little attention or acclaim, except, of course, from other dogs". It's a wonderful image and, despite its obvious irony, it raises another fundamental question: do dogs have culture?

It depends what is meant by culture. Certainly their howls while sometimes musical, could hardly be called symphonies, and their art, when given the benefit of paint, canvas and paw, could not be termed anything other than accidental (despite many people being fooled by that deliciously elaborate hoax, the coffee table book *Why Cats Paint*).

If, on the other hand, by culture you mean the learning that can be passed from one generation to another, then animals do have it. This is the broad church that a number of animal behaviourists have opened for the term "culture". Songbirds gain membership for the beauty and, more importantly, the regional variability of their melodies. Kittens learn from their mothers how to pee in the litter tray instead of on the bedspread, and puppies learn the etiquette of canine society —and that the sound of the tin opener means dinner.

But while the direct transmission of dog culture down the generations probably doesn't go much further than that, there's something more to it. What they've done is gain the use of someone else's culture: ours. And the species *Canis familiaris* certainly knows how to use it.

If we step back and think about it laterally, our animal companions have managed to achieve a very clever thing. They've harnessed *our* culture to teach us how to take care of *them*. And don't some of us work at it! We raise their children. No longer do dog mothers have to suffer the agonies of adolescence — some other poor human does the job for them. Some humans read books on the subject. Some even visit therapists to ensure the satisfactory psychological and physical development of their canine charges — who wants the ignominy of raising a juvenile dog-linquent?

Our pets are living longer (my old cat is nearly 20); their meals are provided (they need to scrounge around in dumps only for fun); they get to visit new places and meet interesting people (and best of all, there are car rides!). In fact, the standard of living is fantastic. It's remarkable how hard they've managed to make us work for them!

Flippancy aside, there is a genuine point to be made here. Ethologist Anthony Barnett, in his paper on pedagogy, points out that one profoundly human feature is our propensity to teach.[23] Not just to demonstrate, so that others can learn by mimicking our actions, but to actively engage with our subject and teach *about* things — keeping at it until we see a change in our pupil. At its fullest, it requires language; so although what the mother cat does in bringing small animals to her offspring (hence providing encouragement and opportunity) could be termed teaching, it can never match our sophistication; what Barnett terms "true teaching". *Homo docens*, he calls us — the teaching species.

Humans have a tremendous power to collect and communicate information, and by writing down what we have learned about dogs — or any other animal for that matter — we can then teach the next generation of people how to teach their canine companions. And it could be said that one of the things that defines domestic animals is their responsiveness to human teaching. It's clearly a trait which has evolved. This way, what is learned in the experience of one animal can be indirectly transmitted to the next and built upon. Cultural transmission does occur from canine generation to generation — by the intermediary of human language. It's an inspiring concept — and one which prompted John Bradshaw to state in his plenary address to the Seventh International Conference on Human–Animal Interactions, "Dogs, in a sense, co-authored the pages of training manuals".[24]

If this were not food for thought enough, there is one other, even more provocative suggestion: human culture has not only changed the shape of dogs' bodies and language, but the shape of their minds.

Professor Daniel Dennett, mentioned earlier as a philosopher specialising in consciousness — human or otherwise — has a startling proposal. He accepts that there is indeed something qualitatively different about the relationship humans have with dogs from that with any other species. His book *Kinds of Minds* does exactly as the title suggests; it attempts to explain from an evolutionary perspective how different minds function according to their structure and available tools — hence, for example, the power of a human mind is magnified a thousandfold by its ability to offload problems or "work" into the environment, such as onto a computer.[25] And in it, he makes a statement about dogs so remarkable that I will include the whole passage here:

> Among other traits we have unconsciously selected for, I suggest, is susceptibility to human socialising, which has, in dogs, many of the organising effects that human socialising also has on human infants. By treating them as if they were human, we actually succeed in making them more human

than they otherwise would be. They begin to develop the very organisational features that are otherwise the sole province of socialised human beings. In short, if human consciousness — the sort of consciousness that is a necessary condition for serious suffering — is, as I have maintained, a radical restructuring of the virtual architecture of the human brain, then it should follow that the only animals that would be capable of anything remotely like that form of consciousness would be animals that could also have imposed on them, by culture, that virtual machine. Dogs are clearly closest to meeting that condition.

In other words, of all the animals, dogs have developed the most human of minds.

A few months ago, my mother's dog Joss stayed at my apartment while my mother was away. He was not really familiar with the surroundings nor particularly with my cat Jezabel. Because I keep Jez's food in the bathroom, I put a low barrier across the doorway to discourage canine thievery. I knew Joss could easily jump over, but hoped he wouldn't. Unfortunately, Jez had great fun teasing Joss from the other side of the post. When Joss could take no more, he put one foot up on the post, then another. I looked over from where I was sitting at the computer, smiled, shook my head (mixed messages) and said, "Uh, uh" — a sound he'd never heard before. If I'd done it with Jez, she'd have completely ignored me. Joss looked at me and took one paw down, and then the other. He didn't try it again.

Our cultural exchange is far reaching. It encompasses the tools of our thoughts — our metaphor, symbols, language — as well as perhaps the architecture of theirs. It has created a shared language so subtle that Joss, who had no prior experience of the situation, was able to read my only half-consciously expressed meaning and stop pursuing both the mischievous Jezabel and her food.

And if there are any doubts, think back to the park scene, or even the last time you had a conversation with a dog. Who initiated it? Dogs, and to a lesser extent cats, are not passive but active participants in the cultural highways and byways of our combined communities. And, as we move on next to look more deeply at what is happening in our cities, bear one thought in mind: being a multicultural society means being a multi-species society as well.

CHAPTER 6

ADAPTING TO CITY LIFE: IN SICKNESS AND IN HEALTH

SOME time in 1991, Dr Warwick Anderson got a surprise. In his heart he had been hoping for just such an outcome all along, but with his analytical head he really hadn't expected it. He simply couldn't see any reason why such a result should be so, and it was partly to debunk what he considered a fairly "woolly" area of science that he originally decided to take the project on. But there it was, at first concealed in the mountain of abstract data: indisputable proof. There was something to it after all.

What Anderson and the rest of his team — Garry Jennings and Christopher Reid — had set out to do was establish once and for all whether there was any basis to the claim "pets are good for you". They were well placed to do it. Although, as we shall see shortly, there was already a plethora of studies indicating some sort of health benefit from keeping pets, the problem was they were generally small-sized samples — and while some were excellent studies, small sample sizes left the field open to accusations of lack of rigour. In part, the size was perhaps due to limited sponsorship for such research — a few dogs parading around a hospital weren't likely to catch the attention of the big funding bodies intent on curing cancer and AIDS, and the subject lacked the lure of a potentially profitable drug, so tended to be of interest only to pet drug and food companies and small not-for-profit organisations. In part, it was due to the backgrounds of the few people interested — psychologists, animal behaviourists — many of whose training favoured small sample methods.

But the Anderson team was coming from left of field. They were not even part of the established human–animal interactions research network. They were cardiologists and epidemiologists, and it was their job to investigate the major risk factors for heart disease in people. And their big advantage was they routinely dealt with huge numbers.

The Baker Medical Research Institute, based in Melbourne, is one of the world's leading cardiovascular disease research units. Through their free screening unit, around 2000 people are tested each year for blood pressure, cholesterol and other indicators of heart disease risk. In addition, participants are asked to complete a detailed list of questions about their lifestyle: their diet, their cigarette and alcohol intake, family history, exercise, and so on. It was Anderson's idea to add one more question — do they have a pet?

Over 5500 people were processed in this way before they started to crunch the numbers. And that's when they found they were on to something.

Across the board, pet owners had significantly lower systolic blood pressure and plasma triglycerides than non-pet owners. In men, plasma cholesterol levels were lower as well. Now, these results could have been due to lifestyle differences between the two subgroups; but the team went back and checked, satisfying themselves that the two groups had virtually identical educational and socio-economic profiles. Perhaps it was because dog owners took more exercise — indeed, when this was examined, they did; but this wasn't the whole answer because owners of other pets proved to have similar health benefits. Moreover, when they looked at other lifestyle factors such as alcohol consumption and diet, it was found pet owners not only ate more meat and takeaway food, but also consumed more alcohol. (A great consolation to many, no doubt.) All in all, the impact of owning a pet was estimated to amount to a 4 per cent reduction in risk factors for heart disease — or the equivalent of starting a low fat, low salt diet. When the results were published in the 1992 *Medical Journal of Australia*, they made headlines around the world.[1]

Why did the outcome provoke such interest? Why did it attract the attention of the major New York newspapers and become so entrenched in the popular imagination that within a few short years the results would trip off the tongues of lay person and medico alike? Well, mainly because it finally gave credence to what many people had privately believed all along. Not to mention a justification for an occasionally embarrassing and irrationally strong attachment. But the reason *I* relate the story is that I think the team's results provided an enormous clue to other, newer functions.

To date, we've looked at several reasons for the presence of cats and dogs in cities. There's the evolutionary advantage they gave us in the lead up to civilisation — admittedly now superseded by machines. There's the fact they've become so entrenched in our culture we'd almost have to excise parts of our language to forget them. And there's the mutual understanding, now so easy and subtle, that it wouldn't occur to us to leave our friends behind. But Anderson's research points us to another reason: to the possibility that their adaptive role with our species is far from over. In fact, they may now be playing a part that is even more important than the defensive or facilitatory function of the past. What scientists like Anderson have shown us is that cats and dogs actually do something to us — something tangible, something which has an effect; and that effect can be measured.

IN SICKNESS AND IN HEALTH

The idea that pets have healing properties is not new.[2] The old wives' tale that letting a dog lick a wound will prevent infection is found in a surprising number of cultures, and goes back at least as far as Ancient Greece. There, the temple of the Cult of Asklepios was populated by a group of sacred dogs that were especially trained to lick the wounds of the sick in the belief they could cure. In Islamic tradition the tongue of a black dog is thought to provide protection against biting things, and various groups including the Gauls believed illness could be cured by holding a young, healthy puppy up close to the body, who would absorb the sickness and draw it away. One ninth-century follower of Islam even managed to describe the therapeutic properties of dog faeces against angina — although the treatment's lack of popularity today is not surprising given that it requires placing the excrement over the sufferer's tongue. Nitro is no doubt more appealing.

Although there are parts of the globe where such applications persist, the modern belief in the health benefits of pets can be traced to a couple of innovative institutions founded in the eighteenth and nineteenth centuries. The York Retreat in Britain worked on the radical assumption that mentally impaired patients weren't prisoners of a hospital, but people with an illness. Part of their therapy was to wander around the extensive gardens and interact with the animals. And at the famous institution at Bethel in Germany, which was originally set up last century for epileptics and now hosts people with a range of disabilities, all patients must participate in running a farm.

While the efficacy of dog tongues is somewhat questionable, the use of animals in these two institutions was heading in the right direction. In a now famous incident in the 1960s, American child psychologist Boris Levinson was sitting in his rooms trying to work out how to get through to a particularly withdrawn patient. The focus of his musings was a young boy. He had been treating the child for months, yet so far had failed to establish even a preliminary relationship. The boy had not said a word, and at this rate, it seemed they would be in exactly the same situation in a year's time. His dog, Jingles, periodically tangling himself around Levinson's feet, was obviously unaware of his master's concerns, simply pleased to be at work where the action was instead of left at home. Ordinarily, Jingles was removed from the office before any clients arrived, but on this particular day, the boy arrived early for his appointment. And this time, the session was different. For the first time, Levinson watched as finally something piqued the young boy's interest — his dog.

This fortunate concurrence was a revelation for Levinson. Subsequently, Jingles was used for every session with that particular boy who started to talk to the dog, and eventually even to Levinson himself. Soon, Jingles became an integral part of the Levinson therapy. The dog enabled the rapid establishment of a rapport with most patients — they would play and interact with Jingles first, and then by subtly insinuating himself into their games, Levinson found the children would start to open up to him as well. In his papers, Levinson termed the process "social facilitation" — and he likened the role of the dog to that of a bridge spanning the social divide between therapist and patient.[3]

Levinson's published reports provoked some controversy at the time; quite a few of his colleagues were sceptical; but it marked the first foray into the scientific literature.

From the time of Levinson's report, the use of animals in therapy or institutional settings has become so well established, it even has its own name. Animal Assisted Therapy — or AAT, sometimes called Pet Facilitated Therapy, or PFT. Thousands of studies have been published recording the influence of pets in any range of situations, from making contact with people with severe dementia, to teaching a "crack baby" how to walk. In Australia in 1995, one such study by psychologist and animal behaviourist Patricia Crowley found that when Heidi the Whippet was placed in an RSL war veterans' home in Queensland, after 18 months residents had significantly less tension and confusion (many of course being sufferers of dementia), and were less fatigued. Today, many nations have established umbrella bodies to coordinate such work, the best known probably being the Delta Society in the United States, which runs the People Pet Partnership program.

Unfortunately, this type of evidence, compelling as it is, is all too often dismissed by scientists as "soft". But the discovery of the link between companion animals and cardiovascular disease really made the medical community sit up and take notice.

The work started nearly 20 years ago with a study by Aaron Katcher who, along with his collaborator Erika Friedman, has since become something of a heavyweight in the study of human–animal interactions (HAI), or anthrozoology. But Katcher claims he fell into the field by accident.[4] A lecturer in psychiatry at the University of Pennsylvania, his interest in the late 1970s was in social support networks, and at the time, he didn't even have a pet. With his colleagues, Katcher was planning a study of survivors of heart attack, looking at their health a year after the attack, and trying to work out the factors contributing to it. Their feeling was that social support in the form of spouse, or family and friendship networks would influence recovery. Of course, when they talked of social support, they were thinking only of humans.

However, they had a new graduate student, a young woman by the name of Erika Friedman, who, after originally wishing to enter veterinary school, had recently completed her biology degree. An ardent animal fan, she suggested they broaden their definition of social support and include an additional question on pets. When the results were analysed, like Warwick Anderson would some years later, Katcher and Friedman received a surprise. Of the 53 survivors of heart attack who had pets, one year later 50 were still alive. Of the 39 without pets, only 28 survived.[5] And these results weren't explicable on any other basis; dog owners walked more, but the results also held for owners of other sorts of pets.

The next step was to start asking why. There were several broad theories put forward about loneliness and depression (which we will explore more fully), but the really interesting question was whether pets produced any physiological change in humans which might explain the extraordinary findings. Blood pressure — fairly easy to read and non-invasive — seemed like a good candidate.

Friedman was fortunate in that recent developments in the technology for reading blood pressure — automated, oscillometric monitoring devices — meant subjects no longer had to be silent while having their blood pressure read. This was just as well because, as the researchers soon discovered, people find it almost impossible to interact with a dog without talking to it.

The team decided to harness the phenomenon that blood pressure increases when people are asked to read aloud (it's obviously very stressful) to find out whether the presence of a pet had any ameliorating effect on this reaction. Two groups of children were organised and asked to read aloud, both in and out of the presence of an unfamiliar but friendly dog. All had higher blood pressure scores while reading than when they were resting, but in the first group, to which the dog was introduced half-way through the experiment, both resting and reading blood pressures dropped markedly after the dog was brought in. In the second group, with which the dog was present from the beginning, blood pressures started at a much lower base point than the previous group. And they remained lower, even after the dog was removed and the children were asked to read aloud again.[6] Clearly the presence of the dog had a calming effect, almost evaporating the tension of the situation. While the effects on blood pressure were not necessarily long term, the results were still exciting.

Throughout the 1980s, Katcher and Friedman continued to work along the same lines, soon joined in their quest by others from the United Kingdom and Europe. They investigated people's blood pressure while talking to pets, or while looking at an aquarium, and how reactions to one's own pet differed from reactions to stranger animals. But the next great leap in understanding was not until the unexpected release of Anderson's work in 1992.

The cardiovascular work continues to be one of the mainstays of the HAI. In 1995, for example, Friedman repeated the original study of survivors of heart attacks, only this time with a substantially enlarged sample group of 369.[7] It was a response to criticism that the earlier work was flawed, and no doubt she was relieved the results were just as favourable. Anderson is meanwhile trying to clarify the physiology of the phenomenon, taking advantages of new techniques in measuring heart nerve activity to discover whether the blood pressure effect is mediated by the sympathetic nervous system.

There are many streams of research I could point to, but other than the cardiovascular work, the most exciting is in general health. One of the problems even with Anderson's large study is that it doesn't demonstrate a cause and effect. In other words, it could be that there is some psychological difference between people who choose to have pets and those who don't, and this accounts for the result. The only way of countering this is to conduct a long-term study, and find out whether the health of people who acquire pets actually changes in some measurable way.

In 1991, Professor James Serpell did exactly that. Nearly a hundred volunteers without pets were recruited and divided into three groups. The first group was given a cat to take home, the second a dog, and the third no pet. At the beginning of the study, all were given a simple test of general health — they were asked to tick a box next to any symptoms of minor malaise experienced in the previous month, including headaches, sleepless nights, colds or flu, hay fever, nerves and painful joints. When the test was repeated one month later, the difference was marked. The no pet group stayed the same, but for both the dog and the cat group the number of minor illnesses or complaints had dropped. At six months, the no pet group remained steady on an average score of 4, the cat group was on 3, and the dog group had dropped to 2. At ten months, although the cat group had rebounded to nearly match the no pets, the dog group continued with their improved general health.[8]

That the health boon is fairly generalised was supported by another major Australian study completed in 1995. A team of specialists, with medical researcher Malcolm McHarg at the helm, were asked to design a comprehensive survey of people's relations with pets. Included in the survey was a series of questions on visits to the doctor and the use of medication. For this National People and Pets survey, 1011 people were duly telephoned and their answers processed. Lo and behold, the same, unequivocal outcome. Pet owners visited the doctor significantly less often, and fewer of them took medication for high blood pressure, sleeping difficulties, high cholesterol or a heart problem.[9] Again, despite everything, and despite the fact other studies in the United States gave a similar result,[10] it came as something of a surprise. I *know* it did because at the time I was a consultant to one of the financial supporters of the survey, and was practically the first person to get the raw data in my hands. As I scanned through the 600 tables of figures in front of me, which no one other than the market research company had yet seen, became more and more excited. Somehow, even

I hadn't believed the survey would "work".

But it *did* work, and with these results, for the first time researchers were able to do something. The team member responsible for the health questions, Bruce Headey, had consulted extensively with Warwick Anderson when coming up with the design. Following the release of the findings, the two came together to work out what it all meant in dollars and cents.

The advantage of the National People and Pets Survey was precisely that it used a representative national sample. This meant the figures could be safely applied to the general population. Anderson and Headey took the difference in mean annual number of visits to the doctor — 4.41 for dog or cat owners as opposed to 5.00 for those without — to represent the total difference in use of the health system. They then calculated roughly what this difference may mean to the national health budget, and estimated savings of between $790 million and $1.5 billion annually.[11]

Some have criticised the analysis for extrapolating too much from limited data. And certainly many studies, such as Jorm et al's examination of the Medicare records of elderly subjects[12] have found no health benefit attributable to pets, or even found a negative impact. And as yet no one has been able to refute conclusively the argument that perhaps only people who are healthier to begin with keep pets. Still, despite the critiques, in the last twenty years sufficient evidence has accumulated to suggest animal companionship does influence the nation's health.

SO WHAT DOES IT ALL MEAN?

It seems that pets are doing *something* to us. And while we can come up with all sorts of reasons for the effect — that rhythmically stroking their silky fur is soothing, that the relationship is undemanding and reliable — underlying it is something else. For all sorts of reasons, our species is undergoing an unprecedented and rapid phase of change. And I believe pets are augmenting our capacity to adapt to that change.

The urbanisation explosion is new. How new is hard to comprehend, because people alive now are almost accustomed to the pace of change, accepting it as the norm. But my great-great-great-grandparents would recognise it as strange. And while that might seem an awful long time ago to me, in the scale of human development, it's like the blink of an eye. Since industrialisation, the steady drain of humanity from farms and small towns towards new work servicing the machine has seen London grow from a modest centre of 18,000 people in 1066, to a city of 1 million in 1801, to a massive agglomeration of 7.3 million in 1994.

Certainly, some of the great ancient cities were quite substantial; Rome in its heyday at about 200 AD had around 1 million inhabitants; and some of the Asian cities like T'ang Ch'ang-an were almost as large. But even then, most people lived close the land which provided for them, and right up until this century, the life for the vast majority of Earth's people was in rural or small communities.

Our future is a purely urban one. By the year 2025, more than two-thirds of us will live in cities, and this number will continue to rise. The largest cities already top 25 million in population, and archaeologist Roland Fletcher, an expert in the rise and collapse of ancient cities, argues that with modern means of communication, we could easily support cities of 100 million.[13] Cities of course vary tremendously in the quality of life on offer: in their amenities, access to garden space, density, and style; but all have one thing in common. They are a far cry from the small hunter-gatherer communities in which we evolved.

The challenges of adapting to city life are many. Not only because of the dramatic alteration to our physical environment

— landscapes with edges sharp instead of tessellated, colours of bitumen and granite clashing with the balm of green or brown — but also because of the equally dramatic and perhaps surprising impact on our relations with other humans. And one of the most important of those seems counter-intuitive. At a time when there are more people alive than at any other in our history, it's getting harder to find anyone to talk to.

LONELINESS

It seems paradoxical. Each of us spends much of the day wading through a sea of people. Yet the number of intimates in our daily lives is dropping.

A hundred years ago, a household of at least five or six people would not be uncommon. That's only two parents and three or four kids — the average number of children (or total fertility rate) at the turn of the century was 3.5. (By comparison, in 1992 it was 1.9.)[14] That's before you add the grandparents, or perhaps a great aunt or a cousin. And then, if your family was of moderate wealth, there were all the servants. In and out all day, washing the clothes, cleaning the houses, preparing the meals; the relentless, time-consuming chores that these days we expect to be done by machines. We forget that in the nineteenth century, the number one source of employment was private service. Since even families without servants had many children, every home must have been an absolute hive of human activity.

Household size has been practically in freefall. According to the International Institute of Applied Systems Analysis (IIASA), in developed countries across the world, the average household size went from 3.6 in 1950 to 2.7 in 1990.[15] The fall continues. And some of us are taking it to the extreme. In 1995, 11 per cent of adults lived alone, a 35 per cent increase since 1982. That means one in every five Australian households is now a lone-person unit. In the nineties, we are rapidly approaching not the small family, not the two-person, but the age of the single-person household. A family unit defined as one.

The reasons are multiple and familiar. Divorce, a rare process in Australia even 20 years ago, is now commonplace. Some rejoin the marriage stakes, some don't. Divorced people make up the second highest subgroup of the people who live alone. Wolfgang Lutz of IIASA, which deals with all the big population issues, argues that divorce may cause more carbon dioxide emissions than an additional birth![16] Divorce invariably means setting up a new household, with all the additional energy and space consumption that goes along.

Other social changes are making their contribution. The freeing up of traditional sex roles and ideas about couple-dom means that people can actually make the choice to live alone without facing social stigmatisation. And attitudes to children are changing, particularly amongst educated women. Partly this is because many of us are so blisteringly aware of population pressures, but mostly it's about financial and time limitations and the fact that both sexes work. Child-bearing, though still preferred by the majority, is no longer seen as the central defining aim of a woman's life. She won't be pitied or castigated if she chooses not to have children.

And we don't have three generations living under the same roof any more. The concept of the extended family is an anachronism to much of the community — when we use the term "extended family" these days, instead of meaning the grandparents and other relatives, we mean the loose conglomeration of people added and lost through divorce and remarriage.

Part of the reason for these changes is cultural, but it is difficult to separate culture entirely from the influence of urbanisation itself. It's all to do with dwelling size. Buying a house in the city is a *lot* more expensive than buying one in the country, or even building one yourself. This is true no matter which historical era, or which part of the world we are talking about. And space, a luxury in medium- or high-density cities, comes at a premium. So in purchasing or renting a home, although you might like to consider room for potential aunts and uncles, incapacitated grandparents, children and their spouses and their children, it may not be economically viable. There's a cost in having space sitting idle in the anticipation of future use. So when additional people come along, the whole family moves, or the newcomers find their own space. Professor Patrick Troy of the Urban Research Program at the Australian National University points out that this is not confined to high-density living.[17] Even with the medium-density urban consolidation policies currently in vogue in Australia, the same pattern emerges. With large backyards, a feature of Australian housing right up until the 1980s, homeowners had the option of extending and building extra rooms, or even building a granny-flat to house the elderly parent or wayward young adult. This option is less and less available. Although it's true that in places like Pakistan, families of six and seven may be squeezed into the same small flat, overall the space pressure in all cities ultimately acts against extended families.

Whatever the reason for the demise of multi-generational households, the result is that the elderly, in particular, face isolation. We don't even put our old in group homes any more — or at least, not for as long as possible. In the Western world, social support policies are moving away from institutionalisation. The aged are encouraged to remain as long as they can at home, supported by a range of home support services. People previously considered too incapacitated to live alone now do so. It's partly for economic reasons, partly a belief in a better quality of life, but still it means that unless both partners die at the same time, one will be left alone. Of the 11 per cent of Australians who live alone, widows and widowers are by far the largest group.

And people who *live* alone spend a lot of *time* alone; according to the 1996 Australian Bureau of Statistics survey, on average 16.9 hours of the day.[18] Admittedly that includes sleep time, but for the elderly the figures are even more alarming. On average, 19.2 hours a day is spent alone. That must mean that for many days and many people, nearly 24 hours passes without any substantial contact with another human being.

Yet the problem is we are an intensely social species. Our sociability is at the base of the evolutionary steps which permanently distanced our brains from those of other animals. We share everything — food collection and consumption, caring for the sick or young, entertainment. Other species do many of these things, but not to the same degree. And certainly no other species will care for a sick or disabled member of the group for years on end. Robin Dunbar, professor of psychology, suggests that we wouldn't have even developed language if we hadn't needed to get better at gossip.[19] Our social drive is one of the defining characters of being human.

So what happens if we spend too much time alone? We get sick. The link between what is termed "social support" and overall health is now well established. People recover more quickly from illnesses, and are less prone to minor complaints such as sleeplessness and headaches if they have company. Admittedly it's complicated by the nature of the relationships (none is better than a bad one), and the strength of our social drive varies (for many, an overabundance of people has the same detrimental effect), but overall, it's undeniable that most of us need some good-quality social contact each day to stay healthy. And we don't all get it. The disease caused by its lack has a simple title: loneliness.

There are many reasons why loneliness is likely to increase in the future. Of course, most of us will continue to have the sort of varied, engaging lifestyle that guarantees the high-quality human contact necessary to meet our social drives. I'm not suggesting that living alone precludes that; far from it. But unless current social trends alter substantially, there are certain significant groups which will not have sufficient human contact. Amongst those, loneliness is set to be an insidious malaise in the twenty-first and twenty-second centuries.

The first reason for greater levels of loneliness is that our increasing mobility spreads families across the globe. Rapidly improving telecommunications compensates to a large extent, but still, the grandmother living a six-hour plane flight away gets far less flesh and blood contact with her children than the grandmother living in the same suburb. Even for the mobile, starting up in a new city is not without its social challenges. It's exciting and fun, but it also takes time and effort to establish a social network. When things go wrong — severe illness, job loss — new networks may not be nearly as supportive as old ones.

Secondly, and most importantly, in the Western world our population is aging. We live longer and have far fewer children — and the rate of change has been nothing short of dramatic. In 1976, the median age of Australians — that is, the age at which half the population is above and half below — was 28.4 years. In just two short decades, it has leaped up by six years — to a median age of 34 in 1996.[20] And proportionately, more and more of us are falling into the "aged" category.

In 1996, 12.1 per cent of Australians were over the age of 65. By the year 2041, it is projected that that figure will be 22 per cent — nearly a quarter of the population.[21] Soon, one in every four of us will be officially an "older person". And for older people who live alone, difficulties in achieving their recommended daily social intake (RDSI) are particularly acute. There are logistical problems. Unlike the younger home-aloners who are quite capable of supplementing their RDSI with trips out and about, the elderly are far more limited in mobility. Failing eyesight eliminates drivers' licences, arthritis transforms a stroll around the block into an arduous trek. Given the disproportionately high incidence of single-person households in the over-65 age group, next century we can expect a *substantial* percentage of our citizens to be living in the "alone for 20 hours a day" category. Or worse.

And then there are the people who just can't cut it in the big city. As many evolutionary psychologists have pointed out, our ancestors evolved within an optimum social-group framework of around 12 adult hunter-gatherers and their offspring. Our intimate social networks continue to be not much larger than this, despite being immersed in a surfeit of social possibilities. Faced with the vast sea of city faces we cannot possibly know as individuals, our minds blank them out. They cease to be people at all. Merely Brownian motion — an endless weaving pattern of particle movements like waves on a seashore, or dust particles tumbling in the light. In smaller groups, they morph back into individuals again, and we can smile and interact and catch another's eye. But in the endless tide, we can't afford to register a presence, lest in some way we become drawn reluctantly into a stranger's life. We've seen the experiments in which a supposedly unconscious human body is strategically placed on the ground. In a small community, people rush out, anxious to know what is wrong and whether they can be of any help. On a busy urban street, the flood of humans barely pauses as it parts and flows around, some of it even over the top of the inert human body.

In the big city, none of us is given an embracing village group identification by dint of simple birthright. All of us, to an extent, have to create our own. This takes effort, advertising, social skills

— an ability to convince others that out of all the thousands of potential anointees, you are one of the few who should be brought to the inner circle. Not everyone can do this. We lack the skills, or the inclination, or the one begets the other. We have all met people like this. Some of us are terribly, terribly lonely.

ANTIDOTE FOR AN AILMENT

There is an excellent remedy for loneliness, and it's an ancient one. And it's the first of the explanations for the benefits of keeping pets.

Anthropologist Stephen Hugh-Jones tells the story of taking his children along on some extensive field research in a remote part of the Amazon.[22] His children, aged five and eight, were thoroughly English, but excited about visiting a place they knew only from stories. After flying to the isolated mission station, the family then clambered into the canoes which would take them on the day-long trip up the Amazon to the village where Hugh-Jones was to conduct his research. About an hour from base, the children noticed two little monkeys running along a branch. No sooner had they cried, "Oh look", than their guide shot the monkeys. The children promptly burst into tears and called the man a murderer. Matters were not improved when they arrived at the village, for the children discovered that they were expected to eat monkey and, on another occasion, caterpillars. Their hostility and homesickness was gradually eased, however, when, over time, the hunters began to bring the children gifts of Toucan beaks and Macaw tail feathers. All resentment was finally abandoned when the hunters gave the children a baby marmoset as a pet. They were very upset when eventually they had to leave the marmoset behind. The point is that the Amerindians realised that the children were nervous, rather lonely, and a long way from home. A pet was their natural cure for loneliness.

While this particular remedy has no doubt been applied since *Homo sapiens* first started acquiring pets, there's now plenty of hard evidence to suggest the Amerindians were right. Companion animals *are* one of the best treatments for loneliness. And, perhaps surprisingly, it's not just that they fill a gap when human company is scarce, but they seem to actually enhance our ability to relate to other *people*.

Let me remind you of the park scene in Chapter 5: I was walking with the Tibetan Spaniels, and on the other side of the rose garden a stranger wandered with her young German Shepherd. If neither of us had had animals, I'd probably have walked straight by her. As it was, we met, introduced ourselves, had a short conversation — almost entirely about the dogs — and then moved on, still smiling. Probably three or four similar incidents occurred on the same day — I don't remember — but that would be a pretty average number for a Tibetan Spaniel stroll.

It's a typical experience, and certainly not confined to Tibetan Spaniels. Any dog walker would note the same. Indeed, the universality of the experience was proven not long ago, in a classic ethological experiment. In the early 1980s, zoologist Peter Messent and a group of students spent many days hanging around London parks. Some of them were simply loitering — actually, more like spying. Others were briskly walking through the colourful gardens, pretending they didn't know they were being spied upon.

As day after day they strolled through the grounds, the spies were busy noting their subjects' conversations. The experiment was to find out how many spontaneous social interactions with strangers — a smile, a nod, a greeting or a full conversation — their test subjects experienced on a typical walk. They were asked to walk first by themselves, then, at the exactly same time on a different day, to take the same route, but this time accompanied by a dog.

The results couldn't have been clearer. When walking without a dog, only 2 per cent of test subjects experienced any form of social interaction. No one stopped to say hello at all. When they walked with the dog, however, nearly one quarter experienced spontaneous social interactions.[23] And the interactions were high quality in the sense that they weren't just nods, but often lasted some minutes. A similar response can be seen when people walk with a baby, but it was interesting that the conversations lasted longer and were more frequent when the subject was a dog. And it's not as though everyone can have a baby. If a man or woman has two children, they have four years of babydom, at the most. Anyone can have a dog.

This invisible force, pressuring people into striking up a conversation is probably one of the most bemusing things about dog ownership. It's almost irresistible. It's very difficult *not* to smile when you see a Golden Retriever bounding through the grass. And once you've smiled, you're history. All the happy hormones are released around the body, and it seems churlish not to make at least some acknowledgment of the dog's human companion. And while for most of us this type of interaction presses our stress-relief buttons and helps us switch off from the pressures of life, for some of us, it is essential.

People with obvious physical disabilities face an additional problem to the simply ambulatory one. Other people don't know how to react to them. Do I smile? Or will that be taken as unwelcome pity? What will I say? Where will I look? What if I accidentally stare? So most of us walk on by, or give a half smile, embarrassed that we can't find the right social graces. There's no such problem when the disabled have a dog.

Veteran human–animal interactions researcher, Lynette Hart

179

studied the interactions of people in wheelchairs and found a striking difference in their social experiences according to whether or not they were accompanied by a pet.[24] During interviews, disabled persons with service dogs were asked to estimate the average number of friendly approaches from other adults when they went on a shopping trip. Without their dogs, the median number was one. With their dogs, they could expect *eight* friendly approaches. The same outcome has been found in a variety of situations — from wheeling along the street to coping with disability in the school playground. The presence of a pet seems to "normalise" social situations, getting everyone through the ice-breaker stage to the point where they can risk directly engaging with the unfamiliar person.

This socially enhancing effect of animal companions doesn't seem to be confined to meeting new people, either. They may also help reinforce existing bonds. And the classic example is the family.

Nienke Endenberg, researcher on the influence of pets on childhood development, has made the suggestion that pets help maintain family harmony.[25] They won't necessarily keep families together, but their role as endless sources of happy, harmless, agreeable family conversation shouldn't be underestimated. In times of high tension and stress, the presence of the cat or dog often helps diffuse the situation — even if it's as simple as the seven year old running off to cuddle the cat in tears after a particularly heavy scolding. In more trying circumstances, pets can mean the difference between whether or not warring parties can communicate at all. A telling example came out of a focus group study designed by social scientist Maree MacCallum to discover "What Australians Feel About Their Pets". The comment was by a middle-aged woman: "When our family was breaking up, a safe topic was the dogs. When my ex-husband rings up I ask him about the dogs. It's safe, neutral territory."

Nienke Endenberg also refers to a US study conducted in the mid-1980s. Researcher A. Cain was keen to discover whether pets did, in fact, make a difference to family cohesion. He asked a group of families several questions about their interactions before and after acquiring a pet. Like zoologist Peter Messent's work, the results were quite clear. Fifty-two per cent of families surveyed reported a substantial increase in the time spent together after getting a pet. A resounding 70 per cent claimed family life was much happier and more fun after being joined by an animal.[26] Although Endenberg comments on the limitations of this kind of subjective data, she notes that we can say, at the very least, that families *believe* their pets bring them closer together.

While generally loving and supportive, the sheer cheek-by-jowl nature of families provides ample opportunities for flare-ups of tension over the long term. The other social setting in which pets have been shown to wield a substantial influence has the opposite problem. Not enough social engagement — neglect, even. Many people living in institutions have little choice in their social exchanges, and with the best will in the world, staff can't give equal time to everyone. And it must be hard coming up with positive topics of conversation when all the resident has to focus on is how long it was since their last visit from family, and how much worse Betty is getting in the next bed. Animals, however, give everyone endless possibilities for long, positive conversations. Patients have generally been found to spend less time alone following the introduction of a resident pet, and both staff and residents mentioned in one study that it gave them something to talk about.[27] The staff are frequently happier, too. This must go a long way to explaining the marked health improvements we see in the many studies of institutions with a resident pet.

In all the examples I've given thus far, the animal has acted as a kind of intermediary object. A "social bridge", as some researchers have termed it, connecting one person to another. A particularly effective bridge at that, but still a role which could be filled by any object — a sufficiently interesting toy, for example. But the effect of companion animals on our social lives may go much much deeper than that. Because it seems they may actually *change* us. They may actually influence our *ability* to relate to others.

Much has been written about the influence of pets on the development of children. Many life skills are thought to be acquired through pets — coping with grief and death, taking on responsibility, learning to care and nurture. Work at the Institute for Psychology at the University of Vienna in the early 1980s, suggests that animal companionship at an early age may contribute substantially to general social skills. The Austrian researchers selected 477 students from a cross-section of different schools, and ranging in age from 11 to 16. The students were then asked: "With which of your classmates would you like to do something during the holidays?" The pet owners came out significantly in front.[28] For some reason, children with pets were more popular.

Now there could be some simple explanation for this — perhaps it was just that children with dogs are more fun to play with; a Nintendo effect, if you like. Except that pet owners also scored significantly higher on another question: "If you have a problem and would like to confide in someone, whom in your class would you choose?"

How could this be so? Well, there are two possible reasons. The first is that other studies have revealed children with pets have better self-esteem. A healthy self-image is critically important in projecting positively to others, so this would obviously have a bearing. The second lies in something else children with pets seem to be better at: empathy.

It's a difficult one to establish, and the jury is still out on the conclusiveness of some studies, but there is enough to suggest that young children may be more open to the needs of others if they live with an animal. In a standard test of empathy towards people, R. H. Poresky found that children aged three to six achieved higher scores if they had a pet.[29] This may be just a simple artefact of being given someone dependent to care for in an era where many children don't have younger brothers or sisters. Or it may be due to another finding that so far has insufficient support: children with pets are better at non-verbal communication.

In the same study that revealed the popularity of pet owners, Professor Giselter Guttman and his colleagues gave their subjects a series of photographs, each one expressing a different human emotion. The pet owners were far better at decoding subtle facial signals, and while the girls generally outperformed the boys, amongst the boys pet ownership made the biggest difference. Other theorists have even suggested pet ownership may enhance a child's development of language — perhaps by pets patiently sitting and listening to babyish babbling, perhaps by providing something kids want to talk *about*.[30] For whatever reason, it just reminds us how fundamentally entwined ours and our ancient animal partners' lives are.

FRIENDS FOR LIFE

Of course, the help we find in getting on with other people is as nothing compared with the friendship animals bring in themselves. Through thousands of years of co-evolution, cats and dogs have developed an emotional responsiveness to humans unparalleled in the animal kingdom. Whether artifice or not, they often seem to hang on our every word. They respond to our signals of sadness with a lick or a flop of the tail. They purr and rub against us with every appearance of total delight when we return home. They come to *us* with unmistakably expressed desire for our company and make us feel as though someone cares. And, for people who live alone, that swelling proportion of the community, the health implications may be profound.

While the National People and Pets Survey found that *all* dog owners went to the doctor less frequently and used less in the way of prescription medication, the health benefits for singles went well over and above that of the general population. This was, in turn, greater again where the attachment was strongest — where high ratings were given to "I feel close to the dog", or "I find the dog comforting when things go wrong", or "I make better social contacts through having a dog". And generally, the attachment between single people and their pets is more powerful than for people who live with others. This is not to say that families do not have a strong bond with their animals, simply that for singles the quality and importance of the relationship slips up one notch on the social support scale. Until in some cases, it is the most significant relationship.

The survey results are not an isolated finding. They have been replicated in many studies in different cultures and communities. A substantial longitudinal study of 1000 older persons in Canada found that those who lacked adequate human social support (such as a good network of friends) but had a pet were better off psychologically than their pet-less counterparts.[31] It's clear that animal companions can, to an extent, compensate for inadequate human contact. They certainly don't replace it, and it would be horrifying to suggest that they could, but if we're experiencing shortfalls in our daily social intake, pets provide a perfectly good supplement. But to suggest that cats and dogs are simply a substitute for humans, a pitiful "second best" when the preferred option isn't available, would be misguided. There appears to be something qualitatively different about the relationship, which means that even when humans are loving and available, the pets provide something else.

It's worth reflecting that the original Katcher and Friedman study, the one which found pet owners were more likely to be alive a year after a heart attack, was originally intended to examine *human* social support. Yet they were struck by this unexpected discovery — that pets gave an additional survival advantage independent of other forms of social support. Even Alzheimer's sufferers, some in such an advanced stage of dementia that they were insensible to human contact, smiled and leaned forward when placed in a room with a dog. They had no such response when the dog handler was there by herself.[32] With the dog, it was as if something deep and inchoate was able temporarily to break through the miasma of their confusion.

This applies to "normal" people as well. Anne McBride of Anthrozoology in Southampton, UK, recently found that people over 65 were markedly less depressed and lonely if they had a pet — and that was despite the presence of a spouse.[33] There is no law which says you won't be lonely just because you live with someone. For that matter, for some it's quite the opposite — trapped in a relationship which doesn't come close to meeting the requirements for quality social contact. And one of the most basic social contact qualities of all is touch.

Yes, we are the most social of species and, like all other social animals, our social drive is manifested in the need to touch. Without touch, infants fail to develop normally, with severe deprivation, they may even die. But in some cultures, in *our* culture, we've almost severed our capacity for touch, except in special, clearly defined circumstances. And even with those whom society gives us sanction to touch, fights, distance, distraction can get in the way.

Except, of course, with our pets. Cats and dogs are both superbly tactile. The cat, with its seemingly infinite capacity for tactile pleasure, perhaps more so than the dog. It's one of the reasons the cat's importance should soar into the next century, simply because it is the pre-eminent supplier of that essential and often all too scarce human requirement — touch. And for both cats and dogs, not only touch, but their emotional responsiveness is unfailingly, unreservedly available on tap.

This is why they provide such a strong buffering effect in times of life crisis. A human partner, no matter how loving, simply cannot *be* there hour after hour, day after day. A recent widow, gratified yet exhausted by the constant stream of concerned well-wishers, longs for the quiet, undemanding balm of sitting with her cat. A year after her husband's death, when the well-wishers still visit but the signs of "get on with it" are imperfectly hidden, her cat still comforts her while she sits and grieves some more. A dying man, whose loving wife and friends visit for hours each day, is calmed by the simple, gentle, constant presence of his dog in the months that it takes to die.

THE GOOD DEATH

There is a final sort of loneliness which we will all face one day. And we will face it on our own because no matter how much we are loved, how cocooned we are by friends, in the end, we can only ever do it alone. For some it will happen quickly, for many others, as medical technology exerts its increasingly elastic influence on our lives, slowly, over weeks or months, with full awareness of what is coming in the end.

The thought of how we die was not something I considered until last year, when I was sent a copy of a seminar paper written by a palliative care nurse who was interested in the benefits of pets.[34] The paper by the nurse (let's call him "Robert") contained a vivid description of a man's death (here referred to as "Tom").

Tom, a highly educated and respected 65-year-old man, was

dying of cancer in small hospital room. Underneath his hand lay the silky head of Sandy, his Golden Retriever, who had been a near-constant and silent companion in the preceding final few weeks. And as Tom finally slipped away, it was Sandy's soft howl which alerted the nursing staff to his passing.

The reason the nurse — Robert — decided to write the seminar paper was that he was determined to share his experience of Tom's case. As a specialist in palliative care, Robert worked almost entirely with the dying. It's obviously not an easy job, and one of the driving philosophical forces behind it is to help the patients achieve what sociologist Allan Kellehear refers to as "The Good Death".[35] The Good Death has a number of qualities. These include the patient being aware that they are dying, and having the time to make personal adjustments, to resolve any outstanding family conflicts, to relinquish former roles, and to become resolved to saying farewell. What struck Robert profoundly about Tom's death was the role that Sandy played in that final resolution.

Tom had been diagnosed with cancer more than three years earlier. Although not yet very ill, he quit his job and, since his wife continued with her work, she decided to buy him a dog for company during the day. Tom and the dog went for long walks together, built sheds and pottered around the house. When the time came for Tom to go to a home, the two were inseparable.

Although officially dogs weren't supposed to be on site, the staff turned a blind eye. Each time Sandy was brought in for a visit, she was duly entered in the visitors' book as Tom's niece. There were plenty of other human visitors too — it became a regular ritual for a group of Tom's friends to turn up and take him around the corner to the local Italian restaurant where they all laughed and drank — for as long as Tom was able.

Towards the end, Tom's family would leave Sandy at the home for hours on end, as much of the time Tom found Sandy's company more restful and soothing than that of other people. To all appearances, Sandy sensed Tom's deterioration, and modified her behaviour accordingly — losing her normally boisterous persona as soon as she walked through the hospital door and lying quiet and dignified with Tom for hours. Even when Tom no longer responded to any other stimulation, the nursing staff noted his thumb gently caressing Sandy as she lay beside him.

The point is it's not as though Sandy was a substitute for any lack of human support. Tom's family was as loving and generous as anyone could wish for. It's just that Sandy was different, and the connection with Sandy was different, and in this time of resolution with death, it was Sandy's type of emotional connection which was often needed the most.

When Tom died, Sandy was the only one in the room. According to Robert, Tom's was a Good Death.

I hope The Good Death is not a metaphor for where our species is heading; I didn't highlight it for that reason. I simply wanted to point out that although death is hardly new, the manner of our dying is. We will not face it in the bedrooms of our birthplace, but in alien function-specific centres for the dying. How those centres are designed, whether they will allow the presence of things we hold dear — our animals — should be of concern to us all.

As we surge forward into the millennium of the mega-city, as a species and as individuals it is true that we face many challenges. Social maladaption and loneliness is one, learning how to die in this age of the institutionalised death, another. In the next chapter we will find others still. The point is, our animal companions are not passive travellers, accidentally swept along for the ride, but are actively helping us meet those challenges.

The evidence is there — pets make a difference, a measurable difference, to our health. Up to 1.5 billion dollars' worth a year of difference, if Headey's analysis is to be believed, in Australia alone. Pets are clearly good for us. Or maybe, as David Paxton suggested to me, we are looking at this the wrong way around. Perhaps what the figures are telling us is not that the presence of animal companions in our communities is good for our health. Rather, that an absence of animals is bad.

CHAPTER 7

BIOPHILIA — OR ARE PETS GREEN?

IF YOU were to look at the pet stories in the media over the last few years, the ones high up into the serious news section rather than the silly pages, you'd be convinced that pets are definitely not green. "Dog poo the number one pollutant of the Yarra"; "Cats kill 200 million native animals a year"; "MP calls for the complete eradication of cats from Australia by the year 2020". These are the types of headlines we've seen in the last few years.

So far it's largely an Australian phenomenon, and it no doubt reflects our passion for the sensitive Australian fauna and flora. But the issue is tentatively emerging in other parts of the globe. A news item last year on the broadcast network CNN featured a biologist on the West Coast of the United States warning against the deadly peril of cats. In the United Kingdom, pets have been pilloried by several scientists. And the apparent rift between conservationist and pet advocate goes to the highest levels. In 1995, Tony Juniper, who heads the biodiversity team and is Deputy Campaign Director at Friends of the Earth, was the source for a particularly scathing article attacking British pets.[1] Amongst his broadsides were accusations that cats are consuming the songbird population of England, and that the number one issue for people

about their local environment is dog poo. And most damning —
that pets consume 55 grams of protein a day, while humans require
only 35 grams a day, and 800 million people in the world are
starving. He does point out that even if pets ate less, the food
would not help the starving millions, but still, he is perfectly serious
in suggesting the number of pets in Britain should be substantially
reduced.

So is he right? Are our animal companions, much as we love
them, part of the pollution problem? Fouling the waterways and
destroying native fauna? Using up the resources which could
otherwise be supporting humans? And if so, should we be doing
without them?

Let's start with dog faeces and water. In 1996, the suggestion
that dog faeces were one of the major pollutants of Australia's
waterways received a lot of coverage. The story caught on in both
Victoria and New South Wales, with the *Age* and the *Sydney
Morning Herald* newspapers running lead features on the issue.
Yet, there was no good evidence for this. The only relevant study
of faecal contamination of waterways at the time had found that
by far the biggest contributor was waterbirds. This was an analysis
of the waterways near Gosford, New South Wales, carried out
by Rhys Leeming of the CSIRO, who was able to use new
techniques to determine which species were the source of the
faecal contamination.[2] In that particular study, he found 80 per
cent of the *E. coli* (a bacterial marker of faeces) in water samples
was from birds. The results couldn't be directly translated to the
more heavily populated areas of Sydney and Melbourne, however
it should at least have given pause for thought. But the media
splash did turn out to have a plus side, even if the environmental
threat of dog poo was wildly overstated. Partly as a result of the
publicity, a number of city councils subsequently improved their
provision of doggy disposal services, and many more citizens

were encouraged to pick up after their pooches.

The charge that cats and dogs are major consumers of resources seems fairly spurious. Cats and dogs don't drive. They don't run offices. Nor do they set up households of their own, complete with television, fridge, central heating and computer. In fact, they fit very neatly into the niche established by humans, making little in the way of extra resource demands. To give you some idea, the average Australian dog costs $352 a year to maintain, the average cat $253.[3] That includes everything — veterinary emergencies, food, grooming, boarding. By contrast, the average cost for a middle income family with a teenage child is $6850 per annum.[4] The relevance of that comparison will become clear soon. As for the food eaten by pets, the vast majority is from protein sources considered unfit for human consumption. Even in the West, cats and dogs generally play the same role they always have — scavenging off the scraps and waste that humans reject.

Predation by cats is a more genuine concern. Biologist Chris Dickman, in his review commissioned by the Australian Nature Conservation Agency, outlined which species are most vulnerable to feline predation — generally small marsupials, especially ones that hop, and especially those whose habitat has been reduced leaving them stuck with small populations on little land islands.[5] The ANCA is busy preparing plans to control feral cats in those areas where it will do the most good.

Meanwhile, even pet cats that live in the city, kilometres away from the nearest endangered fauna, have been redefined as un-Australian. Try the dinner party test. Proclaim loudly that you have a cat and wait and see whether the environment word comes up. It's bound to. It's got to the point where land developers are seriously suggesting pet-free zones as a marketing angle. Amongst young people it's very noticeable, as if it's come down to a choice: do they love cats? Or do they love the environment?

Yet whether cats belong in Australia is a moot point. The fact is they are here. We could wipe out the pet cat population tomorrow and there would still be feral cats inhabiting the bush — as they have done for hundreds of years. The latest evidence is that cats arrived in the north even before white settlement.[6] Again, even if a few of the positions taken seem excessive, the flip side is that the debate has produced some welcome outcomes. Pet owners are now generally far more aware of their animals' activities, and are introducing measures to reduce the chances of their cats catching native fauna.

One intriguing suggestion to come out of the issue is that native animals could be turned into pets, perhaps even replacing cats. The Director of the Australian Museum, Michael Archer, and others point out that animals which evolved in Australia are less likely to be problematic. Moreover, keeping native animals as pets may instil a love of native fauna and help preserve species otherwise threatened. Quolls are a possible candidate — roughly cat-sized, meat eaters, and (so I'm assured) quite friendly. An interesting idea, and one that deserves exploration. Although, of course, the possible repercussions must be considered. As the fox farm experiment demonstrated, reducing aggression and selecting for companionability unleashes the neoteny genie. Fifty generations on, we might not have quite the quoll we started with.

But even if we can quell the quoll, I think it would be a great shame if well-looked-after cats lost their place in Australian society. Given the millennia they've had to evolve with us, it seems unlikely that any suitably interactive pet will be a good substitute soon. And, by all predictions, cats as companions should be increasing in importance into the next millennium. They are better suited than dogs to living in high-density areas. We can see this already in the United States where the number of cats in the country has recently outstripped the number of dogs. By contrast, in Australia cat numbers are dropping.

When it comes down to it, though, all three of these issues are relatively trivial in the overall question of whether pets are green. Where genuine problems exist, they can generally be addressed by sensible management. My real reason for framing the question "are pets green?" is simply to highlight another important point: our evolutionary partners have other functions as we adapt to the twenty-first century — and some of these functions are decidedly "green". The first involves what is probably the most serious environmental issue facing our planet.

THE POPULATION BOMB

In 1968, Paul Ehrlich alerted the world to a problem which had been building steadily for a century. He wasn't the first to notice it, but he was the first to present the issue in a way which hijacked the attention of the media and blasted its way into popular culture. He called it "The Population Bomb", and in his book of that name he argued that if the world's population were to continue doubling at its then rate of every 37 years, in 900 years the world would hold 60 million billion people.[7] Except that it would never get to that stage because well beforehand the soaring death rate — from famine, disease, war — would intervene.

Today the world population is 5.7 billion; when Ehrlich wrote his book in the late 1960s, it was nearly 4 billion. Only 50 years earlier, it was 2 billion. Two hundred years before that, it was 1 billion. What had been merely a steady burn for centuries was rapidly transformed into dynamite for one simple reason: we weren't dying any more. Advances in medicine, health and hygiene meant that from the nineteenth century on, wars and epidemics aside, every child had a more than reasonable chance of surviving to bear children themselves. In the Western world, the drop in mortality rates occurred late last century; in the developing world, not until after World War II. But in either case, it meant that our ancient survival strategy of producing far more children than was needed for replacement, simply to ensure that some lived, was now a hazard.

The disastrous consequences of unrestrained population growth are all too obvious. At some point we surpass the planet's capacity to bear sufficient food. This is the fear which originally stimulated Ehrlich's book. His work with crop plants was telling him there were limits to grain yield improvement. But perhaps even before that point, we run out of water. Certainly this is a major worry in the arid stretches of the Middle East, where populations continue to soar — in Gaza and Oman at nearly 5 per cent per annum, which is amongst the world's highest growth rates.[8] Most countries in the region already consume every drop of rain that falls and are tapping into irreplaceable ground water. Wars of oil and ideology may be as nothing to the wars of water to come, when the 40 per cent of the region's population still under the age of 15 reach their prime.

Population growth also destroys environments. People consume — whole forests, whole seabeds. The more there are of us, the more we consume.

And it makes us violent. The link between density and aggression in other species is well established. Edward O. Wilson, one of this century's most influential biologists of whom we will hear more soon, demonstrated in 1971 that the likelihood of aggressive behaviours evolving in a species could be predicted from population density.[9] Rwanda in the 1950s was apparently a beautiful country with mountains and gentle rolling hills — the "Switzerland of Africa". It was relatively sparsely populated — a comfortable 2 million people — but with family sizes commonly of eight to ten children, the population time bomb was ticking.

By 1994, the formerly almost empty hills were peppered with people — the population in this tiny country had swollen to 7.4 million. And the consequences were soon splattered in gory detail across the screens and headlines of media everywhere. Population wasn't the only factor in the slaughter, but many analysts such as Jared Diamond or the population-control campaigner Dr John Guillebaud claim it was a big one. The reason is pretty simple, really, in human terms. When we don't have the resources to sustain ourselves, we will fight for them.

Fortunately, current forecasts of world population growth fall far short of Ehrlich's truly cataclysmic predictions — and generally without the need to resort to the Rwandan solution. In a large part due to the efforts of Ehrlich and his ilk, sustained, concentrated family planning programs around the world are having an impact, as are the education programs for women, given a boost once it was realised that the best way to reduce fertility was to increase female literacy.

And cities themselves are playing a part. It could be argued that urbanisation is now itself a survival strategy, a means of putting on the population brakes. Not only does urbanisation and concentration reduce the *physical* spread of humans across the planet, it also suppresses our breeding. It's a common finding in the animal and insect kingdoms that at high densities fertility rates drop; and in general the same holds true for humans. For whatever reason — stress, lack of money, lack of space, more education or employment opportunities for women, an intermingling of environment and culture — families are generally smaller in cities than the surrounding countryside. It's an established pattern. Cities act as a natural contraceptive.

Much of the developed world is now approaching zero population growth, and in most of the developing world, fertility rates are high but in decline. The latest projections by Wolfgang

Lutz of the International Association for Applied Systems Analysis, whom I mentioned in the last chapter, are a far cry from the wild imaginings of 20 years ago but still sobering enough. If human fertility rates continue to fall at their current rate, it is estimated the world's population will stabilise some time around the years 2060 to 2070 at 11 to 11.5 billion. Double our current population.

But here's the catch. And to understand that catch we need to move right back to the beginning again, back to the circumstances in which our species first emerged. Like dogs, humans evolved through the process of neoteny, progressively extending the juvenile period until, as modern adults, we have more in common with adolescent chimpanzees than mature ones. We remain playful, curious and friendly throughout life. In the process though, we created something of a burden for ourselves. It takes a hell of a long time for children to grow up.

Humans produce altricial young, which means babies are born at a relatively underdeveloped stage. From an evolutionary standpoint, we had no choice. There is simply a limit to the size of a baby's head that will fit through a woman's pelvis, and consequently much of the brain's growth has to take place after birth.[10] As it is, the current size is hazardous enough, making our birthing process amongst the riskiest in the animal kingdom — it's frightening to recall how recently death by childbirth was such a real and ever-present spectre for women. (An interesting parallel to the human situation occurred not long ago, in the United Kingdom requiring the RSPCA to step in to save the Scottish Terrier breed. Selection for Jock's trademark chunky visage and tapering quarters had gone on to such an extent that the pups' heads were having trouble getting through the birth canal, and many could only be born through Caesarean section. The breeders were forced to start crossing with other breeds to widen the pelvis sufficiently to allow natural birth again.)

Born in such an underdeveloped state, the duration of human childhood dependency has been stretched to almost ridiculous extremes. Human children can't cling to their mother's backs, in fact they can't move about much at all without being carried to the age of three or four — an age when any other self-respecting mammal has already had kids of its own. These days, parents can't even expect their kids to leave home after sexual maturity. They still hang about, relying on Mum and Dad to provide to the age of 25. Or longer.

It's an illogical commitment. So something very powerful must have been operating to ensure parents didn't abandon their kids during this interminable period. And it was. We evolved a compelling desire to nurture.

The strength of the nurturing drive, or instinct, is one of the most powerful motivators of humanity. It's extremely generalised and emerges at an early age — which makes excellent sense from an evolutionary point of view, as there was obviously great advantage in having siblings and others to lend a hand. Caring for a brood all at different stages of dependence was more than could be asked of any woman. Even the men had to get involved from time to time. All humans are born with a capacity for nurturing, and once developed, it doesn't fade with age.

So here's the problem. We *must* achieve zero population growth if we are to avoid the various dooms predicted for us. But if the nurturing instinct is so strongly hardwired into us, what happens when we ask people not to have so many kids?

ASKING THE IMPOSSIBLE

There is a book by a famous English crime writer which describes a horrifying imaginary world. In *The Children of Men*, author P. D. James creates an infertility plague which sweeps the entire planet and stops reproduction overnight.[11] Twenty-five years on, the people are beset by a dreadful ennui. No future, nothing to strive for, nothing to plan but the manner of their own deaths. They manage to find little things to amuse themselves and give a sense of purpose — attending a short course in English literature or creating a wonderful garden. But their response to the lack of babies is the most pitiful. In one compelling scene, a middle-aged woman is wheeling a pram. Inside the pram is a carefully dressed doll, its glassy, azure eyes staring out blankly through thick lashes at passersby. Another woman stops and engages the doll's "mother" in a conversation. They simper and smile and coo at the motionless object. The first woman adjusts the doll's bonnet and tucks in a loose stray of hair. The second woman turns to go, then suddenly reaches back, picks up the doll and smashes it against a nearby wall. The first woman is silent, then she screams and screams. Finally, she falls to the ground sobbing, and tries desperately to piece back together the scattered shards of porcelain. Our prospects are nothing like as bleak as P. D. James's worst imaginings, but still it is undeniable that at no time in our history have societies, particularly in the West, been more deprived of opportunities for nurturing.

Achieving zero population growth brings with it some hard truths. Some of us will not have children at all. Even those that do will likely only have one or two. And children don't remain young and in that irresistible, big-eyed, totally dependent phase for long. With the demise of extended family structures — grandparents no longer living in the same household — exposure to children is even more limited. We can't expect someone else's kids to sustain our nurturing drive into old age. And the constraints of modern housing place further barriers. Increasingly, cities are being sectioned off into specialist child or no-child enclaves. This neighbourhood for the young singles; this for the dual income no kids; this, with its slightly cheaper property rates and larger houses, for the children. This has not been deliberate, but simply a result of choosing the kind of housing that suits the needs of a particular stage in life. But it means that unless we are currently parenting, we may not even meet kids in the street. The windows of opportunity for direct caring of the young are very narrow — and close abruptly.

Of course this will not be a problem for everyone. Like everything else defined as "human nature", the nurturing instinct is subject to the social scientist's best friend, the bell curve. For a proportion of the community, the pull will be very weak if present at all; in the majority, a steady tug; and for some, an urge so overpowering that if not met it literally makes people ill.

The role animals play in meeting this desperate vacuum should be obvious. Just consider that when the whole domestication process took place, the human nurturing instinct we are assuming forged the final link in the chain. Clutton-Brock has even suggested (only slightly tongue-in-check) that domestication was the invention of menopausal women! Wolves may have been able to invade our dumps, enter our villages and scavenge amongst our refuse unasked, but they couldn't cross the threshold and enter our homes without invitation.

The urge to nurture goes a long way to explaining the popularity of pet ownership in general. Cats and dogs stay appealingly doe-eyed, tactile and dependent for their whole lives, and we know that there are certain breeds in which these characteristics have been deliberately exaggerated. It's no accident that the dome-headed, highly neotenised dogs are frequently the preferred companions of older women.

And much of our behaviour towards animals seems to be derived, at least originally, from inbuilt behaviours towards children. It's particularly noticeable in the way we speak, and this was the phenomenon which caught Aaron Katcher's attention while he was doing his work with the survivors of heart attack, and later measuring blood pressure. He decided to explore it further, and after a series of observational studies with his colleague Alan Beck outlined the following characteristics of human conversation with animals:

- Where possible the head of the person is placed close to the head of the animal
- The volume of the voice is reduced, sometimes to a whisper
- The pitch of the voice is raised
- The rate of speech and length of utterances are decreased
- There is considerable verbal play with words, combinations of words and sounds, and stress and length of syllables
- Utterances are terminated with a rising inflection to emphasise or create a question, permitting the creation of a pseudo-dialogue with the animal. In this dialogue, the person may supply a verbal response for the animal, or some response of the animal's may be used as a reply. Appropriate pauses are inserted in the dialogue to permit such replies.[12]

All these features are commonly seen in speech to human babies; Katcher and Beck liken it to a sort of modified "motherese". They found certain differences though, which show we've adapted rather than simply adopted infant talk for animals. When adults talk to babies, the facial expressions are usually highly exaggerated, as if by overemphasising the emotion, the infants will grasp what we are trying to say. The opposite is true of talking to animals. The face is often remarkably tranquil — the brow relaxed, the nostrils flat, and the eyes are frequently partly closed. The smile, when it comes (which is often) is different in character again. Instead of the wide, open smile we might use in talking to another adult, it's a gentle, beatific beam like the "Madonna" smile of parents gazing fondly upon their sleeping child.

Katcher and Beck found further that this smile and the warm, relaxed glow actually makes people more attractive to others when they are in the company of their pets. It may be one of the reasons we are so ready to talk to people with animals, while we will pass the unaccompanied stranger by.

This link between animals, nurturing and human reproduction has some fascinating possible sequellae. Patrick Bateson, Provost of Kings College, Cambridge, and the man responsible for elucidating much of cats' behaviour, speculates whether animals can actually change the hormonal states of their human companions. He tells a lovely story of some friends who were having a great deal of difficulty conceiving. After a few years, and all sorts of tests and interventions, they were more or less resigned to their fate. They acquired a couple of kittens — and then lo and behold, promptly had a child![13] Apparently, it's not uncommon for couples who adopt to subsequently have babies of their own, as if the practice of nurturing helps kick-start reproductive systems into a more readily prepared state. Presumably, says Bateson, pets charge up the sex hormones.

People are also remarkably consistent in their descriptions of pets as "part of the family" or "one of the children". In social scientist Maree MacCallum's focus group work, nearly everyone mentioned something along those lines: "I've got four children — a boy, a girl and two dogs. One of the dogs is called Kelly. Kelly was the first word our two year old said." "My dog is my security blanket, my little child, my baby." "We've got rid of our teenage children and we've got a dog because we missed them."[14]

We also mustn't underestimate the importance of nurturing as an outlet for children. In large families, the older kids always help care for the youngsters, and in play, we often see girls play-acting at motherhood — the boys might too if they weren't so constrained by culture. If youngsters didn't have a strong nurturing instinct, dolls wouldn't be the billion-dollar industry we see today. Yet in the world of 2060, even children will be denied opportunities to nurture as family sizes drop. Elizabeth Paul, based at Edinburgh University and one of the best known researchers on the role of pets during childhood development, believes this is going to be a real issue for small families, and has probably not been sufficiently thought through.[15]

And most importantly, as well as a nurturing outlet, pets provide a training ground. A tendency to nurture isn't enough. It can certainly be suppressed, or even reversed, if children aren't exposed to the right environment — which means experiencing nurturing for themselves. It's worth mentioning, too, the tremendous cultural constraints on nurturing in boys. In a study in which I was involved which looked at the impact of placing a cat to live in a classroom, one of the unexpected but frequently proffered comments from teachers was how wonderful it was for the boys. Animals provide virtually the only socially sanctioned setting in which boys can display anything so soppy as nurturing.

REACHING FOR ZPG

Population growth has also been described using another metaphor — as a giant bucket of water. A tap stands over the bucket, pouring water in — these are the children being born. At the bottom of the bucket is a small hole out of which the water drains — these are the people dying. With rising life expectancy, only a trickle escapes from the hole at the bottom. Unless we want the bucket to fill to overflowing, drowning out the environment in the process, the tap must be turned off.

In all the discussion about achieving zero population growth, few talk about what happens to the people whose taps have been turned off. We're all far too concerned with the logistics of this mind-boggling issue to think seriously about what happens next. Yet the fact that we *haven't* seen mass outbreaks of psychoses in Europe and Australia and North America as a result of nurturing deprivation, suggests Professor Aaron Katcher, can perhaps be put down to our pets.

And turning to pets is a ubiquitous response. In parts of Asia, the many parts with rising incomes and smaller families, pet ownership is growing rapidly. New veterinary schools are being built throughout Asia to meet the demand. And it's far too simplistic to think this reflects only the creeping Westernisation of global culture. Like Westerners a hundred years earlier, Asians are responding to the dramatic decline in opportunities to nurture children with the most obvious alternative.

A friend of mine is in her late forties. She has a daughter, who's grown up now and has moved on. She shares her home with a dog and three cats, and you only have to walk in the door for it to be completely obvious who's in charge.

Last year, the dog, Toby, was hit by a car — my friend saw him bit by bit, disappear under the wheels of the car. She raced to him — he was still breathing, and rushed off to the vet. Fortunately, all vital organs were intact, but his pelvis had taken a hammering and shattered in a few places, and he needed to be kept very still for at least a few weeks. My friend rang her place of work and organised to take semi-leave. For the next month, she worked from home and nursed Toby back to health.

It's the sort of behaviour widely derided in the popular press. For some reason we make fun of people like this — laughing at the childless couple who remember their two cats' birthdays and buy them presents for Christmas, or watching with a faintly contemptuous pity the middle-aged woman who buys smoked salmon for her Silkie Terrier and cooks him a different gourmet meal every night. The very phrase "child substitute" has vaguely derogatory connotations. But what we are looking at is not pathological at all. It's a logical, sensible, adaptive response to the consequences of controlling our population.

By the middle of next century, all nations will have had to adapt in some way to the realities of meeting ZPG. In much of Africa and maybe the Middle East, it's optimistic to think pets will be part of the solution — it's more likely to be recurrent genocide or epidemics. Hopefully, other portions of the globe will opt for more compassionate strategies. Whether anyone realises it or not, underpinning those strategies, probably still unnoticed and underestimated, will sit the companion animal.

OUT OF AFRICA

Our final challenge as we move into the twenty-first and twenty-second centuries is one pets can't overcome, only ameliorate. It's irreversible and it's been happening for the last 10,000 years. We are losing contact with the environment in which we evolved. And no one is really sure what this means.

There are a number of scientists, however, who believe it means something quite significant. They are working on a grand theory. And one of the planks of that theory involves landscape paintings.

Gordon Orians, a US zoologist and environmental scientist, has worked for many years on the phenomenon of habitat selection. It's an attractive subject for a biologist, because the choice of a home is one of the most important any organism will face. Will there be enough food? Is it sufficiently protected from predators? Will it be a safe place to raise young? If the organism gets it wrong, the chances of surviving long enough to reproduce plummet. It's quite obvious, then, that the selection pressure to develop an "instinct" or tendency towards certain types of places would be very strong. And the preferences are extremely specific.

A beaver will fuss about like a houseproud bachelor, finding exactly the right point in a stream to build a dam. A cat searching frantically for a place to bear her kittens will find the darkest quietest place possible, preferably low down and covered by something. (Don't leave the linen cupboard door open!) And clearly such choices can't simply be thought through — "well, if I set up there, it's nice and dark so my kittens won't be bothered by the light, it's secluded in case any predators smell the afterbirth". Even if the mother cat could think in such a human way, a first-time mother has no prior experience on which to base her thoughts. So the most likely mechanism is that certain places evoke some sort of emotional response. A poor environment might evoke a negative emotional response like a feeling of unease; a good one, an emotion like a feeling of comfort or pleasure.

Orians was studying habitat selection in birds, and it started him wondering. Do the same principles apply to humans? Now, there are many ways to test this idea. You could take a lot of humans and place them in different settings and see how they reacted. Or you could simply show them photos of places and see which ones they like (this method has actually been used quite extensively.) But why be confined to these boring experiments, when we already have such an abundance of information about the types of scenery people prefer?

In an inspired bit of detective work, Orians was fortunate enough to obtain a sample of 18 sets of drawings by a famous eighteenth-century British landscape architect, Humphrey Repton.[16] These were delightful "before" and "after" landscape pictures, on which the artist added or removed features to make the scene more appealing, and thereby convince his clients they needed him on the job. Orians reasoned that these "improvements" would give a strong indication of human landscape preferences, and set to analysing the differences.

In about half the designs, Repton had added trees and copses to open fields, and in a quarter of them the copses were placed right at the water's edge. Trees were removed to open up the horizon in 42 per cent of the landscapes and thick woods invariably thinned to reduce their "gloominess". Any sharp transitions from woodland to pasture were eased by the addition of a trickle of trees around the periphery, creating an undulating uneven edge. In most of them, sheep and cows were added, contentedly grazing or just lying down in the sunshine. And water features were pivotal to all Repton's designs; they were added, moved, reshaped, or simply made more obvious. Turgid waterways were transformed into tumbling brooks by the addition of rocks because, to use Repton's own words, it gives "a lively rippling effect which is highly preferable to a narrow stagnant creek".

Orians had a specific idea in mind while he was analysing Repton's pictures. The idea was already being discussed in scientific circles, most notably by Roger Ulrich, whose PhD was obtained in behavioural geography and environmental psychology, and who was trying to understand why it was that certain environments provoke such strong responses from people. The idea was this: that our aesthetic appreciation of landscape is not random, and was not developed in the last 10,000 years of civilisation, gardens and "high culture", but was moulded in the hundreds of thousands, if not millions, of years we resided in the African savannah.

And Repton's work seemed to bear this out. Unlike the dense forests of Britain before it was tidied by human "improvers", the savannah is a land of wide open plains and scattered copses of elegantly spreading trees. The changes introduced by Repton, and many other landscape architects are reminiscent of an ideal human evolutionary habitat. Take the thick woods which were invariably thinned. With thick woods we can't detect predators until they are right upon us; a more open view of the horizon allows constant surveillance. Scattered trees and copses interspersed with open spaces are a typical savannah pattern, and it's interesting how commonly grazing animals help calm a landscape scene. They not only represent available food, but their relaxed state tells us the scene holds no dangers in the form of alert predators or incipient eruptions of threatening weather. Even the types of trees we prefer have distinctly savannah features. In other studies, Orians has shown that the tree shape idealised by humans has low spreading branches, medium leaf canopy (not too thick or too sparse) and a high tree width-to-height ratio. The classic example is the highly pruned and stylised tree of a Japanese garden. We also like our landscapes to have some sort of shelter or refuge — a little hut or a shed, if not a cottage complete with cheerfully smoking chimney. In another fascinating analysis of landscape paintings, Orians found pictures of sunsets were more likely to contain a shelter than pictures of sunrises. He reasons that the coming of night is a threatening setting, so we need to be reassured we have somewhere safe to go. And we are particularly drawn by the features which are essential to survival. In this light, it's easy to understand the overwhelming magnetism of running water. Without food we can last for months, without fresh water we die in days.

Basically, Repton was turning the English countryside into miniature old Africas.

THE BIOPHILIA HYPOTHESIS

The works of Orians, Ulrich and others — even the pets and health benefits research we discussed in the last chapter — have in the last decade been brought together to support a much larger theory, put forward first in 1984 by one of this century's most distinguished biologists, E. O. Wilson.[17] What Wilson proposed is that over the millennia of our evolution, *Homo sapiens* developed certain learning rules, or tendencies, which influence the way we react to natural settings and creatures. These form the basis of our aesthetic sense, and totally artificial settings simply haven't been around long enough to have the same impact. He believes a tendency to seek out natural settings and affiliate with animals and plants is written into our genetic program. He calls these tendencies "biophilia". And the proposal has been extremely controversial.

The derision from colleagues (even supporters unkindly suggested the name sounded like a tropical disease) that his book *Biophilia* occasioned when it was released in 1984 would not have been an unfamiliar experience for Wilson.[18] He went through a far more torrid time a decade earlier with the release of his great work *Sociobiology: The New Synthesis*. Sociobiology was a relatively obscure science at the time, and Wilson, who had been working in it for some decades, conceived the ambitious idea of synthesising all the new information that had come up in the 1960s on kin selection, and the mathematical modelling of social behaviour, into one huge volume which would cover the entire animal kingdom. The problem was, being the thorough researcher he was, in the final chapter he had the temerity to include humans.

The response was extraordinary. A whole society of eminent persons was formed to repudiate his work, and he suffered the ignominy of mass demonstrations, and on one occasion, a glass of water being thrown over his head just before he was about to make a speech. The 1970s was a pretty interesting time to be even suggesting that human behaviour might be influenced by genes — the prevailing radical ideology had so much invested in the idea it was all in the upbringing.

But the principles outlined by Wilson are now more widely accepted, though some remain unconvinced. They eventually led him to the biophilia hypothesis, and they describe the genetic basis for something we often refer to as instinct. Over the aeons of evolution, certain shuffled combinations of genes would have produced chemical states which might have made an organism more likely to react to something in a certain way. If that reaction gave the animal a survival advantage, then the genes which favoured the behaviour got passed on to the next generation. Or the gene combination might make an animal more likely to learn certain things quickly. This is known as "prepared learning". A good example is the human instinct for language. We are primed to learn to talk, whereas learning maths takes a fair amount of applied mental effort.

In this way, over vast expanses of time, every species accumulates a set of learning rules, or inherited tendencies. Of course culture and experience have a profound influence as well. It doesn't mean we are robots, prisoners of our programming, merely that all other things being equal, we are more likely to react in one way than another. These learning rules form the basis of what we might loosely call "human nature".

Once the sociobiology furore had died down, in the early 1980s Wilson started to become more and more concerned about conservation issues (which were just catching on in the popular imagination). He started to think the same learning rules might also apply to human responses to natural settings. Certainly, many of us seem to have an inchoate attraction to trees and animals. Why else do we feel refreshed when we gaze upon the fluttering leaves of a distant tree, and depressed if our office view is of a constant stream of traffic? Why are the high-rise concrete edifices of inner-city dwellings smattered with little colourful pot plants waving forlornly in the breeze? Wilson's biophilia hypothesis would certainly give some sort of valid explanation for these vague but none the less powerful feelings. Wilson is saying what we are experiencing is the emotional draw of ideal habitat selection.

There is plenty of other evidence which appears to back up the biophilia hypothesis. Roger Ulrich's studies show that people who live in vast Asian, European and North American regions consistently like landscapes which look like savannah parklands. And it's interesting that natural light and green spaces definitely affect our emotions and mental states in a way artificial environments don't. In the 1960s and 1970s, there was a trend to constructing buildings with rooms without windows. Alarm bells rang when one researcher discovered that people in windowless post-operative intensive care units were *twice* as likely to be in a confused and hallucinogenic state than patients with windows.[19] We now know that artificial light doesn't trigger the same metabolic responses as natural light, and insufficient natural light can bring on confusion and depression. But it's not just access to daylight; the nature of the view from a window is important as well. Roger Ulrich also found that the wounds from a gall bladder operation healed on average a whole day earlier if the patients had a view of the park from their room.[20]

Others have discovered parks increase people's powers of concentration. The theory put forward by psychologists Rachel and Stephen Kaplan is that we have two types of attention — directed and undirected.[21] Directed attention, the kind we use to focus on work at a desk, is tiring. Undirected attention, the kind that's drawn by rippling waterways or walking through a green space in the sun, isn't tiring and actually allows us time to recuperate. And the difference between human responses to natural settings and urban settings can actually be read in the brain waves. It's interesting how closely the landscape aesthetics research parallels the work on humans and pets.

And you only have to look at real estate prices to feel habitat preference is just as strong an instinct in humans as it is in other animals. What sort of homes do rich people buy? High up, with prominent water views and near parklands with their spreading trees and open vistas. As E. O. Wilson asks — "can it really be just a coincidence, this similarity between the ancient home of human beings and their modern habitat preference?"[22]

The other side of the biophilia coin is the things we don't like. The things which are capable of provoking a fear out of all proportion to their modern risk. And top of the list are snakes.

Many of us are afraid of snakes. Not all, but many of us experience at least the flip of a heartbeat if we see something slithering along in front of us — even if it proves to be a water-animated garden hose. And quite a few develop full blown phobias. E. O. Wilson argues you don't have to look to some Freudian analysis about guilt and sex to explain it — how about considering the fact that the snakes we evolved with can kill us.[23]

In an ingenious set of experiments, researchers looked at how easily people develop fearful responses to a stimulus, and how long it takes for those responses to fade. By pairing a little shock with — say — a photo of a snake or a gun or a chair, scientists can condition a person to react fearfully. Even if the subjects aren't really conscious of it, involuntary responses give them away. Cold sweats and racing hearts. And these can be measured. When the scientists dispense with the shock and just show the photo, they can then measure how these conditioned responses evaporate over time. In this case, what they found was that the fear of spiders or snakes took much much longer to lose than other, more neutral stimuli. In other words, once we learn a fear of snakes, we learn it well — and it takes a hell of a long time (if ever) to lose it. And the interesting thing is, when they tried the same thing with modern, more likely threats — guns and knives — they weren't nearly as effective deterrents.

It could be argued that just about all of these examples of attraction or aversion to natural stimuli could be equally well explained by the force of human culture. And this is the view of Wilson's critics. It's almost impossible to exclude the influence of culture from any theory involving humans, because to do so would require removing a young child from all the care and social interaction which nurtures them into functional adults — totally out of the question. Other cultures, particularly those which have only been in contact with European culture for a relatively short time may be different. In Papua New Guinea, for example, the locals aren't afraid of all snakes, they just say the white people are too stupid to tell the harmless from the dangerous ones. And it's hard to believe that the Amerindians of the Amazonian jungle, surrounded by their towering pillars of trees and dense, glowing green canopies, would suddenly express a preference for Central Park.

Wilson does have responses to these criticisms. For example, he notes that humans are not the only ones to respond strongly to snakes — Old World monkeys also have aversions and fascinations for snake-shaped objects, and vervets (monkeys) seem to use a special shout which means "snake". And he is convinced that there is more than enough information to suppose that millions of years of evolution in a particular setting with particular benefits and threats has left our species imprinted with certain learning rules. Even if they have been weakened and, at this point in our development, can be easily overturned, they are still detectable.

So how should we read all this? Well, if Wilson is right, then to a greater or lesser extent we all have a tendency to respond to certain natural things in a positive way. Like the nurturing instinct, some will have it more strongly than others, some won't develop it at all. And what happens if we miss out on opportunities to respond to these natural settings? Well, again it will vary from person to person. Plenty won't even notice, and about all you will be able to say is that they are perhaps missing out on reaching their full potential as human beings. But for others, it could be a destroyer. In the urban translocation, we are moving faster and faster away from the landscapes in which we evolved. And unfortunately, or so psychiatrist Aaron Katcher, who's now a staunch supporter of the biophilia hypothesis, believes part of what he treats is the pathological consequences of that move.

UNFIT FOR CITY LIFE

Attention deficit hyperactive disorder, or ADHD, is *the* childhood disease of the 1990s. It's the most common behavioural problem in US children today, with up to 5 per cent of children under the age of 18 thought to be affected. These kids are impulsive, finding it almost impossible to control their behaviour, and their short attention spans and seeming indifference to punishment sorely stretch the patience of any teachers or parents. They often do poorly in school as a result, and are notorious truants. They lack social skills, have trouble making friends and are particularly prone to aggression. And in the worst cases, they are institutionalised or ripe fodder for lives of crime or substance abuse or both.

Aaron Katcher's interest in human–animal interactions eventually led him to ADHD. It's a difficult condition, often complicated by poor family circumstances, but in the main, the only successful treatment has been stimulant drugs. From the beginning of the nineties, prescriptions of Ritalin in the US went up 390 per cent in just four years. By the time Katcher got to ADHD, he'd been working already for a decade with the idea that the human relationship with animals was special. So he decided to find out whether animals could do something for these kids.

Katcher worked with the Brandywine Center, a specialist institution for children with psychiatric disorders. The children were already receiving all the standard therapies, but Katcher and his colleagues set up two additional programs. The first they called the Outward Bound. One group of children were taken on regular outings to learn rock climbing, canoeing, and water safety. This went on for six months, and then they swapped with the other group. The second group they called the Companionable Zoo. A large building was equipped to house a collection of small animals — hamsters, mice, chinchillas, rabbits, lizards, goats and more. This group was taken to the zoo once a week for five hours, although they had free access in their spare time because it was thought unfair to separate the kids from their pets. The children were encouraged to adopt one special pet, but only after they had first learned the unique care requirements of that species. Following adoption, they then had to learn 21 skills associated with their animal. Many of these skills were designed to exactly mimic the areas in which the kids were having trouble learning in class — weighing and measuring their pets, calculating their daily feed intake. And running through the whole program, they had to follow two rules. First, to be gentle with the animals and speak softly while in the zoo. Second, to respect the animals and their classmates and not make derogatory remarks about either. Precisely the type of self-control ADHD kids find so impossible.

The zoo program achieved by far the best results. Its attendance was always extraordinarily high: 93 per cent for the summer program as opposed to 71 per cent for the Outward Bound. And this was still true when the groups swapped. And it provided a superb setting for learning. The average student learned eight new skills, and partially learned several more over the six months. There were students who had achieved virtually nothing in the last four years of schooling who rapidly picked up new skills. And all were surprisingly self-controlled. It was estimated there should have been at least 35 incidents requiring some sort of restraint by the teachers over that period, yet not one child required restraint in the zoo. They were also given tests to measure overall behavioural pathology — that is, their behaviour during the whole day, not just for the hours spent on the program. It was substantially reduced for the whole time the kids were on the zoo program. Once they were taken off the program, their general behaviour worsened again.[24]

Katcher's results are bittersweet. While it was obviously tremendously beneficial for the kids involved, we know it's unlikely many such kids will have the opportunity for an experience like it. I witnessed a similar outcome in a program with which I was involved — a sad story with a positive ending. Called Cats in Schools, the program involved placing a kitten to live in a classroom for the school year, and nearly 40 schools and more than 900 children took part. These were perfectly normal kids, and even with this group the evaluation showed that long term, the cat had a remarkably calming effect. But there was a case that particularly bore out Katcher's theory.

Towards the end of the program, I visited one of the schools where I was met by a boy almost pushing over the other kids in his eagerness to show a stranger their wonderful cat. His behaviour was a little disconcerting but very appealing. Later I learnt that he had some pretty awful family problems.

For various reasons he'd been in and out of foster homes almost all his life. He'd joined the class that year after moving to yet another home, and initially was impossibly disruptive — perhaps borderline ADHD. But just as Katcher discovered, the boy relaxed once he bonded with the cat, becoming calmer, more engaged and socialising better with the rest of the class. It was soon found that his outbursts could be anticipated and could be headed off simply by suggesting he go and sit with the cat.

The reason Aaron Katcher is rather pessimistic about our future is that to him the results of such experiments suggests that there is more to ADHD and its treatment than just a chemical imbalance in the brain. He thinks ADHD is a symptom of a deeper problem. That within us all sits an array of genes which, to a greater or lesser extent, equip us for life in the countryside. And that some of us just aren't designed to make a living in cities.

The sweep of human potential allows an array of different kinds of intelligence. Some of us are artists, some mathematicians, some physical, some spiritual, some think with their heads, some with their hands. Seventy years ago, more than half the people in the United States worked on farms. Today, that figure is 2 per cent. Katcher is afraid that by forcing the whole of humanity into urban life, we are restricting the kinds of people who can make a living to a very narrow range of human potential. A proportion of our population will never be able to find gainful or satisfying employment. It's certainly not true for all people, and indeed the high suicide rates among rural men show that it is a far from simple equation. But for some city dwellers, argues Katcher, they will be lost in the mental opacity of the person without purpose — turning to the destructive crutches that can prop up a life without direction. As Katcher says, " It takes a different kind of intelligence to work with earth or animal or craft from the one it takes to punch numbers into a computer."[25]

Are pets green?

Not everyone is convinced that biophilia actually exists. Even Wilson says he's not irreversibly committed to the idea; he just thinks it's a reasonable hypothesis which deserves to be properly tested. But the point on which everyone agrees is the need for an _ethic_ of biophilia. Literally, love of the biota. Because if we don't all develop an overwhelming empathy for the natural world, will we have the will to protect what's left of our planet?

And the question is, can we ever learn a conservation ethic without direct experience? Is it possible to develop true empathy for the other than human if we don't, at least at some point, live closely with such other? Perhaps we can. Perhaps nature films are enough. Perhaps the views from the information highways and the television screens are enough. Perhaps the infrequent visits, for those of us that have the opportunity, to parklands and nature reserves and zoos are enough. However, the little evidence we have would suggest they are not the whole story. Not a lot of work has been done on it, but Elizabeth Paul, the English researcher who specialises in animals and childhood, has found enough to pique her interest. Recently, she surveyed a large group of university students, asking about current membership of conservation and animal welfare groups. She also inquired about pet ownership as a child. And she found there was a significant correlation between pet ownership and the likelihood of membership of both groups.[26] But it only held true for what she called "important" pets: the animals with which the students recalled a close bond. In this case, only dogs and cats. She suggests this is a classic example of what the psychologists call "generalisation" — the phenomenon of learning about one thing and being able to generalise and extend the knowledge or the emotion to all things like. Animal companions may be lending a paw, not just as a necessary focus for an instinctive biophilia, but by helping to create the very biophilia ethic which will motivate us to conserve.

The ecologists have a beautiful term for the interconnections that bind each cell, each organism, each community on this planet together. They call it the "web of life". Over the last 10,000 years, humans have been diligently working on the periphery, spinning a new web. Dense and matted — more like a ball of yarn than an airy lattice — and it's getting bigger and denser and more and more matted. Several threads still connect us to the old web —

threads made up of the plants, the animals, even some of the genes developed in the world in which we evolved. But they are starting to fray. First one, then another thread has snapped: we no longer see the horses that carried us, the grains that gave us bread, we don't know the animals we eat. For the vast majority of city dwellers, the only real cords still connected to the web of the natural world are the little pot plants sitting gaily in windows and gardens, and the animals with whom we share our homes.

Elizabeth Paul's research recalls to mind a wonderful quote by Karl von Frisch, one of the most famous ethologists of the century, and whose work revealed the strange dances of bees: "The layman may wonder why a biologist is content to devote 50 years of his life to the study of bees and minnows without ever branching out into research on, say, elephants, or at any rate the lice of elephants or the fleas of moles. The answer to any such question must be that every single species of the animal kingdom challenges us with all, or nearly all, the mysteries of life."[27]

We can't all be biologists, and we won't all have access to the kinds of natural landscapes that inspire. But we can all spend a lifetime studying, however unconsciously, the lives of the animals in our midst. And perhaps they too challenge us with all, or nearly all, the mysteries of life.

So are pets green? Well, in the wrong place and at the wrong time they can undoubtedly do "un-green" things. But without them, zero population growth may be a really difficult ask. Without them, perhaps we lose the will or the skill to understand anything not human. Without them, perhaps we miss one of the few remaining opportunities to express the potentials which are sitting there, however weakly, in our own genes — genes selected over the millions of years before we started weaving our *own* separate web.

CHAPTER 8

PLANNERS FORGOT THE PETS

IMAGINE a place, a place very much like the one in which you live now. Perhaps this place is in the future, perhaps it is one of those parallel universes beloved of science fiction writers, but it is very familiar, and you are visiting it as a sort of observing ghost.

At first as you waft from corner to corner, you become convinced this really *is* your home. It certainly *looks* like it. But soon you start to notice there is something slightly strange. The pattern of city noise is a little different. Drifting randomly as only spirits can, you hear the wind whistling through the trees in the parks, and the sounds of city traffic and construction work. In a schoolyard children are shouting; the occasional car alarm goes off. There's something missing which you can't quite put your finger on.

The people also look a little odd — grumpy, even. Joggers in the park keep their eyes dead ahead (well, there's nothing odd about that) but even the walkers seem to stare fixedly as if nothing exists except their own internal universe, and no one at all stops to say hello.

Drifting past the hives of inner suburbia, your penetrating spectral eyes reveal rows of blank-faced people sitting quietly in ones and twos, watching television or preparing the evening meal. Intrigued, you zoom in to have a look at what's on TV — even ghosts can't resist the appeal of the flickering light — and settle in to watch. First on is *Gilligan's Island*, then a banal but entertaining program full of evil people in suits. All is right — but not *quite* right.

Eventually, you reach what looks very like your own front gate. The floating gently comes to a halt, and your toes reach down to make contact with the earth. Crunch, crunch, up the path. Pull the door open. Silence. A silence which is palpable, because the air should be filled with something *so* familiar. A snuffling, or barking — a greeting ritual as predictable as the rising of the sun. All of a sudden you realise what's wrong. The city contains not a single animal.

The vision of an animal-less city is absurd. They are so integral to our lives; their sounds and movements so familiar to our subconscious that their absence is more noticeable than their presence. Yet, in parts of the world, it's the direction we are heading. Believe it or not, as we move into the next centuries, it is not only our contact with "wild animals" which is at risk from the bulging imperative of human populations. The animals which throughout our history have been closest to us, whose very presence helps define human "nature", face the squeeze as well.

You may think I'm joking, or needlessly hyperbolising. After all, the pet ownership figures in Australia are nothing to worry about — 42 per cent of households with a dog, 31 per cent with a cat, most children having some experience of pet ownership during childhood.[1] Hardly the statistics to send a pet marketing manager searching for the nearest tall building. Yet even here we are beginning to see the effects of the change. After steady increases paralleling the increase in human numbers during the 1980s, absolute dog numbers have now plateaued. Cat numbers have already traversed the plain and are slipping down the far slope of decline. Although in the case of cats, other confounding factors such as the redefinition of cat ownership as "un-Australian" complicate the interpretation, it does seem as though something is happening. Maybe, just maybe, it is the earliest warning of yet another fundamental shift in our relations with the non-humans — only this time not just away from the "wild", but from even our most ancient symbiotic partners. And, as we shall see later in this chapter, internationally the signs are already there. Despite popular opinion to the contrary, they are flagging us from the "pet-loving" cities of London and Paris. The problem is that in parts of the world we're running out of room. And the fact is, somehow, despite everything we've discussed in the previous seven chapters, city planners forgot the pets.

A SMALL MATTER OF SPACE

The "hunger for land", it's been called. It's an inevitable progression, born of the inexorable tide of humanity as it swamps, floodwater-like, every hospitable lowland.

The population figures themselves tell the story. One billion people alive at the beginning of the last century; five billion now; an expected 11 billion by the end of next century. To many, the idea of living in a world with double the number of humans already here is inconceivable.

Yet we must plan — for it will happen. Just feeding, watering and clothing a world population of 11 billion humans will be a herculean task and its practicalities are already inducing global managerial migraine. Not to mention how we're going to process the waste products when we don't even do a good job of it now. Or to mention where we're going to *put* everyone.

And it seems that the majority of us will be put in cities. The

United Nations predicts built-up urban areas will *double* in size in most developing countries over the next 20 years. Forty-five per cent of the world's population lives in cities now; by the year 2025, it will be 66 per cent.[2] And unless we intend to completely obliterate all remaining countryside, ultimately higher densities will mean many of us can expect less personal space. As can the city animals, if we make any room for them at all. How those cities will look, how their inhabitants will live, whether they will have access to the sorts of things we associate with the "good life" — variety, space, green things, fresh air — are to a large extent already being determined. And these are the sorts of quality-of-life issues, amongst others, which will be substantially shaped by today's urban planners.

Urban planning is as old as the settlements which spawned it. From the time permanent communities first appeared on the landscape, intrinsic rules about personal space and utility governed the distances between dwellings and gave the semblance of design even if the process itself was haphazard. Structure followed not far behind — witness the graceful complexity of ancient Babylon. The Roman planners had no patience for disorder, steam-rolling all in their path with the clean lines of basic grid work. While the Middle Ages saw a return to a more organic urban growth, the Renaissance of fifteenth century Italy produced perhaps the most tightly structured and in some ways beautiful city designs. It was the era of the geometric "ideal city", with streets radiating from a central hub to terminate in glorious star-shaped walls. Towns like the patterns of a snowflake.

Nevertheless, urban planning was more often observed in the breach than in the act. Settlements which grew up organically worked perfectly well when reasonably small, but upon reaching a critical mass, required urgent attention to infrastructure: sewage disposal, roads, a clean source of water. Many of the most interesting cities in the world developed this way. London, a small trading centre at the time of the Romans, underwent a series of renovations, including those that followed the Great Fire of 1666. Christopher Wren's artistry in Saint Paul's Cathedral or the airy rooms of Hampton Court remain key tourist attractions to this day. Yet even without the fire, seventeenth-century London had already reached a severe state of dilapidation, congestion and pollution, and required urgent attention. The impetus for many urban reforms has been incipient infrastructural collapse.

Modern town planning grew out of just such a crises. The problems of Christopher Wren's day were nothing compared to those of post-industrialisation. Working-class ghettoes, built purely to house the slaves of the production line within walking distance of the factory, were dark, dirty, disease-ridden places. The sheer unpleasantness of these slums prompted the humanitarian movements of the nineteenth century, and part of their platform was the push for "air for the working classes". Like many nineteenth-century "improvements", even though it was a health issue, this one was tied to morality. The philanthropic idea was that if cities were better ventilated, the lower classes wouldn't be such a godless lot. Its adherents were strong believers in "physical determinism". They argued that if the environment determined the moral fibre of the inhabitants, then fresh air, space and green areas would make them holier, thriftier, harder working and more productive. It all made good economic sense and the generously proportioned boulevards and parklands of Melbourne — largely laid out in the 1860s — owe a great debt to planning's influence.

By the twentieth century, urban planning was well and truly an established discipline. In Australia, city plans were being drawn up in the late 1940s, but it was not until the 1960s that local government began to plan in earnest. By the 1980s, no local government body could function without urban planners.

And this is where we reach the nub of the problem.

Throughout this book, I have argued consistently that dogs in particular, but other domestic animals too, are part of a mixed-species community. Wherever there are people, there are dogs. So the question is: what does urban planning have to say about this? And the answer is: nothing. A resounding silence. It's as if dogs don't exist.

In all the work on sustainable cities, all the conferences on the future of our communities, dogs don't rate a mention. *Living Suburbs: A Policy for Metropolitan Melbourne into the 21st Century*, published in 1995 by the State Government of Victoria, has zero to say about dogs.[3] It mentions cultural development, economic growth, children, infrastructure, wildlife corridors, parklands, dwelling size but nothing about the non-humans which also use the city. *Building a Better Future: Cities for the 21st Century*, the New South Wales equivalent, also has zero to say about dogs.[4] For that matter, around the world, in all the policy documents governing all the cities, you'd be hard pressed to find anything about dogs. (I must note that in the short time since this book was first published, I am delighted that in Australia, at least, the situation has started to change. A number of councils in Victoria and New South Wales have taken up the challenge and conducted extensive reviews of the use of their parks by dog walkers. In New South Wales, the recently tabled Companion Animals Act requires councils to provide at least one off-leash park. The success of these pro-active approaches will, I hope, encourage others to follow suit.)

But does it actually matter? If dogs are so well adapted to living with us, if they are as much a part of human existence as making friends or going for a walk, then surely plans for humans will automatically cater for the needs of dogs? Well up until now, in Australia at least — which is where we are going to focus our attention for the moment — they probably have. But the space crunch is now on. And the results of failing to plan are already being felt.

URBAN PROTEST — THE SYMPTOMS OF NEGLECT

On 28 May 1995, page three of the *Sunday Age* in Melbourne carried the headline "Blame the owners who unleash the dogs of fear". The opening to the story was equally dramatic: "Elizabeth Lazaro knew the dogs would be coming for her seven-year-old son, Roberto, again tonight. After tucking him into her double bed she sat back and waited for the screaming to start."

Young Roberto had been attacked by a Rottweiler dog in Fawkner Park, a popular destination for the denizens of inner-city Melbourne. It was a nasty incident — the child required surgery on his mauled arm and shoulder, although was fortunately spared permanent damage. But the real story that unfolded had little to do with whether the boy was emotionally scarred by the experience or ever recovered from his nightmares. The real story had to do with how the community and the council reacted.

The *Sunday Age* was unequivocal in its slant. It attacked the "common practice among dog owners of leaving their pet unleashed in public streets and parks", citing the shocking discovery that in Fawkner Park on the Wednesday previous, the reporter had spotted no fewer than 34 unleashed dogs compared with 12 leashed ones over three hours. The editorial in the same paper was equally pointed. It concluded: "The community is, perhaps, too tolerant of dogs roaming free, being a nuisance, or in extreme cases, a public menace. Let's get our priorities straight. The rights, safety and amenity of people in the streets, in parks and on beaches must come before the freedom of dogs and their irresponsible owners."

The City of Melbourne, the council responsible for Fawkner

Park, went into a spin. They faced a public relations disaster, particularly as the story followed so soon after the horrifying attack by four dogs on an elderly woman in Perth which resulted in her death. Urgent talks were called, and the council moved fast. On 7 July, the new policy was announced. All dogs were to be leashed at all times in the City of Melbourne.

Across the way a little, although for less dramatic reasons, the pretty bayside suburbs of the City of Port Phillip, Melbourne, were heading in the same direction. Tossed to the surface by the upheaval of council amalgamations, all local laws were up for grabs. Although unnoticed by most people, for they had never been enforced, the old laws already said that effective control of dogs at all times meant being leashed. The council officers re-presented the existing by-laws, including this one, in mid-May. Soon after, the draft was advertised. That's when, as one of the officers involved put it, all hell broke loose.

Both councils were shocked by the reaction: huge public protest. Submissions flooded in and the Australian Veterinary Association as well as the RSPCA thundered about the importance of allowing dogs to run free. The *Age* felt compelled again to editorialise — this time, condemning the City of Melbourne's failure to acknowledge the needs of dogs and their owners.

In the City of Port Phillip, whole communities were mobilised. Anna, a Port Phillip resident and professional dog trainer, went into total panic when she heard the news. Then she became angry, convinced, as she was, that restricting dogs to a leash permanently actually *caused* aggression — with dogs failing to learn the basics of communication and social etiquette. Within two to three days, she and her friends had encouraged around 80 people to contact the council directly, by telephone or fax. A petition was arranged, which quickly gained 500 signatures, and a small rally held in a local park. They didn't have long, for by the time Anna heard of the proposals, the council meeting to ratify the new by-laws was only days away.

The meeting, as it turned out, was quite important — for other reasons. The council was to decide how it would manage the transition back to an elected version (Port Phillip had been run by appointed commissioners during the council amalgamations) and the meeting attracted an unusually large turnout. First on the agenda were the by-laws. When they turned to the by-laws about dogs, one after another of the assembled group of more than 100 observers stood to talk. According to the then Chief Commissioner, Des Clarke, they spoke with intelligence, eloquence and passion.[5] In fact, council had already responded to the month-long community protest and consultation by modifying their proposal to include an extensive array of designated free-run areas. But few of those assembled were aware of this. As they then moved on to the key items of the agenda, one by one the observers filed out until there were only two people left to hear the discussions about the return to elected government. Des Clarke relates this story rather ruefully. By his count, it was 98 per cent for dogs, 2 per cent for democracy!

Facing similar public outrage, the City of Melbourne followed suit — only it took more than a year of consultation and debate, partly because its decision had been made more for ideological reasons than simply by default. It was more complicated to back down, but eventually in August 1996, a new plan was announced.

The interesting thing was that out of all the issues thrown up in Melbourne during the tumultuous years of council amalgamation — barring the Grand Prix car race — in the city of Port Phillip it was the dog question which provoked the most comment from the public.

So what does all this have to do with urban planning? Surely what we are looking at was a simple, isolated overreaction? Yet similar things are happening in other parts of the world. In May 1996, dog owners staged a public protest in Central Park, New York. They were reportedly "sick of being victimised" by not being allowed to let their dogs run free. Tensions were so high that the story crossed the Atlantic to make the evening news in the United Kingdom. A few years ago, a group of Californian residents became so angry at the steady erosion of opportunities to walk their dogs, they initiated a comprehensive lobbying campaign, and ultimately succeeded in establishing one of the world's first parks specifically for dogs. In Beijing, with unsurprising heavy-handedness, the government responded to the growing number of dogs in the city by imposing a dog registration fee equal to the average worker's annual salary.

These are not isolated incidents, but symptoms of something larger. Each innocuous display seems trivial enough — the friend who is running with his dogs on an empty rural beach and is told by an officer to leash his dogs or face a fine; the relative who, when asked about the lovely long walks on her recent holiday, replies she kept being blocked and having to walk home in the face of the "no dogs allowed" sign. Yet in the past 20 years, even though inspired in many places by the highest of motives, we've seen the steady erosion of the easy-going integration of dogs into the community. When presented with obvious conflict, the local government body, reacting in the only way it knows how, tightens up the rules and blames the "irresponsible owner". The rhetoric of "irresponsibility" is everywhere — the term tripping off the tongues of officials at every opportunity, until it simply becomes a shorthand for whichever code of behaviour the agent disagrees with now. Of course the term is terrifically useful, and there are many cases I wouldn't hesitate to call irresponsible. It helps set the codes of behaviour essential for the smooth functioning of any community. But in its power and usefulness as a tool of social order, this "blame the owner" mentality runs the risk of blinding us to another essential element of what is going on. Because some of what we are dealing with is not a people or animal problem at all. It is structural.

As I've said, we have a problem with space. Even here, in Australia, one of the most "underpopulated" nation in the world, we have a problem with space. And to understand why that is going to get worse over the next hundred years, we need to look at what our urban planners are doing now.

The urban consolidation push started in the early 1980s, and there were a number of factors driving it. The original one, according to Professor Patrick Troy, Head of the Urban Research Program at the Australian National University in Canberra (who is a long-standing and outspoken critic of such policies), was simply financial.[6] The spread of suburbia is expensive. The infrastructural cost of each new development — providing sewerage, electricity, roads, communications — is borne by the state. Faced with a shortage of money for capital development, planners within the New South Wales Department of Environment and Planning came up with the idea of decreasing lot size and encouraging dual occupancy. The rationale was that the greater the number of dwellings per hectare, the less the overall capital cost per dwelling. This seemingly logical equation was enshrined in the New South Wales State Regional Environment Plan 1, gazetted in 1980, which amended ordinances to allow dual occupancy and increase site coverage. As the idea took hold, further arguments in its favour were added. Reducing the rate of urban spread would be good for the environment. It also reflected a mature approach to changing social structures. Families were getting smaller, people were increasingly living in ones and twos. They needed choice in housing — other than the traditional quarter-acre block with room for three kids and a pony. Modifying limits on block size would encourage the necessary housing variety. The official drive for urban consolidation had begun.

By the mid-1980s, most Australian authorities had come on board with some version of urban consolidation. By the 1990s, the virtues of higher density housing were more or less established wisdom, challenged only by the handful of adamant critics, such as Professor Troy. To quote from a policy for *Metropolitan Melbourne* published in 1995, "One way of catering for the changes occurring in the way Melburnians live is by providing more medium-density housing. Already about 20 per cent of Melbourne's housing stock is medium density, and this figure is likely to be higher in the future, as more people seek alternatives to the conventional detached dwelling."[7] Guidelines for excellence in medium-density housing have been prepared to complement the policy.

It is not my intention here to comment on the pros and cons of urban consolidation. But what I do want to comment on is the effect it is having on the dogs.

FACING THE URBAN SQUEEZE

The 1950s "ideal" is certainly not one to which I aspire. Mum in the kitchen, Dad at work, kids and dogs playing in the street. But it certainly made a dog's life easy. There was plenty of room in the backyard for the family mutt along with the Hills hoist and barbie, and anyway, dogs weren't confined to the yard — they were more or less free to do their doggy business as they pleased, their only impediment the occasionally alert eye of the dog catcher. Cartoons such as "Ginger Meggs" and "Marmaduke" evoke this supposedly carefree age — with both kids and animals seeming to enjoy a freedom barely remembered. These days, the law insists dogs may not roam — and excluding escape, they don't.

The problem facing dogs no longer allowed to roam is not, as you might expect, one of insufficient exercise. It's actually about mental stimulation. Dogs have active brains — brains in so many ways like our own — which need interest, variety, purpose even, to keep them occupied. The majority of dogs no longer have the stimulus of work. On the one hand, over the last 20 years we have taken away their ability to seek additional interest independently. On the other hand, we have reduced the area in which they must find what activity they can. Just to give you an idea, soon after World War II, the average block size was 1000 square metres. This was the age of the true quarter-acre block — before universal sewerage, when each house maintained a separate septic tank. With sewerage upgrades during the 1950s, the average block size dropped to 700 square metres; by the 1970s it was down to 600 square metres. Today, with urban consolidation policies in force, you can find block sizes as small as 250 square metres or one-sixteenth of an old acre.[8] What's more, house size has not necessarily dropped correspondingly. The same four-bedroom home may be plonked on a tiny block, leaving little outside space for the yard. And even that small amount of open space may not be entirely available to the pet. If front and back yards are separated, either by gate or house, then the animal may only get the run of the back. The chances of finding something interesting to do are reduced in tandem.

And what happens to unoccupied canine brains? They seek out their own amusement. Melbourne-based animal behaviourist Dr Robert Holmes refers to it as the BAD behaviour complex: Barking, Aggression, Destructiveness.[9] And while the latter two behaviours may cause great heartache to the owner, it is the first which has community-wide implications.

Dogs bark for many reasons, but let's just confine ourselves here to the boredom and loneliness factors, for these are the ones which produce the rhythmic, relentless barking of the sort which starts community feuds. And it is this type which is favoured by urban consolidation. To compound the problem, increasing density doesn't just mean there is less space for canine amusement, it also reduces acoustic separation. More households per kilometre means more dogs as well. The barking dog in the distance may be easy to ignore, the cochlear-grating sound of the dog 3 metres away not so. At higher densities, the chances of there being a bored or lonely dog within your vicinity is proportionately increased.

This is no small issue. It may surprise readers to discover that this problem is the number one cause of complaint to local government. Consistently across Australian councils, barking dogs are the source of around 30 per cent of *all* complaints.

And it's hard to imagine the figures improving if future housing developments in any way reflect the new suburb Patrick Troy took me to see in Canberra. There, medium-density ordinances had been followed by developers to the letter, but the result was unsettling. Great tracts of bitumen covered the multi-dwelling entrances to allow complicated car access. Huge houses had been dumped cheek-by-jowl on adjacent blocks. Public open space requirements had been fulfilled by drainage routes and power lines. I asked Troy whether there was room for dogs, and he said there was hardly room for kids — those that had moved already into the area were finding the kids played on the street with the cars because there was nowhere else. Looking at the slotted rows of tiny backyards, I could imagine them soon filled with bored cattle dog crosses barking their hearts out, with absolutely no sound barrier to a hundred neighbours. There seemed to be no coordination, so the overall effect was stifling.

As Professor Troy ruefully pointed out to me, things would be greatly improved if all developers applied one simple test: *Would you want your grandmother to live in there?*

So the crunch is on private open space — what about public? Even more so. Increasing density within established areas (for every house knocked down, a duplex or complex springs up in its place) is not accompanied by a commensurate expansion of parkland. As for new subdivisions, forcing developers to set aside a proportion of land for public open space, say 5 per cent, is undermined in practice by there being no specifications for its *quality*. More people are using the same limited open space — in fact, their need is greater, as many lack gardens or green space of their own. And just as more people are sharing parkland, so too are more dogs. Like the humans, they need it more than ever; their one or two walks a day being the sole source of excitement other than what can be contrived within their four fences. Who knows, maybe, like us, they even gain pleasure from frolicking across the green on a sunny day? They certainly seem to — and it is difficult to argue in the same breath that humans have a deep attraction to "natural" spaces without also feeling that animals might have the same. Moreover, parks aren't just a place to wander and commune with nature. They play another critical role in our mixed-species communities — a social one. We know that dogs are amongst the most social of species, and while human-only interaction may be sufficient, if they enjoy the company of other dogs (well at least they speak the same language) then the only opportunity for it is generally at the park.

This build up of pressure leads inexorably to one thing — tension. Open space planners are certainly no strangers to this type of conflict because they deal with it all the time. It's their job to recognise the often polarised needs of sporting interests, children's play space, formal gardens, and native flora, and try to balance everyone's expectations in the design of parks. But surprisingly, they too seem largely to have overlooked the dogs. It stands to reason that if 42 per cent of Australian households have a dog which should be walked each day, then dog walkers must be one of the heaviest park users. Shouldn't park designers recognise this when preparing their "needs based" recreation plans?

And without plans, we see the kind of ad hoc responses which occasionally border on the ludicrous. A Canadian acquaintance relayed the tale of a popular bayside walk in Vancouver where the council had recently decided dogs were not allowed on the bay portion of a boulevard, but *were* allowed on the other side of a high fence. Because the dog walkers liked to walk along the water, they resorted to letting their dogs run wild off the lead on one side of the fence, while they walked serenely along the other side. It was bedlam!

This kind of wilful protest occurs commonly when the public perceives measures as impractical or unfair. Surely if anyone within the City of Melbourne had sat down and thought about it, they would have realised that requiring dogs to be leashed at all times flew in the face of normal behaviour.

Actually they wouldn't even have thought about it. An assumption that dogs are accommodated passively within human open-space needs was fine at low densities. At high densities, it doesn't work. The response from authorities is too often to tighten laws, treat dogs as pests which must be controlled, ban them when their interests conflict with others, or define them as "recreation tools" — which, like bicycles or rollerblades, are catered for by setting aside a few special-purpose areas. It is to call the owners "irresponsible", and denigrate protesters with the label "animal rightists" (as an *Age* newspaper article did, whatever *that* means). It is to eat away imperceptibly at opportunities to participate in a public life — a *shared* public life — where, with our symbiotic partners, we meet and mix in an open arena, so that when finally we notice what is going on, anger spills over in the town halls of Melbourne or the footways of Central Park in New York. It is to force dogs into smaller and smaller, more isolated enclaves, where frustration at their narrow world finds relief in the anodyne of incessant barking. Without active recognition, in the tough competition for resources, the voiceless lose. It strikes me (and I'm not entirely being melodramatic) that the neighbourhood splitting staccato of the lonely dog *could* be read as the forlorn cry of the politically mute!

SQUEEZED OUT

If this were all there was to it — a few confrontations, a bored dog, annoying "no dog" signs which everyone ignores — I wouldn't be worried. In the end, such things can be resolved, albeit with needless anger and heartache. Port Phillip got its free-run areas (although some would argue, insufficient), Melbourne is trying for a please-all policy, the New Yorkers got back their part of the park. And despite my fanciful turn of phrase, I'm not actually suggesting dogs get the vote. If all we were dealing with were the irritating rumbles of urban life, then I wouldn't have written this book. What I am concerned about is something far more insidious.

Slowly, imperceptibly, living with other animals is getting harder. For most animals, in most large cities, it is already *too* hard. Cattle, sheep, horses; the animals we relied on for at least 6000 years can't live in cities. Yes, there will always be birds and rodents and other happy urban dwellers, but of the creatures which evolved the most complex relationships with us, there is really only the dog and cat left.

Rather than the company of animals being a passive thing, easily accommodated within the rhythms of daily life — you do the washing and pour the cat some milk; you head off to the ironmonger's and the local dog comes too — their presence is increasingly a conscious decision. More work must be done to compensate for constricted freedoms. It is certainly possible to keep a dog happily in a small apartment, but it takes a lot of effort — four or five visits to the outside a day. A trip to a suitable park may involve a care drive; a hassle with heavy traffic before and after work. Men and women are both employed outside the home these days, often for long hours, and the strict separation of work and homelife — a feature of human lives since the Industrial Revolution — tends to preclude the direct care of animals for much of the day. (Children too, for that matter.) It's possible that the current Information Technology revolution may reverse this trend, blurring the spheres of work and home, but even so, it's likely that the majority of workers will still spend a significant amount of time outside the home in special work places.

The very demographic trends which make animal companionship more important are also working against pet ownership. Our population is ageing, yet the elderly find it increasingly difficult to care for pets without home support. When they move to retirement homes, they face further barriers. Most nursing homes still won't take animals, and even in those that do, you are not allowed to replace your pet once it dies. We can see the impact on pet ownership figures. Surprisingly, the over 65s have the *lowest* pet ownership of all groups in the community: 35 per cent of households, as compared with 66 per cent overall.[10]

And with the shift towards one and two person households, people won't necessarily have the housing or the back-up to make animal ownership easy. Quite apart from the fact that unless they own their own home, finding a place to live which allows pets is very difficult due to widespread rental restrictions. It all adds up.

At some stage, it gets too difficult. People decide against it — "it would be irresponsible to own an animal with my lifestyle". And they are probably right, but that's not the point. The worry is that these days — and into the future — the *only* way to continue any relationship with the non-human is to have a pet. And people are choosing not to.

In Australia, this is not readily apparent. At 42 per cent of households, we have the highest dog-ownership figures in the world. But that in itself tells us something.

Why does Australia have the highest dog-ownership figures? Let's look at the United Kingdom — surely with their history of dottiness about dogs, the numbers must at least equal or outstrip Australia? Not so. In England overall, dog ownership sits at 27 per cent of households. In London, 16 per cent of households. The same pattern holds for France — in Paris, 16 per cent of households have dogs. In Manhattan, it's just 12 per cent.[11] Why?

I chose the examples of the United Kingdom, France and the United States because culturally they are quite similar to Australia, so I find it hard to believe the answer is simply that Australians "love their dogs" more. The only thing to which I can attribute this disparity is the relative availability of space. And as we double our world population over the next hundred years, space will come at even more of a premium. Some will have plenty, but many more won't. And the "space-poor" will have little in the way of room for any animal larger than a bird or fish.

It could be argued that this is just a Western issue. After all, around the word, few cities even have the luxury of planned growth. Sao Paulo, for example, enjoyed the dubious honour of leading the world population-growth stakes in the 1950s, going from a modest city of 1.7 million people in 1940 to a seething sprawl of 16.4 million in 1995. Asian cities like Jakarta and Karachi continue to grow at between 4 and 5 per cent per annum, while by comparison, Melbourne and London are both experiencing a net annual loss in population.[12] All these cities, even Tokyo and Beijing, have far more important concerns on their plates than worrying about a few mutts. Nor do they even have a strong tradition of dog ownership; dogs are more likely to be street scavengers or food than companions. So am I being Anglo-centric to see this as a world issue rather than just a local cultural one?

I don't think so. As we have seen, the same forces which made pet ownership for affection so integral to Western culture over the last hundred years, are now occurring elsewhere in the world. Family sizes are dropping, and humans increasingly are cut off from daily interaction with animals and plants. And it's not only that they lose the physical relationship, but they are also losing the cultural one of *how* to live with animals.

Maybe it doesn't matter — just because we lived with dogs for tens of thousands of years doesn't mean we need them around now. And I'm certainly not saying that cats and dogs and other pets are under threat in any *real* way, like the Sumatran tiger or the white rhino, so it may seem trite to speak of them in the same terms. But if animal companionship were largely to become restricted to an elite, it would still represent a fairly radical shift in a relationship which for so long formed part of human existence. Human communities — cities — are becoming more inhospitable places for dogs to live.

In Beijing, a special dog farm has been set up for city people to visit. In Tokyo, you can rent a dog by the hour to take for a walk. This is the direction in which parts of the world are heading.

CHAPTER 9

THE URBAN SEXTIPEDE

SO WHAT'S to be done? Is it hopeless? Not at all. What it requires is a little shift of focus; a sideways step. What is required is for urban policy makers to close their eyes for a moment, then slowly open them, and this time to see — really see the animals standing there in front of them. Who were there all along. When they return to their chart or their draft or their discussion paper, somewhere in the back of the mind will float the recognition that this work shapes the future of a mixed-species community.

Veterinarian David Paxton has an evocative phrase: Urban Sextipede.[1] He says we must start viewing our communities as being populated by a single, indivisible unit — the one part with two legs, the other with four: the Urban Sextipede. Then every decision, every plan, can be subjected to its test: how does this affect the Urban Sextipede? Can the Urban Sextipede survive? And once this concept is taken on board, it is easy to see how it can be simply and practically applied.

Around the world, a few groups of innovators are doing exactly that. And some of the most original work is being done here in Australia, so this is where I'm going to start.

CHANGING THE APPROACH TO "ANIMAL CONTROL"

This was the situation in a northern Queensland town in 1975: for as long as anyone could remember, the job of managing the dogs within the community had fallen to the dog catcher, who held the lowest position within the local council. No training, no resources. The person who "couldn't do anything else" got to drive around the streets, picking up the roaming dogs and taking them to the pound — there to be claimed by reluctant owners or, more often than not, shot. Records from the early part of this century show it had ever been thus, and nothing had changed, let alone improved.

In the early 1980s, Dick Murray, a veterinarian in Townsville, was one of a number of people around the world beginning to appreciate there was something wrong. For Murray, the clincher was one day observing the dog catcher's truck trundling down the urban street — chased all the way by a pack of excited, barking dogs. It was farcical — there had to be a better way.

After some research, and with the assistance of Jenny Brennan from Mt Isa, he managed to convince the local council to institute some changes. The key, Murray and Brennan thought, was to raise the profile of the dog catcher. A name change was tried — Animal Control Officer — and resources and training were, for the first time, allocated to the job, which took on an educative as well as punitive role. And it worked. Within three years of the door-knocking campaigns, which were initiated as part of the push for universal dog identification, dog registrations had gone from 30 per cent to 80 per cent, people had started to comply with other laws, and the "wandering dog" problem had significantly abated. Murray then wrote *Dogs in the Urban Environment: A handbook for municipal management* — the first real guide local governments had ever had.[2]

By 1983, Murray was convinced the problems he saw were not confined to his small patch of Queensland, but were universal. He contacted the Queensland branch of the Australian Veterinary Association, of which he was a member, and convinced them to hold a conference. Prepared with the title "Animal Control Conference", a friend pointed out that "animal control" sends out the wrong message. You need to call it an "urban animal integration symposium", or something positive, he advised. They tossed it back and forth, then came up with "Urban Animal Management".

A successful symposium was followed by a ten-year hiatus and then, in 1992, the term re-emerged with renewed vigour. The Australian Veterinary Association initiated the National Urban Animal Management Conference, now an annual event.[3] In 1995, Terri Ann Pert from Warringah Council in Sydney won the inaugural Animal Control Officer of the Year Award for the following programs: her "reward a good citizen" scheme, whereby patrol officers carry gifts they present to registered dogs they may see walking quietly with their owners; the establishment of "pooch patches" throughout municipal parks (a short telephone-type pole next to a dog litter bin), out of which they are now collecting over 150 kilos of dog faeces a week; the renting out of anti-barking collars which emit a citronella spray every time the dog barks; special education days for owners of Rottweilers and German Shepherds (these followed a series of high-profile dog attacks); and the decidedly lateral decision to seed four harbourside parks with dung beetles — the idea being that whatever dog poo is not taken to the litter bin can be rapidly removed underground by these industrious insects. She was promoted by her council and awarded a brand new title — Animal Management Officer — and a full-time position. A far cry from "dog catcher".

This little story illustrates the power of words. "Dog catcher" has obvious problems — it is not only demeaning, but implies that dogs are a menace that must be incarcerated. "Animal control", while an improvement, still casts the authorities and dogs in an adversarial relationship. By changing the emphasis, replacing the pejorative "control" with the more neutral "management", Murray and his friends subtly shifted the dog from community pest to participant. By adding the word "urban", they stated baldly that dogs and other animals are not invaders, but normal residents of the city. It's a classic example of applying the philosophy of the Urban Sextipede test.

The Urban Animal Management (UAM) Conference is unique in that it is the only forum with the exclusive purpose of bringing together local and state governments, animal welfare groups, vets, obedience clubs and others to discuss the integration of animals in the community. Over the five years it's been going (and I have attended four of these conferences) you can *feel* the change. The participants, mostly from local government, have a sense of excitement about what they are doing, and ideas which are floated as pie in the sky one year come back as implemented programs the following. And many of the most exciting examples I am going to give of Urban Sextipede planning either came as a result of a discussion at a UAM conference, were presented at one, or both.

In pockets around the world, similar reasoning has prompted some new approaches. San Francisco, for example, is home to one of the most innovative and successful animal welfare shelters in the world. Driven largely by the vision of its director of 20 years, Richard Avanzino, the San Francisco SPCA has an excellent relationship with the city managers. For years the SPCA did all the animal management work, then later helped the authorities establish a proper pound, staffed mainly by ex-SPCA employees.[4] In the SPCA's own shelter, all dogs are socialised and retrained before being placed with a new human. And their approach to parks, rental accommodation, allowing pets in hotels, and more, is formulated around one word: *integration*. The integration of animals into human communities. And the city and the people are listening. One in every three households in San Francisco contributes money to the SPCA.

In France, the French Association for Information and Research on Companion Animals (AFIRAC) also uses the word integration.[5] It runs a Club de Ville — towns sign up to receive a practical newsletter, access to literature on education or the design of "dog comfort stations" (more on those later), and to attend four seminars a year. One town, Nantes, is developing a "pact with the city" to plan for the integration of animals in the community for the decades to come. In Australia, the Petcare Information and Advisory Service, which also works extensively with local government, in 1995 produced guidelines for local government strategic planning — a previously unheard of concept.[6] Again, integration featured in the title. The suggested mission statement sums up the philosophy: "Recognising that companion animals are part of the community, contributing to its quality of life, and ensuring that the needs of animals and their owners are accommodated while recognising the differing needs of all members of the community."

Instead of seeing animals as a pathology of urban living, the Urban Sextipede shift sees them as a sign of the health of the society.

DON'T CASTIGATE, EDUCATE

As a direct result of an entrenched control mentality, local authorities have occasionally made some pretty stupid decisions. Passing a law has in the past too often been their first, rather than last, response to problems — and Melbourne City Council's move, as we saw in the last chapter, is the classic example. But there are plenty of other less obvious bad decisions. Take fines for barking dogs — yet do owners have the appropriate help to cure barking? Or fines for dog litter — yet has the council provided facilities for people to dispose of litter? Or banning dogs from urban parks — yet has the council considered whether dog use will be more concentrated and cause problems in another park?

Laws alone are usually not the most effective way of resolving these kinds of problems. And in many councils, the focus *is* shifting. The laws are still there — but they are the last-line rather than the first-line response. Instead of issuing a fine for barking, for example, why can't councils work with animal behaviourists to offer retraining for the dog? The Animals Management Resource Extension (AMREX) program in Western Australia is trying out a barking "hotline", which takes people making complaints through a series of steps to identify and resolve that problem, all before getting to the local laws officer.[7] In the first 12 months, over 1200 calls were handled in this way, and the council estimates that the number of complaints progressing to council have dropped by 60 to 70 per cent.

Prevention as a tool of animal management is finally creeping up councils' priority lists. And it includes the fundamental platform of education — for dogs as much as their owners. Many councils are now forming strategic alliances with vets, animal welfare groups and obedience clubs to develop public education programs covering issues ranging from the choice of a suitable pet for the urban environment, to basic animal behaviour, to animal management and personal responsibility. And at the state government level, new Acts in New South Wales, South Australia and Victoria have seen these initiatives carried up into the state-wide arena.

Another concept seeping into council mentality is that animal control or management officers have an enormous educative potential. They are out there on the streets, dealing with the public constantly, and in a prime position to dispense literature and advice. Education of the officers themselves, over the last five to ten years, has been a great step forward. And the education of dogs is being re-evaluated also.

The problem with traditional obedience training is that for most people it doesn't "go" anywhere, directed as it is at achieving ever higher levels in competition. Nor does it prepare animal or owner for the realities of urban life. To remedy these deficiencies, in the late 1980s a US dog trainer invented a program called Canine Good Citizens, designed to train good citizens "on both ends of the lead". It is a ten-week course with a definite "graduation" (your dog even gets a special striped lead in honour of its achievement), at which dog and fellow human learn *useful* things. Like how not to chase bicycles or skateboards; how to cross a street; how to sit quietly while tied up with other dogs at the shop; how to greet strangers; as well as the important "sit, come, stay, drop". With its emphasis on small classes and individual attention, it can also treat canine behavioural problems, such as separation anxiety (surprisingly common in this era of the empty house, and a source of problem barking).

The other wonderful US export is "Puppy Preschool". Puppies trot off with their owners to the vet once a week for four weeks and there start learning the basics of training, as well as the skills of canine and human communication which can only be absorbed during the all-important socialisation period. Kersti Seksel, the animal behaviourist who introduced Puppy Preschool to Australia, is so delighted with the program she recently started up "Kitty Kinder". Could sending pups to school become as natural and inevitable as sending the kids? Half the problems with dogs in the community might be solved overnight.

BUSY PEOPLE, BUSY LIVES

Even if we change substantially the government's approach to animals in the community, the Urban Sextipede is still faced with a problem. People's lives are full with the challenges of work, housing, or even old age, and this makes it difficult to take on a pet. Here again, there are ways and means. Consider these two people.

Sarah loves animals but she doesn't live with one. She hasn't since she left home eight years ago. Her partner is adamant that they don't have the time or the space to keep a dog. After yet another gruelling ten-hour day, she thinks he's probably right. Anyway, if she wants to rent a halfway decent place, she knows it will be impossible to have a pet. Everyone is in the same boat; none of her contemporaries keeps animals. She's stopped asking.

A few blocks away, Maude has trouble keeping her spirits up. It's not like her — even after her husband died, she stayed active and positive. But it's hard not to feel miserable now. A few months ago, her hip broke, shattered as she slipped on the welcoming surface of her own front porch. It's mended, but she will never again be capable of more than a careful and painful hobble to her front gate. And the worst of it is looking into her little black companion's eyes. She's convinced they reproach her, a heavy resentment that they no longer venture further than the gate. It's probably her imagination, but she can't bear it. She is seriously considering giving him up. She doesn't know what to do.

The two scenarios are typical. You could find them enacted in any urban street, in fact I've adapted them from the stories of people I've met. And when juxtaposed like that, the solution seems obvious.

The drivers behind a new social program in the City of Port Phillip, Melbourne, have identified a way of serving the needs of people like Sarah and Maude. Worldwide, the thrust of social services is shifting away from institutionalisation towards maintaining people for as long as possible in their own homes. Apart from anything, it's cheaper. Meals on Wheels, home help, home nurse, "garden-mates"; these sorts of services are provided by a combination of paid coordinators and volunteers. But with the recognition that keeping people happy and healthy takes more than providing enough to eat, at last attention is being paid to the "social" end of social support. And for the first time, perhaps in the world, in 1996 the Department of Social Services in Victoria recognised and funded the social support of animals.

The program is called Petlinks.[8] It's such a simple idea: a coordinator, paid on a part-time basis, organises the matching of people like Maude and Sarah. Volunteers have a choice of commitment — they might decide, like Sarah did, to become a "petmate" to Maude and take her dog for a walk three times a week, or they might offer transport to the vet, or foster care in the event of emergency hospitalisation of the pet owner or death. For Sarah it has meant the childhood companionship she remembers — and something she'd more or less lost hope of. For Maude, it has meant the difference between keeping her companion or giving him up.

This is exactly the sort of lateral solution our society will need to look at in the next century lest whole swathes of the population break the animal connection. Ideally, it will be conducted with strong institutional support. Similar volunteer programs *are* being run elsewhere in the world, but what is so significant about Petlinks is that it has permanent government funding. It is not dependent on the goodwill and dedication of concerned individuals; it will not fall over once the visionary zeal of its founder fades. Furthermore, it makes one very powerful statement. It says that the social services client is not the human, but the human–animal unit.

Indivisible. You cannot service the part without the whole. It remains to be seen whether this high ideal will filter through the rest of the community support network, but if it does, it will be a great leap towards the policy of the Urban Sextipede.

Even without an official stamp, there is no reason why similar concepts can't be run at the individual, local level. For every young couple that works all day and likes to go away for the odd weekend, nearby lives an elderly person who is afraid of the financial and other responsibilities of owning an animal, but would be delighted to care for one during the day and overnight occasionally. Not only does it allow both a companionship they could not otherwise manage, it also fosters a level of local community interaction which is fast disappearing from our often isolating and impersonal neighbourhoods.

You might call it "dog pooling" — a move almost back to the notion of communal animals, the pattern which dominated for most of our history. All it takes is a bit of quid pro quo, and it can assume many forms. Local pet owners could get together and arrange reciprocal care — I'll look after your dog when you're away, if you do the same for me. And why not during the day as well? Try taking it in turns to have the dogs over to keep each other company. I know of a few people with informal arrangements like this, and it works wonderfully.

The separation of workplace and life is another artificial barrier which could do with some shaking up by the Urban Sextipede. Admittedly it is difficult to anticipate the impact of technology on the workplace — whether in 50 years time we will still turn up *en masse* to the work factory each day — but suppose that many of us do, why shouldn't our animals come too? It wouldn't be possible in all circumstances, but I'm quite sure there are many workplaces which could easily accommodate, even greatly benefit from, the presence of a pet. The Blue Cross in the

United Kingdom recognises this, and runs a popular annual "take a dog to work" campaign.

How about one more lateral step? We already accept the concept of creches for children; why not one for dogs? This isn't a flaky idea. The San Francisco SPCA has recently started a "doggy daycare" centre. The animals are guaranteed amusement and company during the day, and as an added bonus, they can receive training or remedial work while they are there. So when the person gets home drained, desperately needing to relax, the energy levels of the dog are more or less the same. It is not "anthropomorphic nonsense", as I heard one commentator describe it, but a sensible response to the challenge of integrating dogs with frenetic human urban lives.

And it's all the more significant when you realise that the number one cause of death in dogs in the Western world is not parvovirus; it is not being hit by cars; it is bad (read "inappropriate") behaviour. Contrary to popular belief, studies from around the world show consistently that half the dogs given to animal welfare shelters are not abandoned, but are taken there by their owners who cannot cope with the barking, destructiveness, or sheer energy of their pets.

To give some idea of the success of the San Francisco SPCA's approach, when director Richard Avanzino first took the helm 20 years ago, the city was putting down 60,000 animals a year. In 1996, it was 4000 — and that was only those animals which were dangerously aggressive or had fatal medical conditions.[9] It is the lowest euthanasia rate in the United States. The SPCA has recently signed a pact with the City of San Francisco stating that no animal which is capable of being re-homed will be put down. Workers call their workplace a "no kill" shelter. I doubt there is any other welfare organisation in the world which could claim such a record.

BUILDING CITIES WHERE ANIMALS LIVE

This is all the easy stuff. The trimmings — the steps that can be taken to accommodate what we have now. But in the overall scheme of things, in 50, 100 years, their impact will be marginal. That is, unless we decide to tackle the hard stuff — the infrastructure; the way we shape our physical environment. And in particular, our public open spaces. More than any other factor, their design and use will determine the "livability" of cities. The need of parks for a brush with the Urban Sextipede is urgent. For the two-legged urban residents, it's about quality of life; but for the four-legged, it's about whether they can live in cities at all.

As we have seen, at the present time animals in parks are a prominent cause of community tension. The people in charge worry — about aggression, dog faeces, and potential conflict with other users, such as sporting clubs and children playing on equipment. They worry and they crank up the restrictions on animal access. But again, viewed through the prism of the Urban Sextipede, the problems look different. For Virginia Jackson, they look like a breach which is crying out for the application of her craft.

A town planner and urban policy analyst by training, Jackson was made all too aware of the difficulties facing urban animals by a painful childhood experience. Her father was a vet and she grew up on a farm. When they moved to the city, they had such trouble finding rental housing that would also take animals, they were faced with the very real prospect of leaving her friends behind. Eventually they found somewhere, but Jackson remained acutely sensitive to the issue of pets in the city.

In 1994, Jackson did a search to see what literature was available to help urban planners accommodate dog use. The result should be no surprise — she found virtually nothing, anywhere in the world. In response she released her own report, *Public Open Space and Dogs: A design and management guide for open space professionals and local government*.[10]

The opening premise of her 1995 document is simple: that dog owners should be given access to open space because they are substantial users of the park, and that they should be integrated with other park users, not separated off in some dog-only zone. The report develops a regional-based model, arguing that until the whole network of open space is assessed, it's pointless looking at specific parks. This holistic view allows planners to ensure, for example, that every resident can visit a suitable park within 15 minutes' walk of home — critical for those who lack transport or have limited physical mobility. Or that overall, there is an attractive combination of opportunities within the community for Urban Sextipede outings. Only then should individual parks be examined.

And at that level, there are so many ways in which good design can dramatically improve the enjoyment of the park for everyone. Take the issue of conflict. Instead of dealing with it by banning dogs or restricting access, why not harness the natural topography to minimise it? Jackson's suggestions seem so obvious. If a wide open space just beckons dogs to run, then ensure it is a free-running area. If free-run areas border ovals where kids play sport, then use a steep incline to separate the two groups, or plant a line of shrubs. If you want to keep dogs and children's play equipment separate, place an attractive fence around the playground; it keeps the kids in as well as the dogs out. "Visual literacy" is the technical term — using natural features to "show" people how they can use that part of the park.

The structure of the park substantially determines behaviour, and this can be harnessed to foster compliance. If there are areas where you would like the dog to stay on a lead, then create a meandering linear path — people are far more likely to keep their animals by them if they are purposefully walking somewhere. A circular route around a water feature or some other natural pivot gives a wonderful sense of achievement, and it's interesting enough that Urban Sextipedes are happy to use it every day.

Jackson's guidelines are comprehensive and practical. The report is the first of its kind. Since 1996, she has been commissioned by many Australian councils to review their open space policies. She is getting phone calls from Pretoria to Vancouver.

Other common problems start to change when viewed through Urban Sextipede eyes. Take the issue of dog faeces. It's usually seen as a sin committed upon the environment by irresponsible owners — rather than a biological inevitability for which cities have never catered. This is changing. I've noticed even in the last two years the furious sprouting of dog bags and litter bins all over Australia. I mentioned Warringah Council's introduction of pooch patches and dung beetles. David Paxton has made the obvious suggestion that if it's the look of dog poo that people find offensive, why not instruct the garden staff to leave the grass a bit longer in some areas and allow it to decompose naturally — a perfectly safe method of disposal, and appropriate in medium to low density areas.[11] (At one stage Paxton became so annoyed by the dog poo debate, he measured the output of his own dog, then calculated the per-square-metre deposition in comparison with the packet recommendations for spreading an expensive, prepared version of chicken poo. He found that they worked out the same!) Paxton's proposal to leave the grass longer made its way into Jackson's guidelines. In similar ways, the English and the Americans have been tackling faeces with litter bins and poop scoops for years — far more of an issue when great tracts of urban land are at very high densities. But probably the most impressive people about dog poo are the French.

In an intriguing experiment conducted in Nantes in northwest

France, visitors to the clinic at the veterinary school had to manage one little task.[12] With their dogs, they were asked to walk onto a large circular platform, surrounded by a fence and potted plants. There they had to wait until their dog selected one of the eight different surfaces and set to its business. As the study to find the dog's favourite surface drew to a close, the contest narrowed to three frontrunners: grass, sand and pine bark. Which would win? Well, although grass was the most popular, it was ruled out on the basis of being impractical for heavy use. Sand, though a bit of a sentimental favourite, was no good because kids might mistake it for a sandpit. This left pine bark the clear winner. It was easy to replace, looked attractive, had the advantage of being a nice dark brown colour for faecal disguise, and most importantly, with its capacity to retain smells and be scratched about, popular with the pooches.

Facilitated by AFIRAC, a number of towns in France have gone the route of creating dog "comfort stations". They are a terrific idea in high-density areas. Pains have been taken to make sure they look attractive, and dogs are quite easily trained to use them. Depending on the situation, the faeces may be placed in a bin by the owner, or collected daily and burned by the council. Of course, such facilities are useless if sparsely located, but when laid out in an extensive network, they become viable. The Nantes study was conducted to improve their design and appeal.

The other distinctly French feature is the vacuum-mobile. Racing through the rues of Paris, its dexterous trunk whooshes up any loose substance in its path, including poo.

Why not go out of our way to create a park which is especially appealing to dogs and their human companions? AFIRAC has produced hints about this, and Virginia Jackson has proposed in her guidelines for open public space[13] that in every region, at least one park should be designed specifically with the needs of dogs in mind. Instead of paving, use dirt paths, which retain smells; don't mow so regularly, rather keep the grass long so dogs can race around; provide water access for splashing and swimming; agility courses for human and dog to play on. Not on the least attractive piece of real estate in the area, but a place so appealing it is worth the extra effort for person and animal to drive a short distance to visit.

All of this seems like commonsense, but represents a radical departure from existing notions — of authorities and in the community. Recently revisiting Perth for a holiday, I saw dogs and humans mingling freely and joyfully in the cool waters and on the white sugar sand of the local dog beach, versions of which occur every few kilometres. It's a delight. But mention the possibility of a dog beach in Sydney, and they look at you in horror: "Oh no, we have far too little waterfront to allow dogs." Or, "Yes, we'd like to allow them, but then all the dogs in Sydney would come here and it would just be too crowded." Precisely. Isn't that proof of the extent of the need?

We've tackled public space, but the other side of the equation is private space, and in many ways it's more problematic. Developers and property managers have numerous priorities, and making room for the family mutt is not one of them.

The most obvious place to start is the pet ownership restrictions common to rental and body-corporate accommodation. In general, keeping pets requires the written permission of the landlord — which is often not forthcoming. The example of the Victorian Residential Agreement is fairly typical: "The tenant shall not keep any animal, bird or pet on the premises without the written consent of the Landlord".[14] In the United Kingdom, all public housing has generally had a "no pets" clause. The sheer absurdity of this was only too apparent when, as occurred in an outer London housing estate, a fire alarm prompted the exodus of Noah's Ark. One woman had been smuggling her dog to and from the apartment in a shopping bag for years.

The Pathway group in the United Kingdom is currently lobbying hard for a policy shift, and it has had some success in freeing up these restrictions by drafting a model animal ownership agreement for tenants. Similar strategies are starting to work elsewhere. In 1996, the US House of Representatives passed an amendment to its controversial housing bill, which freed up pet ownership in public housing — but only for seniors or people with disabilities. The San Francisco SPCA not only drafted guidelines but publicly offered $5000 compensation to property owners to cover any damage caused by a tenant's pet. Since the offer first went out in 1991, it has never had a claim. The SPCA calls it the "open door" program. Its current project is to convince hoteliers and restaurateurs to free up all accommodation to pets. Of course, this has long been the situation in France, where the poodle calmly nibbling on a bone while its human companion whips through her coq au vin seems, to many visitors, confirmation the French are insane. Hardly. In France, where renting accommodation is common, in the early 1980s a law was passed prohibiting property owners from discriminating against tenants on the grounds of animal ownership.

The most difficult area of all is the design of high- and medium-density housing, a trend that has spread worldwide. As it stands currently, such housing's inadequacy as homes for animals actually causes many of the distressing behavioural problems common to urban life. We've discussed the link between mental stimulation and destructiveness or barking in dogs, but the same is true of cats — only it's less obvious to neighbours or local authorities. They scratch the furniture, pee in the wrong place, rip out their own fur or start eating the carpet. Bored animals behave badly.

The solution is something the animal behaviourists refer to as "environmental enrichment". Translated, the jargon essentially means "putting back what you took away". If space is restricted, then extra effort must be made to provide the interest and variety a cat or dog might get if living on the street or farm. Toys, excursions out of the home, human companionship are critical, but the structure of the home is also important.

According to urban planner Virginia Jackson, the typical medium-density dwelling has an inordinate amount of dead space.[15] By this, I mean space which is not available to the animal — often not even to the humans. And when space is so limited, not making the best use of it seems wasteful. To give an example, in Canberra some years ago it was decided that houses would not have a front fence. The rationale was that this would foster a more open community, but what it means in practice is that residents don't get the full use of the front yard — often a substantial proportion of the free space of the property. Young children cannot be allowed to play there because it fronts onto a road, and as for dogs, they have to be locked out back — away from all the interesting street activity. (I call the slatted front gate at my mother's house "dog television" — peering through the slats at the street scape engages the Tibetan Spaniels for hours.)

In multiple housing units, the garages, which belong to the property, are often sited in a separate block, grouped together a short distance from the units. If they were placed alongside the dwelling, they'd dramatically increase the available space and form an excellent shaded area for dog use. In many medium-density developments, the amount of space available only to the car is ridiculous. In Canberra Professor Pat Troy took me to see minute patches of garden totally overwhelmed by the mosaic of bitumen built to accommodate the cars. Surely people would be better off with a fenced communal garden in the centre (which could hold dogs), and the cars spaced around the outside.

The way the houses are aligned on a property often pays little account to acoustics. All dogs will bark at some stage — we helped them evolve that way. Jackson makes the point that there are ways of positioning the home on the site which not only maximises the space for a yard, but creates sound barriers to the neighbouring property.

Inside the home, wide ledges on windows provide a wonderful resting place for cats or dogs to laze in the sun and enjoy the street scene. They love it! And bay windows are even better, with their literally panoramic views. Internal light wells, free access between yard and house, all these maximise interest and variety for the home-bound animal.

Again, these are all very simple suggestions — the result of a collaborative work by Virginia Jackson, "Pets in Urban Areas: A guide to integrating domestic pets into new residential developments", which was released in 1993.[16] The guide is just now reaching the international journals. And the Victorian Department of Planning and Heritage recently decided to display the report prominently alongside their guidelines for medium-density housing.

Convincing developers to take on these reforms is another matter, however. The best hope is probably the economic argument. If you bear in mind that two-thirds of consumers in Australia live with an animal, then designing "pet friendly" homes should yield a market edge. This is certainly the tack a few advocates have chosen; an editorial in a popular dog magazine by Leslie Wilson of the San Francisco SPCA began: "Are you looking for a way to make your rentals more competitive? Would you like to attract more responsible and stable tenants? If you want an edge in the rental market, consider allowing pets. In San Francisco, more and more property owners are renting to responsible pet owners, citing benefits such as higher profits, lower vacancy rates, and more satisfied tenants."

True high-density housing of the type typical of Hong Kong or London is more limited in scope, but even here, a bit of lateral thinking could make an enormous difference. Why couldn't every development include a communal organic disposal unit for animal excrement? Why couldn't part of the garden space be available to dogs? Common courtyards, if suitably enclosed, could provide a wonderful "daypen" for the building's canine residents. Perhaps one of the residents might like to supervise during the day — another version of an informal "doggy daycare".

My wish list is preliminary only. No doubt there will be many more creative solutions when good designing minds are applied to the problem.

We have academic policy centres for all kinds of weird and wonderful topics; why not a Policy Centre for Animal–Human Integration in Cities? Such a centre would provide a nexus for urban planners, architects, local governments and others to exchange ideas, receive expert advice and develop innovative programs. One such is the Tufts Centre for Animals and Public Policy in Massachussets in the United States — but we need others. Moreover, a university-based centre can act as the "honest broker" in assessing policies advocated by industry and other vested interests.

If there is an area pleading for the touch of the Urban Sextipede, it is this one. It is time we recognised that when we build homes for people, we are also building them for animals.

You wouldn't let your dog live in it

The visions I've given so far are practical, do-able, and firmly rooted in the here and now. But we can, if we wish, let our fancy fly and dream up the future city we would really want our children to enjoy.

For Professor Aaron Katcher, the man who has spent a lifetime studying the effects of animals on people's wellbeing, that dream would see the return of the "village" common.[17] Perhaps we would all live in high-rise apartments with little private space of our own, but within walking distance of every dwelling would stretch vast tracts of communal land. Tangled native forest, home to the "wild" creatures, would abut glorious sculpted gardens. Scattered plots of urban farmland would yield seasonal vegetables and delicious fresh fruits. And all would be tended by everyone. Each city dweller, perhaps concentrating on a special interest carefully cultivated over a lifetime, partaking daily in the preservation and nurturing of our urban sanctuary. And in that shared responsibility, we would rediscover public dialogue and a deep, soul-filling empathy for the common good.

Colin Tudge, a leading science writer at the London School of Economics, has an even more captivating vision. His London of the future has no concrete at all — that is, none visible.[18] All the buildings are coated with a thick fringe of living vegetation, like enormous green cliffs. Butterflies hatch in the lower levels, spiders weave their sparkling nets, songbirds nest and raptors swoop suddenly from the upper levels on their unsuspecting rodent prey. The old London waterways, bricked over generations ago, are restored and clear, twinkling brooks amble alongside grassed streets and gardens. The zoos cease to be penitentiaries, open their gates and let the wild animals out. Wandering more or less freely through the fertile urban landscape, they are looked after by groups of like-minded individuals who work and learn alongside specialist carers. He calls his vision Arcadia.

To these inspirational visions, I will add only one provision: when we open our minds to sharing cities with the "wild", let's not make it at the expense of the "non-wild". Mine has all of the above, but climbing happily through the vegetation outside my window is my cat, and walking contentedly by my side to a workplace with big welcoming buckets of water and other four-legged mates is my dog.

Arcadian dreams indeed, but I fear they are exactly that: dreams. When I look as far as I am capable into the future — 100, maybe 200 years — I am not optimistic, despite the positive steps I outlined at the beginning of this chapter. In many parts of the world, I doubt we have the will to achieve even many of the practical reforms which would allow the easy continuation of human–animal cohabitation in cities.

In places like Australia and Canada, the outlook isn't too bad. Some government bodies will continue to ignore the animal component, mopping up the consequences with greater or less insight and success. Many others, though, are now acknowledging the needs of the Urban Sextipede — particularly in parks.

However, developers and property owners are certainly not convinced of the need to consider animals. Quite the opposite. Economic arguments may work eventually for rental restrictions, but whether they are enough to shift bricks and mortar remains to be seen. And while such nations will of course never lose dog companionship, for they are relatively space-rich, housing and lifestyle restrictions may mean the proportion of the community that can manage dog ownership in the future will decline.

In other parts of the world, the outlook is bleaker. Within the next century two-thirds of the population will be living in cities. A proportion of those will face circumstances similar to those of Australians. Urban sprawl is the pattern everywhere, as the rich abandon city centres and reach for the "good life" of low to medium density. As problematic for the environment as that will be, such areas will remain hospitable to dogs. But for the rest of the population, the "space-poor", living in their vast concrete conurbations, the prospects of maintaining any meaningful relationships with the non-human seem slim.

In the last couple of years I have met many policy makers — theorists and practitioners, global thinkers and local. For a few, discussion of the Urban Sextipede is like a light globe switching on. Not long after I met Emeritus Professor Stephen Boyden who edits *Nature and Society*, he forwarded a note saying he realised the issue on Sustainable Cities had a serious deficiency — there was nothing on pets. But others like Alexander Cuthbert, Professor of Urban Planning at the University of New South Wales, and an expert on the development of Asian cities, are quite blunt in their dismissal. For him, the only context for the discussion of animals in high-density areas is as pests. They have no place in city environments. They were not designed for it — keeping a dog 40 storeys up in a Hong Kong apartment of 500 square feet simply cannot work. The thing is, I wonder if living in such places works for people.

In Isaac Asimov's *Caves of Steel*, our future world is one of order and safety.[19] Great domed cities stretch high into the air and kilometres below the ground. The natural patterns of light and shade are almost absent — everything is bathed in a diffuse, regulated light. No rain, no animals, nothing living but humans. The people seem happy, or at least, no more unhappy than anyone you might meet now. In fact, when taken out of their regulated environment to feel wind on the cheek, they panic. Yet even here, we are aware of the author's discomfort with the scenario. His hero, Lije Bailey, ultimately rejects the safety of the City, resolving to abandon the womb. And by the way, Asimov's Earth had a population of only eight billion. We are now facing 11 billion.

It's true that the notion of "physical determinism", that the personality of an individual is determined by the city environment and that high-density urban environments are detrimental, has been largely discredited by urban planners after the failure to find any scientific evidence in its support. But why is it then that even the proponents of this view seem vaguely uneasy when discussing their personal experiences of cities like Hong Kong or New York? Why this faint sense of something awry, something absent, something perhaps not consciously missed, but diminished?

E. O. Wilson notes that if we simply look at tangibles, like measuring stress indices, even feed-lot cattle appear perfectly happy.[20] I wonder if our unease is not a subconscious rejection of a human-only environment. A human monoculture. And of the final severance of the frayed cord which binds us to the "natural".

It seems to me that in a very meaningful way, our own species' future is tied to the viability of the Urban Sextipede. Yes, we can move to a place which is too confined for our most ancient partners, but the point is, would we want to? If we can't even find the space to take the dog for a walk, are we sure there is enough there to meet human needs? If we make our cities too hard for the dog, are we really making them too hard for people?

The fortunes of our world's cities will differ. Some will be successful, creating vibrant, exciting communities, where the cost of reduced personal space will be compensated for by wonderful public amenities. Others will create Caves of Steel with battery people, isolated although immersed in a sea of other humans, fitting fodder for the machines. I believe the Urban Sextipede test is a simple and practical means of distinguishing between the two types of city. A litmus test, if you like, of urban viability.

In other words, if you have the power to shape a city, a community, a home, don't just ask the Pat Troy question, "Would you want your grandmother to live in it?". Ask yourself another, more basic question: *Would you let your dog live in it?*

ENDNOTES

Chapter 1

1. Barker, S. B. and Barker, R. T., "The human–canine bond: closer than family ties?", *Journal of Mental Health Counseling*, no. 10, pp. 46–56, 1984.
2. Thomas, K., *Man and the Natural World: Changing attitudes in England 1500–1800*, Allen Lane, London, 1983.
3. Bradshaw to Newby, interview, May 1996.
4. Lorenz, K., *Man Meets Dog*, Methuen, London, 1954.
5. Clutton-Brock, J., *A Natural History of Domesticated Animals in England*, Cambridge University Press and The British Museum (Natural History), Cambridge, 1987.
6. Clutton-Brock to Newby, interview, May 1996.
7. One of the best discussions of this process is to be found in Clutton-Brock's more recent publication: Clutton-Brock, J., "Origins of the dog: domestication and early history", in *The Domestic Dog: Its evolution, behaviour and interactions with people*, ed. James Serpell, Cambridge University Press, Cambridge, 1985.
8. ibid.
9. Morey, D. F. and Wiant, M. D., "Early Holocene Domestic Dog Burials from the North American Midwest", *Current Anthropology*, vol. 33, pp. 224–229, 1992.
10. Background setting for the scenario kindly provided by Juliet Clutton-Brock.
11. Coppinger, R. P. and Kay Smith, C., "The Domestication of Evolution", *Environmental Conservation*, vol. 10, no. 4, pp. 283–291, Elsevier Sequoia for the Foundation for Environmental Conservation, Switzerland, 1983.
12. Dunbar, R., *Grooming, Gossip and the Evolution of Language*, Faber and Faber, London, 1986.
13. Fox, M. W., *The Wild Canids: Their systematics, behavioural ecology and evolution*, Von Nostrand Reinhold Co., New York, 1975.
14. Clutton-Brock to Newby, interview, May 1996.
15. Coppinger to Newby, interview, July 1996.
16. ibid.
17. Marshall Thomas, E., *Reindeer Moon*, Pocket Books, New York, 1988.
18. Clutton-Brock to Newby, interview, May 1996.

19. Paxton to Newby, interview, August 1996. Also: Paxton, David W., *Urban Animal Management: A naturalistic perspective*, PhD thesis, National Centre for Development Studies, Australian National University, 1998.

20. Colin Groves kindly provided a picture of the community's surroundings.

21. Adams, G. J., "Sleep-wake cycles and other night-time behaviours of the domestic dog *Canis familiaris*", *Applied Animal Behaviour Science*, no. 36, pp. 233–48, 1993.

22. Groves to Newby, interview, August 1996.

23. Vila, C., Savolainen, P., Maldonado, J. E., Amorim, I. R., Rice, J. E., Honeycutt, R. L., Crandall, K. A., Lundberg, J. and Wayne, R. K., "Multiple and Ancient Origins of the Domestic Dog", *Science*, vol. 276, pp. 1687–89, 1997.

Chapter 2

1. Shepard, P., "On Animal Friends" in *The Biophilia Hypothesis*, eds Stephen R. Kellert and Edward O. Wilson, Island Press, Washington, 1993.

2. ibid.

3. Hemmer, H., *Domestication: The decline of environmental appreciation*, Cambridge University Press, Cambridge, 1990.

4. Gould, Stephen Jay, *The Panda's Thumb*, Norton, New York, 1980.

5. Coppinger to Newby, interview, July 1996.

6. Coppinger, R. and Schneider, R., "Evolution of working dogs" in *The Domestic Dog: Its evolution, behaviour and interactions with people*, ed. James Serpell, Cambridge University Press, Cambridge, 1995.

7. Boith, V., Wright, J., and Danneman, P., "Is there a relationship between canine behaviour problems and spoiling activities, anthropomorphism, and obedience training?", *Applied Animal Behaviour Science*, vol. 34, pp. 263–272, 1992.

8. Freedman, D., King, J. and Elliot O., "Critical periods in the social development of dogs", *Science*, no. 133, pp. 1016–17, 1961.

9. Ruvinsky to Newby, interview, August 1996.

10. Trut, L. N., "Early Canid Domestications: The Farm-fox Experiment", *American Scientist*, vol. 87, no. 2, pp. 160–69, 1999.

11. Clutton-Brock, J., "Origins of the dog: Domestication and early history" in *The Domestic Dog: Its evolution, behaviour and interactions with people*, ed. James Serpell, Cambridge University Press, Cambridge, 1995.

12. ibid.

13. Darwin quote cited in Coppinger, R. and Schneider, R., "Evolution of working dogs" in *The Domestic Dog: Its evolution, behaviour and interactions with people*, ed. James Serpell, Cambridge University Press, Cambridge, 1995. Both this chapter, and that by Juliet Clutton-Brock (op. cit.), provide a comprehensive overview of the history and science of the development of dog breeds.

14. Wayne to Newby, interview, October 1996.
15. Vila, C., Savolainen, P., Maldonado, J. E., Amorim, I. R., Rice, J. E., Honeycutt, R. L., Crandall, K. A., Lundberg, J. and Wayne, R. K., "Multiple and Ancient Origins of the Domestic Dog", *Science*, vol. 276, pp. 1687–89, 1997.
16. Menzel, R. and Menzel, R., "Observations of the pariah dog" in *The Book of the Dog*, ed. Brian Vesey-Fitzgerald, Nicolson and Watson, London, 1948.
17. MacDonald, D. W. and Carr, G. M., "Variation in dog society: Between resource dispersion and social flux" in *The Domestic Dog: Its evolution, behaviour and interactions with people,* ed. James Serpell, Cambridge University Press, Cambridge, 1995.

Chapter 3

1. Much of the discussion in this chapter draws on the following two (excellent) books. For readers interested in a more detailed account, I heartily recommend them: Clutton-Brock, J., *A Natural History of Domesticated Animals,* Cambridge University Press and The British Museum (Natural History), Cambridge, 1987; and Diamond, J., *The Rise and Fall of the Third Chimpanzee,* Random House, London, 1991.
2. Clutton-Brock to Newby, interview, May 1996. Also, Clutton-Brock, J., 1987, op. cit.
3. Diamond, J., 1991, op. cit.
4. Zeuner, F. E., *A History of Domesticated Animals,* Harper and Row, New York, 1963.
5. Schwabe, C. W., "Animals in the Ancient World" in *Animals and Society: Changing perspectives,* Routledge, London, 1994.
6. Perkins, D., "Fauna in Çatalhüyük: Evidence for early cattle domestication in Anatolia", *Science,* vol. 164, pp. 177–79, 1969.
7. Grigson, C., "Size and sex: Evidence for domestication of cattle in the Near East" in *The Beginnings of Agriculture*, eds Milles, A., Williams, D., and Gardner, N., Symposium of the Association for Environmental Archaeology, 1989.
8. Lobban, R., "Cattle and the rise of the Egyptian State" in *Anthrozoos*, vol. ii, no. 3, pp. 194–201, 1989.
9. Malek, J., *The Cat in Ancient Egypt*, British Museum Press, London, 1993.
10. Clutton-Brock, J., *The British Museum Book of Cats: Ancient and modern,* British Museum Press, London, 1988.
11. Groves to Newby, interview, August 1996.
12. Clutton-Brock, J., 1987, op. cit.
13. Diamond, J., 1991, op. cit.
14. Brown, D. and Anthony, D., "Bit Wear, Horseback Riding and the Botai Site in Kazakstan", *Journal of Archaeological Science*, vol. 25, pp. 331–47, 1998.

15. Jones, B. and Dixon, M. V., *The Macmillan Dictionary of Biography*, Macmillan, Melbourne, 1986.

16. Diamond, J., 1991, op. cit.

17. Clutton-Brock, J., 1987, op. cit.

18. Diamond, J., *Guns, Germs and Steel: The fates of human societies,* Jonathan Cape, London, 1997.

19. Diamond to Newby, interview, September 1996.

20. Paxton, David W., *Urban Animal Management: A naturalistic perspective,* PhD thesis, National Centre for Development Studies, Australian National University, 1998. Also, Paxton, D., "Community involvement and urban dogs — some ideas" in *Urban Animal Management: Proceedings of the national conference, Canberrra 1994,* Australian Veterinary Association, Canberra, 1994.

21. Bradshaw, J. "Social interactions between people — a new evolutionary framework", Plenary address to the 7th International Conference on Human–Animal Interactions, Geneva, 8 September 1995. Also, Paxton, op. cit.

Chapter 4

1. Serpell, J., "From Paragon to Pariah: Some reflections on human attitudes to dogs" in *The Domestic Dog: Its evolution, behaviour and interactions with people,* ed. James Serpell, Cambridge University Press, Cambridge, 1995.

2. Copies of orginal transcripts of the witch trials were kindly sent to me by James Serpell.

3. Serpell, J. A., *In the Company of Animals,* Basil Blackwell Ltd, Oxford, 1986.

4. Serpell to Newby, interview, July 1996.

5. Menache to Newby, interview, May 1996. Also, Menache, S., "Dogs: God's worst enemies?", *Society and Animals,* vol. 5, no. 1, pp. 23–44, 1997.

6. Geering, W. A., Forman, A. J., and Nunn, M.J., *Exotic Diseases of Animals: A field guide for Australian veterinarians,* Australian Government Publishing Services, Canberra, 1995.

7. Menache to Newby, interview, May 1996.

8. Serpell, J., 1995, op. cit.

9. ibid.

10. Evans, E. P., *The Criminal Prosecution and Capital Punishment of Animals,* Faber and Faber, London, 1987. First published 1906 by Heineman.

11. Cohen, E., "Animals in Medieval Perceptions: The image of the ubiquitous other" in *Animals and Human Society: Changing perspectives,* eds A. Manning and J. Serpell, Routledge, London, 1994.

12. Serpell, J., 1995, op. cit.

13. Serpell, J., 1986, op. cit.

14. Hugh-Jones, S., "Bonnes raisons ou mauvaise conscience? De l'ambivalence de certains Amazoniens envers la consommation de viande" in *Terrain,* no.

26, pp. 123–148, March 1996.

15. Hugh-Jones to Newby, interview, May 1996.

16. Ritvo, H., *The Animal Estate: The English and other creatures in the Victorian age,* Harvard University Press, Cambridge, MA., 1987. Also, Ritvo to Newby, interview, May 1996.

17. Arkow, P., "Cruelty to Animals and Child Abuse" in *Animals and Us: Sixth international conference on the relationships between humans and animals,* HABAC Canada, Montreal, 1992.

18. Evans, E. P., 1987, op. cit.

Chapter 5

1. Morris, D., *Animal Days,* Jonathan Cape, London, 1979.

2. For a wonderful morning spent touring the National Gallery, I thank Dr Andrew Edney, veterinarian and art afficionado extraordinaire.

3. Taken from a collection of myths by James Serpell in: Serpell, J., "From Paragon to Pariah: Some reflections on human attitudes to dogs" in *The Domestic Dog: Its evolution, behaviour and interactions with people*, ed. James Serpell, Cambridge University Press, Cambridge, 1995.

4. Shaw, R. "Squatter's Rights", *The Cat Book*, Frederick Warne & Co., New York, 1973.

5. Rowan to Newby, interview, August 1996.

6. Ammer, C., *Raining Cats and Dogs ... and other beastly expressions*, Paragon House, New York, 1989. (Kindly forwarded by Andrew Rowan.)

7. Serpell, 1995, op. cit.

8. Leach, E., "Anthropological Aspects of Language: Animal categories and verbal abuse". Reprinted in 1989 in *Anthrozoos*, vol. II, no. 3, pp. 151–65.

9. MacCallum, M. and Mackay, H., *What Australians Think About Their Pets*, Petcare Information and Advisory Service, Melbourne, 1993.

10. Katcher, A. H. and Beck, A. M., "Health and Caring for Living Things" in *Animals and People Sharing the World*, ed. Andrew Rowan, published for Tufts University, University Press of New England, 1988.

11. Katcher to Newby, interview, September 1996.

12. Stamp Dawkins, M., *Through Our Eyes Only?: The search for animal consciousness,* W. H. Freeman, Oxford, 1993.

13. Katcher, A. H. and Wilkins, G. G., "Dialogue with Animals: Its nature and culture" in *The Biophilia Hypothesis*, eds Stephen R. Kellert and Edward O. Wilson, Island Press, Washington, 1993.

14. Masson, J. M. and McCarthy, S., *When Elephants Weep: The emotional lives of animals*, Delacorte Press, New York, 1995.

15. Stamp Dawkins to Newby, interview, May 1996.

16. Dennett to Newby, interview, January 1997.

17. Stamp Dawkins to Newby, interview, May 1996.

18. Kennedy, J. S., *The New Anthropomorphism,* University of Cambridge Press, Cambridge, 1992.

19. Goodwin, D., Bradshaw, J. W. S., and Wickens, S. M., "Paedomorphosis affects agonistic visual signals of domestic dogs", *Animal Behaviour,* vol. 53, pp. 290–304, 1997. Also, Bradshaw to Newby, interview, May 1996.

20. Cameron-Beaumont, C., material for PhD thesis at the University of Southampton.

21. Cameron-Beaumont to Newby, interview , October 1996.

22. *The Faber Book of Science,* ed. John Carey, Faber & Faber Ltd, London, 1995.

23. Barnett, S. A., "Humanity as *Homo docens*: the teaching species" in *Interdisciplinary Science Reviews,* vol. 19, no. 2, 1994.

24. Bradshaw, J. W. S., "Social Interactions Between Animals and People: A new evolutionary framework", Plenary address to *Animals, Health and Quality of Life,* the 7th International Conference on Human–Animal Interactions, Geneva, 8 September 1995.

25. Dennett, D. C., *Kinds of Minds,* Weidenfeld and Nicolson, London, 1996.

Chapter 6

1. Anderson, W. P., Reid, C. M., and Jennings, G. L., "Pet ownership and risk factors for cardiovascular disease", *Medical Journal of Australia,* vol. 157, no. 5, pp. 298–301, 1992.

2. Serpell, J. A., *In the Company of Animals,* Basil Blackwell Ltd, Oxford, 1986.

3. Levinson, B. M., *Pet-orientated Child Psychotherapy,* Charles Thomas, Springfield, ILL, 1969.

4. Katcher to Newby, interview, September 1996.

5. Friedman, E., Katcher, A. H., Lynch, J. J., and Thomas, S. A., "Animal companions and one-year survival of patients after discharge from a coronary care unit", *Public Health Reports,* no. 95, pp. 307–312, 1980.

6. Friedman, E., Katcher, A. H., Thomas, S. A., Lynch, J. J., and Messent, P. R., "Social Interaction and Blood Pressure: The influence of animal companions." *Journal of Nervous and Mental Disease,* no. 171, pp. 461–65, 1983

7. Friedman, E. and Thomas S., "Pet ownership, social support and one year survival after acute myocardial infarction in the cardiac arrhythmia suppression trial (CAST)", *American Journal of Cardiology,* 76: 1213–17, 1995.

8. Serpell, J. A., "Beneficial effects of pet ownership on some aspects of human health", *Journal of the Royal Society of Medicine,* no. 84, pp. 717–20, 1991.

9. McHarg, M., Baldock, C., Headey, B., and Robinson, A., *National People and Pets Survey,* Report to the Urban Animal Management Coalition, Sydney, 1995.

10. Siegel, J. M., "Stressful life events and the use of physical services among the elderly: The modifying role of pet ownership", *The Journal of Personality and*

Social Psychology, 58, pp. 1081–86, 1990.

11. Headey B., "Health benefits and health cost savings due to pets: Preliminary estimates from an Australian national survey", Social Indicators Research, 47, pp. 233–43, 1998. Also Anderson, W. P., "Medicine and the Community: The benefits of pet ownership", letter to the Medical Journal of Australia, vol. 164, p. 441, 1996.

12. Jorm, A. F., Jacomb, P. A., Christensen, H., Henderson, S., Korten, A. E. and Rodgers, B., "Impact of pet ownership on elderly Australians' use of medical services: An analysis using Medicare data", Australian Medical Journal, 166, pp. 376–77, 1997.

13. Fletcher to Newby, interview, September 1996.

14. Australian Bureau of Statistics (ABS):Australian Social Trends, Australian Bureau of Statistics, Canberra, 1995.

15. Lutz, W., MacKellar, F. L., Goujon, A., and Prinz, C., "Population, Number of Households and Global Warming" in Popnet: Population network newsletter, no. 27, International Institute for Applied Systems Analysis (IIASA), Vienna, 1995.

16. ibid.

17. Troy, P. N., The Perils of Urban Consolidation: A discussion of Australian housing and urban development policies, The Federation Press, Sydney, 1996. Also, Troy to Newby, interview, August 1996.

18. ABS, 1996, op. cit.

19. Dunbar, R., Grooming, Gossip and the Evolution of Language, Faber and Faber, London, 1996.

20. ABS, 1996, op. cit.

21. ibid.

22. Hugh-Jones to Newby, interview, May 1996.

23. Messent, P. R., "Social facilitation of contact with other people by pet dogs" in New Perspectives on Our Lives with Companion Animals, eds A. H. Katcher and A. M. Beck, University of Pennsylvania Press, Philadelphia, 1983.

24. Hart, L. A., Hart, B. L., and Bergin, B., "Socializing effects of service dogs for people with disabilities", Anthrozoos, vol. i, no. 1, pp. 41–44, 1987.

25. Endenburg N. and Baarda, B., "The Role of Pets in Enhancing Human Well-being: Effects on child development" in The Waltham Book of Human – Animal Interaction: Benefits and responsibilities of pet ownership, ed. I. Robinson, Pergamon Press, Oxford, 1995.

26. Cain, A. O., "Pets as Family Members" in Marriage and Family Review, no. 8, pp. 5–10, 1985.

27. Hogarth-Scott, S., Salmon, I., and Lavelle, R., "A dog in residence" in People —Animals —Environment, no. 1, pp. 4–6, 1983.

28. Guttman, G., Predovic, M., and Zemanek, M., "The influence of pet ownership

on non-verbal communication and social competence in children." Proceedings of *The Human–Pet Relationship: International symposium on the occasion of the 80th birthday of Nobel Prize-winner Professor Konrad Lorenz*, Institute for Interdisciplinary Research on the Human–Pet Relationship, Vienna, 1983.

29. Poresky, R. H., Hendrix, C., Mosier, J. E., and Samuelson, M. L., "The Companion Animal Bonding Scale: Internal reliability and construct validity", *Psychological Reports*, no. 66, pp. 931–36, 1987.

30. Condoret, A., "Speech and companion animals: experience with normal and disturbed nursery school children" in *New Perspectives on Our Lives with Companion Animals*, eds A. H. Katcher and A. M. Beck, University of Pennsylvania Press, Philadelphia, 1983.

31. Raina, P., Waltner-Toews, D., Bonnett, B., Woodward, C. and Abernathy, T., "Influence of companion animals on the physical and psychological health of older people: An analysis of a one-year longitudinal study", *Journal of the American Geriatric Society*, 47, pp. 323–29.

32. Batson, K., McCabe, B., Baun, M. M. and Wilson, C., "The effect of a therapy dog on socialization and physiological indicators of stress in persons diagnosed with Alzheimer's disease", in *Companion Animals in Human Health*, eds C. C. Wilson and D. C. Turner, Sage Publications, London, pp. 105–122, 1998.

33. McBride, A., unpublished data from the Anthrozoology Institute, Southampton, personal comment.

34. Saunders, L., "Get that dog out of here — this is a hospital, not a park", 1995. (Permission kindly granted to refer to a paper given as part of a Master's degree in Health Science. Names and some details in the story have been changed to protect anonymity.)

35. Kellehear, A., *Dying of Cancer: The final year of life*, Harwood Academic Publishers, Melbourne, 1990.

Chapter 7

1. Juniper to Newby, interview, May 1996.

2. Leeming, R. and Nichols, P., "Use of faecal sterols and bacterial indicators to discriminate sources of faecal pollution in urban creeks and lakes of Wyong, NSW", Report to the Wyong Shire Council, CSIRO Division of Oceanography, 1995.

3. BIS Schrapnel, *Contribution of the Pet Care Industry to the Australian Economy*, industry study, 1995.

4. Lovering, K., "Cost of Children in Australia", *Working paper no. 8*, Australian Institute of Family Studies, Melbourne, 1984.

5. Dickman, C. R., *Overview of the Impact of Feral Cats on Australian Native Fauna*, Report for the Australian Nature Conservation Agency, Commonwealth of Australia, Canberra, 1996.

6. Paul Wagner, personal comment.

7. Ehrlich P., *The Population Bomb*, Ballantine Books, New York, 1968.

8. Jessica Mathews of the US Council on Foreign Relations. Reprinted article first appeared in the *Washington Post*, 1996.

9. Wilson, E. O., *Naturalist*, Penguin, London, 1996, p. 315.

10. Katcher, A. H. and Beck, A. M., "Health and Caring for Living Things" in *Animals and People Sharing the World*, ed. Andrew Rowan, published for Tufts University, University Press of New England, 1988.

11. James, P. D., *The Children of Men*, Faber and Faber, London, 1992.

12. Katcher, A. H. and Beck, A. M., 1988, op. cit.

13. Bateson to Williams, interview, June 1996.

14. MacCallum, M. and Mackay, H., *What Australians Think About Their Pets*, Petcare Information and Advisory Service, Melbourne, 1993.

15. Paul to Newby, interview, May 1996.

16. Heerwagen, J. H. and Orians, G. H., "Humans, Habitats and Aesthetics" in *The Biophilia Hypothesis*, eds Stephen R. Kellert and Edward O. Wilson, Island Press, Washington, 1993.

17. Wilson, E. O., *Biophilia*, Harvard University Press, Boston, 1984.

18. Wilson, E. O., 1996, op. cit.

19. Wilson, L. M., "Intensive care delirium: The effect of outside deprivation in a windowless unit", *Archives of Internal Medicine*, vol. 130, pp. 123–45, 1972.

20. Ulrich, R. S., "View through a window may influence recovery from surgery", *Science*, vol. 224, pp. 420–21, 1984.

21. Kaplan, R. and Kaplan, S., *The Experience of Nature*, Cambridge University Press, Cambridge, 1989.

22. Wilson to Newby , interview , November 1996.

23. ibid.

24. Katcher, A. H. and Wilkins, G. G., "Helping children with attention deficit hyperactive and conduct disorder through animal-assisted therapy and education", *Interactions*, vol. 12, no. 4, pp. 5–9, 1994.

25. Katcher to Newby, interview , September 1996.

26. Paul, E. W. and Serpell, J. A., "Pets and the Development of Positive Attitudes to Animals" in *Animals and Human Society: Changing perspectives*, eds A. Manning and J. Serpell, Routledge, London, 1994.

27. von Frisch, K, quoted in the preface to *The Biophilia Hypothesis*, eds Stephen R. Kellert and Edward O. Wilson, Island Press, Washington, 1993.

Chapter 8

1. Reark Research, *Research Report: Pet care industry statistics*. Prepared for the Petcare Information and Advisory Service, Melbourne, 1994.

2. Figures supplied by Wolfgang Lutz of the International Institute for Applied Systems Analysis, Vienna.

3. *Living Suburbs: A policy for metropolitan Melbourne into the 21st century,* Department of Planning and Development, Government of Victoria, Melbourne, 1995.

4. *Building a Better Future: cities for the 21st century,* New South Wales Department of Planning, New South Wales Government, Sydney, 1995.

5. Clarke to Newby, interview, November 1996.

6. Troy, P. N., *The Perils of Urban Consolidation: A discussion of Australian housing and urban development policies,* Federation Press, Sydney, 1996.

7. Government of Victoria, 1995, op. cit.

8. Troy, P., 1996, op. cit.

9. Dr Robert Holmes, personal comment.

10. Pet industry research figures, 1996, personal comment.

11. ibid.

12. "The Challenge of Urbanisation: The world's largest cities", Department for Economics and Social Information and Policy Analysis, Population Division, United Nations, New York, 1995.

Chapter 9

1. Paxton to Newby, interview, September 1996.

2. Murray, R. and Penridge, H., *Dogs in the Urban Environment: A handbook of municipal management,* Chiron Media, Mount Pleasant, Queensland, 1992.

3. See *Urban Animal Management: Proceedings of the first national conference on Urban Animal Management in Australia,* ed. Richard Murray, Chiron Media, Mount Pleasant, Queensland, 1992.

4. Avanzino to Newby, interview, November 1996. Also, Avanzino, R., "The importance of companion animals to society" in *Urban Animal Management: Proceedings of the national conference, Sydney 1996,* ed. Sandra Hassett, Australian Veterinary Association, Canberrra, 1996.

5. *La Lettre de l'afirac,* no. 7, Association Francaise d'Information et de Recherche sur l'Animal de Compagnie (AFIRAC), Paris, February 1994.

6. Laysell Consulting, *Guidelines to Developing an Integrated Urban Animal Management Strategy,* Petcare Information and Advisory Service, Melbourne, 1995.

7. Garth Jennens, personal comment.

8. Eidelson, M., "Petlinks — a new service for home and community care" in *Urban Animal Management: Proceedings of the national conference, Sydney 1996,* ed. Sandra Hassett, Australian Veterinary Association, Canberra, 1996. Also, Grant, J. and Miller, E., *Companion Animals: A model for providing companion animal support services in the community,* report for the Victorian Home and Community Care Program, Melbourne, 1995.

9. Avanzino to Newby, interview, November 1996.

10. Jackson, V., Blackshaw, J. K., and Marriott, J., *Public Open Space and Dogs: A*

design and management guide for open space professionals and local government, Petcare Information and Advisory Service, Melbourne, 1996. Also Jackson, V., "Guidelines for designing and managing public open space" in *Urban Animal Management: Proceedings of the national conference, Melbourne 1995,* Australian Veterinary Association, Canberra, 1995.

11. Paxton to Newby, interview, August 1996.
12. Gaultier, E., "Experimental Study of a Dog Comfort Centre", 1996, unpublished data, available from the veterinary school, University of Nantes, Nantes.
13. Jackson, V. et al, 1995, op. cit.
14. Victorian Residential Agreement put out by the Real Estate Institute of Victoria.
15. Jackson to Newby, interview, December 1996.
16. Jackson, V. and Holmes, R., *Pets in Urban Areas: A guide to integrating domestic pets into new residential development,* Petcare Information and Advisory Service, Melbourne, 1993. Also, Jackson, V., "Facilitating pet ownership through improved housing design", *JAVMA,* vol. 209, no. 6, pp. 1076–79, 1996.
17. Katcher to Newby, interview, September 1996.
18. Tudge to Williams, interview, June 1996.
19. Asimov, I., *The Caves of Steel,* Panther, London, 1958.
20. Wilson to Newby, interview, November 1996.

INDEX